What Others Ar[...]
More Taste Be[...]

"From pimples, PMS and braces [...] teen sometimes seems more than I [...] —and relief—to read that other teens often feel as I do, and to learn how they're sorting out life and making good choices. This is a very positive and uplifting book. It makes me proud to be a teenager today."

Ashleigh Thomas, 16

"One of the ways we keep our communities healthy is to make certain our youth are healthy. *More Taste Berries for Teens* helps provide the nourishment needed to support the values, emotional well-being and positive direction required to assure such health in today's youth. Its value is in its approach: Teens sharing their experience, strength and hope with other teens—what a profound way to effect positive change."

Senator Roy Herron
Tennessee

"Sometimes I feel like half my life is a big setup for doing something that's going to make me look like a fool, or worse, a geek! It was great to read that other teens face this same problem, and that they survived the ultimate embarrassments—and even learned something from it. Besides, their stories were just hilarious—and they made you think."

Toby Schultz, 17

"You're going to love this book. This past year, Rotary put *Taste Berries for Teens* in the hands of many of our youth teen leaders across the country (as well as its companion journal). After reading this follow-up book—another real winner—I can vouch that it will be of great use to teens. A genuine treasure trove of actual stories from real-life teens."

Darrell Marshall
Rotary Youth Leadership International

"I swear my sister is boy-crazy! Just ask her and she'll tell you who's who in the hunk category in her class. I got her this book because I thought the section on love would help her put into perspective some of her issues and shed some light on the subject. So far she's dumped three guys off the hunk list . . . and I've made some important decisions about some girls I've been interested in, myself!"

Derek Anderson, 15

"This book is brilliant! The authors have given teens an ideal forum for processing their experiences, thoughts and feelings about life, love, faith, the future and so much more. What a gift, or as they say, a taste berry!"

Debbie Thurman
author, *From Depression to Wholeness*

"When I read the unit on friends in this book, I thought about just how important my friends are to me. It was good to read what other kids had learned about keeping and making really great friends."

Tyanne Rhodes, 13

"When I read this book, I found it inspiring that teens were so open with each other and the world. When I gave it to my daughter to read, she came to me pointing out one of the stories and said, 'I felt exactly like this the time. . . .' She then proceeded to tell me all about her own most embarrassing moment. I'm certain that any teen who reads this book will find the encouragement and comfort of being able to say over and over again, 'I felt exactly like this. . . .'"

Karen Mayheim
educator, Minneapolis

"I love this book because it was a way for me to really trust that other teens aren't ashamed to talk about how their faith is central to keeping them on track."

Corey Bandy, 16

"Today's teens are looking for the answers to some heavy stuff— everything from how do you want to define your life to how do the people you hang out with redefine your life, from who do you want to be in the world to is there a source of strength outside of this world. This book offers teens the assurance they're not alone in their search, and helps them sift through and discover the answers they're seeking, wanting and needing."

Nancy Rivard
founder, Airline Ambassadors International

"Most teenagers today have heard about the importance of having good self-esteem, but having it presented as an outcome of acting in ways you can be proud of and being your own best friend made it clear to me."

Daniel Matthews, 15

"I got this book for my sixteen-year-old niece, who has been struggling with her parents' divorce. She loved it. The stories of other teens finding their way through their own 'tough stuff' give teens both the comfort of knowing they're not alone, as well as tools on how to cope and survive the perils in their lives."

Karen DeSilva
parent

"The *Hopes and Fears* section was my favorite because I believe in my future and I want to be all I can be! Reading the stories gave me an even larger perspective on how I want to handle myself and *my attitude* when my *hopes* get confronted with some of my *fears*."

Melissa Albright, 15

More Taste Berries™ for Teens

A second collection of inspirational short stories and
encouragement on life, love, friendship and tough issues

With contributions from teens for teens

Bettie B. Youngs, Ph.D., Ed.D.
Jennifer Leigh Youngs

Authors of the national bestseller
Taste Berries™ for Teens

Health Communications, Inc.
Deerfield Beach, Florida

www.hci-online.com

We would like to acknowledge the following publishers and individuals for permission to reprint the following material. (Note: The stories that were penned anonymously, that are public domain or were previously unpublished stories written by Bettie B. Youngs or Jennifer Leigh Youngs are not included in this listing. Also not included in this listing but credited within the text are those stories contributed or based upon comments by teens.)

Member of the Gang, Free Speech, The Pheasant and *Mailboxes,* by Bettie B. Youngs. Reprinted with permission by publisher Health Communications, Inc., Deerfield Beach, Florida, from *Values from the Heartland* by Bettie B. Youngs, Ph.D., Ed.D. ©1995 Bettie B. Youngs, Ph.D., Ed.D.

New—and Late and *Mirror, Mirror,* by Leslie Hendrickson, Ph.D. Reprinted with permission of the author.

(Continued on page 335)

Library of Congress Cataloging-in-Publication Data

More taste berries for teens : a second collection of inspirational short stories and encouragement on life, love, friendship, and tough issues / [compiled by] Bettie B. Youngs, Jennifer Leigh Youngs ; with contributions from teens for teens.
   p.   cm.
   ISBN 1-55874-813-X
   1. Teenagers—Conduct of life.   I. Youngs, Bettie B.   II. Youngs, Jennifer Leigh, date.
   BJ1661 .M86 2000
   158.1'0835—dc21

                             00-040821

Publisher: Health Communications, Inc.
            3201 S.W. 15th Street
            Deerfield Beach, Florida 33442-8190

Cover illustration and design by Andrea Perrine Brower
Inside book typesetting by Dawn Grove

In memory of our mother and grandmother,
Arlene Berniece Burres,
a "taste berry" to every soul she encountered—
and then some.

Also by Bettie B. Youngs

Taste Berries for Teens Journal: My Thoughts on Life, Love and Making a Difference (Health Communications, Inc.)

Taste Berries for Teens: Inspirational Short Stories and Encouragement on Life, Love, Friendship and Tough Issues (Health Communications, Inc.)

Taste-Berry Tales: Stories to Lift the Spirit, Fill the Heart and Feed the Soul (Health Communications, Inc.)

A String of Pearls: Inspirational Stories Celebrating the Resiliency of the Human Spirit (Adams Media Corp.)

Gifts of the Heart: Stories That Celebrate Life's Defining Moments (Health Communications, Inc.)

Values from the Heartland: Stories of an American Farmgirl (Health Communications, Inc.)

Stress & Your Child: Helping Kids Cope with the Strains & Pressures of Life (Random House)

Safeguarding Your Teenager from the Dragons of Life: A Parent's Guide to the Adolescent Years (Health Communications, Inc.)

How to Develop Self-Esteem in Your Child: 6 Vital Ingredients (Macmillan/ Ballantine)

Self-Esteem for Educators: It's Job Criteria #1 (Jalmar Press)

Keeping Our Children Safe: A Guide to Emotional, Physical, Intellectual and Spiritual Wellness (John Knox/Westminster Press)

You and Self-Esteem: A Book for Young People (Jalmar Press)

Developing Self-Esteem in Your Students: A K–12 Curriculum (Jalmar Press)

Getting Back Together: Repairing Love (Adams Media Corp.)

Is Your Net-Working? A Complete Guide to Building Contacts and Career Visibility (John Wiley)

Managing Your Response to Stress: A Guide for Administrators (Jalmar Press)

Stress Management Skills for Educators (Jalmar Press)

Also by Jennifer Leigh Youngs

Feeling Great, Looking Hot and Loving Yourself: Health, Fitness and Beauty for Teens (Health Communications, Inc.)

Taste Berries for Teens Journal: My Thoughts on Life, Love and Making a Difference (Health Communications, Inc.)

Taste Berries for Teens: Inspirational Short Stories and Encouragement on Life, Love, Friendship and Tough Issues (Health Communications, Inc.)

Goal-Setting Skills for Young Adults (Learning Tools Press)

A Stress-Management Guide for Teens (Learning Tools Press)

Contents

PART 3: BEING FRIENDS WITH THE FACE IN THE MIRROR

PART 4: LOVE IN OUR LIVES!

PART 5: EXPRESSIONS OF LOVE!

PART 7: TOUGH STUFF

PART 8: FAITH AT WORK IN OUR LIVES

Acknowledgments

We would like to thank some of the "taste berries" in the development of this book. First, to the many of you teens who became a part of our everyday lives, in person and via your stream of letters and emails: We hear you! Thank you for your willingness to share what's on your mind and in your hearts. A bushel of berries to our publisher, Peter Vegso, and the talented staff at Health Communications, Inc.—especially those with whom we work most closely: Lisa Drucker, Matthew Diener, Christine Belleris, Susan Tobias and Erica Orloff—a very special thanks. As always, your professional assistance, encouragement and support makes for a real team. And to bride-to-be Maria Konicki, Kim Weiss and the many others who transport the words within these pages into the hands and hearts of our read-ers. And, of course, it's always an experience filled with pizzazz to work with Andrea Perrine Brower, who designed the gor-geous covers of six of our other books. Her designs are, quite simply, "berry beautiful"! A very special thanks to Tina Moreno of our staff. She not only keeps us functioning, but is in the truest sense of the metaphor, a taste berry.

And to the many important taste berries in our personal lives: We never take your love for granted; it is much honored. We'd like to acknowledge our mother and grandmother Arlene Burres, who died in December 1999, just twelve weeks after being diagnosed with ovarian cancer. Thank you Mom and Grandmother for your love and belief in us, for providing us with a sense of community and unity, and now for being our guardian angel. To our staunch confidant, Everett Burres, our dad and grandfather, for being such a wise old sage and a very loving one. Thank you for holding us so tight these past few months; it's helped free us to move about more than we would have been able to without such a binding anchor. To the "guys" in our lives: for Jennifer, the latest squeeze—you know who you are; and for Bettie, the "perfectly good Texas boy," husband, David Kirk. TBF! (Taste Berries Forever!) And to our many *brothers and sisters everywhere*—your love and soothing over the past months will forever be felt within our hearts. Thank you for sharing the journey—and holding our hearts—in such a touchingly human way.

As always, we give thanks to God from whom all blessings flow.

Introduction

Welcome to *More Taste Berries for Teens!* If you haven't yet had a chance to read *Taste Berries for Teens* or the *Taste Berries for Teens Journal* you're probably asking, "What is a taste berry?" A taste berry is a glorious little fruit that, when eaten, mysteriously convinces the taste buds that all food—even food that is distasteful—is delicious! The bright little berry has been used around the world for countless years to make the sometimes necessary eating of bitter foods, such as roots, tolerable. On some days, we could all use a taste berry! Luckily, people can be taste berries to each other. Has someone cheered you on or been extra kind to you at a time when you needed it most? Has someone paid tribute to you, or congratulated you, making one of your victories even sweeter? If so, that person was acting as your taste berry! When we reach out to others in thoughtful ways, we flavor each others' life with greater joy and buffer the bitterness of heartache and disappointment.

Teens know a great deal about needing—and being—a taste berry! We work with teens worldwide, and from these connections, as well as from the thousands of letters we receive from teens, we learn firsthand how you teens are making a difference to others—in your homes, schools and communities, even to the planet! We began sharing that heartening news in our first *Taste Berries for Teens*, and continue it here in *More Taste Berries for Teens*. Central to the goal for both books is to share what teens have to say about life, love, friendship and tough issues. As always, most life lessons arrive in the day-to-day living of life. Many of the teens we heard from said that sometimes they learned they needed to lighten up and laugh at themselves, such as when seventeen-year-old Tony Johnson sat on his date's delicate sequined purse—and crushed it—then struggled with when and how to tell her!

Sometimes the lesson was about the need to find courage, such as when fifteen-year-old Shannon Tucker came upon a couple of girls scribbling nasty words about a classmate on the paper towel dispenser in their school's bathroom. And sometimes it was about the need to come to terms with a crisis and learn healthier ways to get through it, such as when nineteen-year-old Sarah Jane Keller found herself labeled a "violator" by everyone—including the law. And sometimes it was a matter of understanding that hopes and fears can be the same thing.

While many of the teens profiled in this book found creative and positive ways to come to terms with the growing pains of growing up—and are thriving as they do—you will also meet teens who are still in the process of sorting out some of life's tougher blows. Central to the theme of this book is the reminder that it is always our honor to help others see their lives in the most positive light possible. So if some of the issues for the teens in this book seem a bit removed from your life—even foreign to you—may we suggest that you read their words keeping an open mind and hear their voice with an open heart—and then react to their plight by doing something kind and considerate for the first person you come across who looks in need of comfort or simply a moment of soul.

For those of you facing struggles that seem overwhelming, rather than suffer alone or resort to doing things that are self-destructive, we urge you to confide in an adult you trust. This is especially true in cases of physical or sexual abuse, suicidal feelings, eating disorders, depression, pregnancy and/or using drugs or alcohol. If you're uncertain where to go for counseling, turn to an adult (whether a parent, teacher, school guidance counselor or clergyperson) whom you feel you can trust to direct you to the proper place. Also, many schools provide peer crisis counseling, and there are toll-free hotlines (some are listed in part 7 in this book and may also be listed in the Yellow Pages of the phone directory) that offer teens valuable information and can direct you to other sources of help as well.

This book is divided into eight parts, with some fifteen stories per unit. Each part opens with *A Word from the Authors*, which is our chance to give you a brief overview of what teens have shared with us on the subject collectively—both through their letters and in our workshops. This opening is also our opportunity to point out some key "taste-berry" lessons to be gathered along the trail through "Teenville" (as a few teens called it). We'd also like to remind you that the stories in this book represent the personal opinions of the diverse group of teens, both males and females, of varying ages (twelve to twenty) and backgrounds. As such, their views do not necessarily reflect our own opinions, nor are we suggesting that you must agree with them. We also recognize that the stories in this book do not represent the full range and scope of the many issues which today's teens face. In our first *Taste Berries for Teens* we covered specific topics teens told us were of great interest to them, and in this book, we've covered yet others. Still, there isn't space to cover all the many things you had to say, which is why we are now working on an upcoming third edition, *Taste Berries for Teens III*. So if you have a story that you'd like to submit for consideration, please send it to us at:

Taste Berries for Teens III
c/o Tina Moreno
P.O. Box 2588
Del Mar, CA 92014

We hope you enjoy this book! We look forward to hearing which of these stories touched you and which ones you liked best—and why. We'd also love to hear about the "taste berries" in your lives—or how you've learned to be better "taste berries" in the lives of others.

"Taste Berries" to you!

Part 1

Embarrassing—but Funny—Moments

*If you're going to be able to look back on
something and laugh about it,
you might as well laugh about it now.*

—Marie Osmond

A Word from the Authors

In our first *Taste Berries for Teens: Inspirational Short Stories and Encouragement on Life, Love, Friendship and Tough Issues,* we told the story of the young woman who decided to treat herself to an ice-cream cone after a vigorous workout at her gym one day. Exhausted and sweaty, wearing her workout clothes, with her hair pulled haphazardly up in a ponytail, she walked into the ice-cream parlor. There, sitting at a table near the counter, was movie star Paul Newman. Here she was, face-to-face with Paul Newman—handsome film idol and local (as well as international) celebrity—and only having the flu could have made her look worse! The woman cringed at her timing, embarrassed to be seen by someone so famous, looking as she did. "Don't be nervous," the woman told herself. "Be cool. Be calm. Be collected. He's just a person who happens to be a movie star—one who happens to be in the same ice-cream parlor as I am. Just be gracious and graceful." So she walked past Mr. Newman, smiled a warm but casual smile, and in a friendly voice said, "Hello." Mr. Newman returned her smile, tipped his head and said, "Hello."

Though her heart was pounding with excitement, she walked to the counter and ordered her ice-cream cone. She paid for her cone, took her change, turned and walked out of the ice-cream parlor, smiling again at the movie star as she passed him. When she reached her car, she breathed a sigh of relief, then looked down at the car keys in her hands and realized she didn't have an ice-cream cone! "Oh, no," she groaned. "I must have left it in the ice-cream rack at the counter—or maybe even in the hands of the clerk behind the counter!" The woman had been so preoccupied with trying to act calm while feeling so nervous, she'd walked out without her ice-cream cone.

"What should I do now?" she wondered, and then decided to just go right back in and get her ice-cream cone. Hopefully, no one would even notice that she had forgotten the cone. Maybe it was right there in the rack at the counter, waiting for her. So, the woman took a deep breath, turned around and walked back in the ice-cream parlor. She smiled casually at Mr. Newman and then looked towards the counter. Paul Newman, knowing what she'd returned for, calmly informed her, "You put it in your purse."

Teen readers loved this story and told us so. "Putting an ice-cream cone in your purse—in front of someone you'd like to impress and while you're trying to be cool—ranks right up there," teens said, "but wait until you hear what happened to me!" Then you told us of your own funny incidents, many of which seemed humorous only when looking back on them. At the time these incidents occurred, teens admitted they usually seemed a lot more disastrous and embarrassing than funny.

Most of us have moments when we want to sink through the floor, or run and hide. Never is this more true than in the teen years when looking cool and in command of life is all-important. You think you've got it all worked out, an idea of how things will be, but then, as it unfolds, it doesn't entirely play out the way you had planned. This can leave you feeling silly, dumb, embarrassed—even out of control. Though difficult to accept at first, eventually we learn that things don't always go as planned, no matter how cool and in control we think we are, or how we think we've planned things down to the most minute detail. Take Tony Johnson (whose story is included in this unit), for example. Tony planned and planned for a date with a special someone, wanting everything to go so smoothly. It did for a while; everything was right on schedule—until he got to his lovely date's house to pick her up. Then, after a series of small bungles getting out of the house with her, Tony did something even more extreme: He sat on his first date's delicate sequined purse. But if that wasn't bad enough, he found himself in an even more precarious predicament: How should he tell her? You'll have to read the story for yourself to see how things turned out, but Tony, like so many other teens, discovered that things will probably be *different* from what you had imagined they would be.

Something else became evident: In retelling incidents and situations that teens found hilarious, many times it was often a case of "you just had to be there" to get the full impact of the comedy in it. For example, Marty LaBauer and his brother, Brent, rounded up a couple of little grass snakes and strategically placed them among the overstuffed pillows of an unsuspecting neighbor—who comes to their house to watch his favorite team, the Dallas Cowboys, on their big-screen TV. You probably had to be in the same room with the guys to completely enjoy the excitement—and humor—of the moment when the little snakes make their way out from under the pillows and across the neighbor boy's lap. One thing was clear: It was *hilarious* to Marty and his brother. (Since we haven't heard from the neighbor, we can't report on him. Yet, so many teens report finding humor in retrospect, so maybe he now sees it as funny, too.) When they told us their story, it took them twenty minutes to relay it to us because even in telling, they hooted and howled so much just remembering. Jennifer and I found ourselves laughing not so much *at* what the brothers found funny, as much as *with* the two of them because they were laughing so hard. Our teen reviewers found the story funny enough to include in the stories in this section; we hope you will enjoy it, too.

So what does it take for a moment to be "funny"? Perhaps like the saying "beauty is in the eye of the beholder," humor, too, is in the eye of the beholder. Certainly, some people have a bigger funny bone than other people do. Teens find that "new" and "first-time" situations made for a lot of "embarrassing yet funny moments." These times when teens were just getting the hang of things (which is maybe why we heard about so many *first* dates) were almost always coupled with high expectations for everything turning out "just right." Alas, things didn't necessarily go according to plans. This common ground for producing an embarrassing yet funny moment also produced a lesson: While at first inconveniently embarrassing, in retrospect at least, it was not as disastrous as it first seemed. And so, as time went on, even an embarrassing situation became the fodder for seeing humor.

The good news is that the sting of those times passes, along with all the uncomfortable feelings they bring. And in the end, teens said that sharing funny moments with each other is more than a point of conversation. Being able to laugh at yourself is, in the words of teens, "an ice breaker," "a great way to be considered a regular guy (or girl)—one of the group," and "an indication of being a real person." Hear, hear! Teens also realized something more: Seeing themselves caught in their own moments of embarrassment pointed the way to having compassion for others. And that's what being a "taste berry" is all about.

The gifts of humor don't end there. Being able to see the humor in a situation, to laugh at ourselves and not take ourselves too seriously can also be one of life's great coping skills. It's another way we get to choose our attitude and perspective. Laughter, when it's not forced or mean-spirited, feels great and can help us move on—and to love rather than berate ourselves. To be able to look back at something that seemed catastrophic, like tripping in front of someone you really wanted to impress, and to chuckle and make light of it is so much healthier than saying, "I'm such a klutz!" or "I'm always doing stupid things"—not to mention what you may say to yourself that you don't repeat out loud. Such messages are self-defeating and keep you caught in the web of low self-esteem.

Presented here are some of the many stories teens rated as their favorite embarrassing yet funny moments. Enjoy them. May they help you recall your own moments, and revisit them in a new light. And as always, may they sweeten your experience of the often unpredictable and sometimes capricious times of, in the words of our teen reviewers, "Teenville."

Finally! A Date with Rosalee Whitamore!

Finally! It was almost like reaching one of those big goals you hear about—I had a date with Rosalee Whitamore. It had taken me forever to build up the courage just to ask her. Rosalee Whitamore was one of the most popular girls in my high school—and as far as I was concerned, she was without question the most cool. My hands were actually sweating when I asked her if she wanted to go the Spring Formal at our school. She said, "Sure," as quickly and easily as if I were asking to sit down next to her in the cafeteria! I was a million miles off the ground! Finally, a date with Rosalee Whitamore.

The night of our first date, I wanted everything to be perfect. I spent so much time getting showered and dressed for the date that my older sister accused me of taking *twice* as much time as she took to get ready for her prom. Once I was sure I looked cool, suave and my very most debonair, I hopped in my older brother's car—a silver Volvo—which I had begged to borrow and washed until it gleamed just for the occasion. I parked down the street from her house fifteen minutes before I was supposed to be there, put on my favorite CD and sang along with it, keeping a constant tab on the time. I wanted to make a really good impression, and I knew being punctual was a good start. After that, I'd let my charm take over!

When I figured the time was *exactly* right, I pulled up in front of her house, and strolled up the walkway with a confident stride and my warmest smile. Compliments on how great she looked were running through my mind as I searched for the best one possible. I was in the middle of considering whether "Wow, you look really beautiful," was better than, "You look awesome tonight," when her mother opened the door. "Hello," I said, exercising the dazzling smile I'd been practicing. "I'm here to pick up Rosalee."

At the sound of my voice, Rosalee came rushing to the top of the stairs. The sight of her literally took my breath away. It must have taken my mind with it. Her mother reached out her hand to introduce herself: "I'm Rosalee's mother," she said with a cordial smile. Having seen Rosalee's beautiful smile—and having seen her in a great dress, and with the magic of her perfume wafting about—I was spellbound and wanted nothing more than to continue gazing upon her. Then I remembered I was in the midst of shaking her mother's hand. Rosalee's mother looked at me, expecting me to introduce myself or pass out— after all, it was my turn to say *something*. "Glad to meet you," I responded, but I was so dazed by the sight of Rosalee that for the life of me, I couldn't think of Rosalee's last name! "Mrs. . . . uh . . . Rosalee's mother," I bumbled. "I'm . . . ," and then I forgot my own name. My mind a complete blank, I said simply, "I'm Rosalee's date."

"Yes," Rosalee's mother laughed, "I'm sure you are."

"I'll be down in a minute, Tony," Rosalee called, taking mercy on me from the top of the stairs where she had seen the whole embarrassing scene! My confident, highly practiced, best smile now stiff, I cleared my throat, and tried to recover lost ground by saying to her mother, "I'm a classmate of Rosalee's—eleventh grade." Then, realizing how stupid it was of me to have added the eleventh grade—as though Rosalee's mother needed to be reminded what grade her daughter was in, I added, "I'll graduate next year." Once again, her charming mother smiled and then remarked, "Yes, Rosalee, too!" She wavered between looking concerned for my sanity and her daughter's well-being for having agreed to go out with me. I'm sure the woman thought I was a complete idiot! At this point, I certainly felt like one. Luckily, Rosalee came sailing down the stairs.

No doubt to release me from my bumbling agony, Rosalee's

mother turned our attention to admire Rosalee's delicate, little beaded purse in the shape of a ship (supposedly the Titanic—the theme of our Formal), one Rosalee had purchased for just this occasion. After we all duly admired this little "production," Rosalee quickly kissed her mother good-bye and we were off.

Determined to make up for lost ground, like a perfect gentleman I walked my beautiful date to her side of the car and opened the door for her. So that she could devote herself to lifting her exquisite dress into the car, Rosalee handed me the elaborately decorated and fragile little purse. So I could completely dedicate myself to helping this celestial being get into the car, I did what seemed logical: I tossed the little ship over to my side of the car seat. Like a graceful angel, Rosalee glided into the seat, and I closed the door, my heart thankful that God had created such a work of art—one who had agreed to be my date. Practically floating around the car to get in, I then bounded with gusto into my seat. The only thing is, I forgot the delicate, little sequined purse was on my seat!

Needless to say, I smashed it—smashed it flat! Now sitting on her prized work of art that doubled as a purse—and the possessions in it—I wondered *when* I should inform her of this. I mean, I didn't want the first words out of my mouth to be, "By the way, I'm sitting on your purse!" I wondered if I should just pretend I didn't know about the purse, let her search her side of the car and then my side and "find" it beneath me. Or should I question aloud what on earth was making my sitting so uncomfortable, feel around to see what it could be and then act surprised that it was the purse? Or should I just produce the purse and apologize? Or should I just wait until she got out and then toss it back on her seat and let her think that she had been the one who sat on it? In the midst of my deliberation, she asked, "Where's my purse?" There was nothing I could do but produce the purse right then and there. "I'm sitting on it!" I declared. Then I scraped it out from under me and, holding it by its slinky little chain, dangled the mangled mess in front of us.

Looking as shipwrecked as it did, the purse was downright ugly, and no amount of dazzling beads or glittering sequins could change that fact. Rosalee, looking stunned, said nothing. Humiliated, and quite sure I'd blown all possibilities of a great evening, I began to offer an apology, when suddenly, my lovely date began to giggle. Then she laughed, and soon we were both laughing. It was a great moment—especially when she then announced, "Looks like your pocket will have to serve as my purse tonight."

Imagine, Rosalee on my arm and her lipstick in my pocket!

It just goes to show that you can never really predict how everything is going to turn out, even when you've planned things down to the last detail. Certainly my evening with Rosalee didn't play out the way I expected. But for an evening that began with a series of disastrous moments, looking back on it, things weren't nearly as "Titanic" as they seemed at the time. In fact, in a way the purse ordeal was an ice-breaker, paving the way for a relaxed and fun-filled evening. Maybe what they say about being able to see the humor in a situation, to laugh at ourselves and not take ourselves too seriously can be a good thing. I know Rosalee and I had such a good time all evening. I especially liked the times she reached her lovely hand into my pocket for her lipstick!

Rosalee and I dated for four weeks, the sweetest weeks I've ever known. Then she decided to go steady with another guy she had also been seeing. That's the bad news. The good news is that I've had some really great dates with some very wonderful girls since then. And, I haven't sat on any date's purse ever again!

Tony Johnson, 17

If *You* Want to Date My Daughter . . .

I go to a small school in a small town. There are only about ninety kids in my class, so just about everyone gets asked out. Almost all of my friends have someone with whom they are going "steady." It's just how things work around here: You always have a date. Except me. Even by the end of tenth grade, I still hadn't been on a date. Not even to the prom—and that's a bad sign. It means you are really unpopular, or worse, a nerd. Nor did I have a date in the summer between my tenth and eleventh year. So when eleventh grade got swinging, for most events—dances, class plays, sports games at night and all the other stuff—I'd find myself tagging along with a couple of friends in the same boat as I was—dateless. We played it off pretty well, like we wanted it that way, but believe me, it was not the original plan. And then one glorious day, things changed. I met Jeremy Knight!

Jeremy is cute. He's smart. And, he wasn't even going with anyone. Three out of three! Imagine that. So when I was finally asked out—and by Jeremy Knight!—I was ecstatic!

Jeremy asked if I would go to Homecoming with him, an event that is a *really* big deal at my school. Homecoming is an all-afternoon and late-evening affair, starting off with a school assembly and the crowning of a king and queen, and then the parade and floats down through the town, followed by the big football game, and then a school dance afterwards. I told my parents that Jeremy Knight had asked me to attend the evening football game and the dance afterwards with him, and asked for their permission to stay out until 1:30 A.M., which is about the time the dance ends. They said yes! I thought I'd "died and gone to heaven!" Homecoming, and I had a date—my *first* date! Suddenly everything about my life seemed perfect.

Going out on a date was about the most important thing in the world to me, and I wanted everything to go just right. So when the day of my first date arrived, you can just imagine how nervous I was—and how nervous I stayed all the way up until my date arrived. When Jeremy came to the door, my father, just out of the fields (he farms), stood there beside me to meet him—with his boots and cap still on! My father is a handsome man, and when he cleans up he's really nice-looking. But just out of the fields, well, let's just say he looked a little rough. Not that this bothered my father. He greeted Jeremy at the door, asked him to step up into the kitchen, pulled out a chair, and then directed him to sit down. I quickly opened the refrigerator and retrieved the mum boutonniere (dyed and sprayed in our school colors) I had gotten for Jeremy to wear. As I did this, Jeremy and my father exchanged a few words between them, but I couldn't hear what was said. Then, my father handed Jeremy a piece of paper and a pencil and said, "Well, I'll need a little information, then." I just about died! Was my poor date being pressured to fill out information for my father about where we were going? Knowing my Dad, he probably wanted the phone number and address of where we'd be every step of the way.

I thought Jeremy looked a bit tense and decided my standing there was making him even more nervous. So I excused myself, telling him I needed to go upstairs for a minute, but I'd be right back. I paced in front of the mirror to calm myself down, hoping and praying that after this, Jeremy would even want to ask me out again. I'd wanted a date for so long, and now my dad was ruining it all for me. I stayed in my room several minutes so poor Jeremy wouldn't have to be grilled by my father in front of me. Feeling I'd given poor Jeremy sufficient time to provide a detailed list of our activities, I went back downstairs to rescue him. Needless to say, he was relieved I had returned. We left as quickly as we could.

I wasn't necessarily surprised that Jeremy was a little reserved for the rest of our date. I chalked it up to his tête-à-tête with my father. So I was extra nice to him, which wasn't hard; I was already ga-ga over Jeremy—and hoping he'd ask me out again, especially after the fiasco of meeting up with my father.

All my wishful thinking paid off. After a great first date, Jeremy asked if I would go to the movies with him the following weekend.

When Jeremy came to pick me up for our second date, I saw him hand my father fifty dollars. I was surprised—and also relieved! So that was it. Jeremy had probably forgotten his money on our first date and had to ask my father if he could borrow some. Now, he was paying my father back. My father had no doubt asked for an IOU. That would be fair; I could see why my father asked him for information. Not wanting to embarrass Jeremy, I didn't question him about the money I saw him hand my father.

Well, I'm pleased to report that Jeremy and I continued dating! But seven months later, I learned my assumption about the fifty dollars was wrong! I was over at Jeremy's house for a Sunday evening dinner when I discovered what really happened that first night in the kitchen between Jeremy and my father. Just as Jeremy and I were getting up to help his mother clear the table, Jeremy's mother remarked, "Thank you, but don't worry about these, I'll get them. You need to get going so Rachel won't be home too late." To this Jeremy's father chuckled and added, "Yeah, or you'll be out the fifty dollars from Mr. Burres." All of them laughed, including Jeremy. I found the comment odd, so when I got to the car, I asked Jeremy, "What did your father mean, 'out fifty dollars'?"

"Oh, it's an agreement I have with your father," Jeremy replied.

"An agreement you have with my father?" I questioned. "What sort of an agreement?"

"A deposit," he answered. "A fifty-dollar deposit."

"A deposit for what?" I asked, completely baffled.

"It went with the application," Jeremy explained good-naturedly.

Feeling even more confused, I prodded, "The application?"

"Yes, the application to date you," Jeremy said matter-of-factly and then asked, "You mean you haven't seen it?"

"No!" I replied, at the same time reminding myself to breathe.

"Not ever?" Jeremy asked, laughing.

"Do you mean to tell me that my father made you fill out an application to date me?" I gasped, wishing I could disappear into the biggest black hole in the universe. "I can't believe you ever asked me out again!"

"At first I thought your father was a little weird," Jeremy admitted. Then he added, "But then I thought it was refreshing to see that there were other parents who checked up on their kids as much as my parents look out for me. It's not so bad, you know. In fact, it's made me think of you as someone very special. When I date you, I'm asking out someone who is very loved and important to someone other than me—like her family."

"But even your parents know about it! How embarrassing!" I groaned.

"To tell you the truth, it's been the reason my parents allow me to go places with you during the week and not just on weekend dates," Jeremy explained, not at all deterred by the chain of events. "My mom and dad had questions about you because you'd just made cheerleader, and they worried you might run with a fast crowd or something. After they saw that your father wanted to know who I was, and who *they* were—hence the application—they were much more relaxed about me going out with you. They said that any parents who had 'guidelines' for someone dating their daughter were serious about their daughter's well-being and she must be well-raised. It was very reassuring to them. And, they were comfortable knowing their son had to honor a girl and her family in this way. That's what my having to fill out *the application* meant to them."

So that explained the money I'd once seen Jeremy give my father. Even though I was relieved that Jeremy was okay about "the application," the second I got home, I marched right into the house and asked my dad to show it to me. "Sure, honey," he said, going into the living room and returning with it. Looking it over, I asked, "Are you serious about this, Dad?"

"Absolutely," he said, smiling. "I consider it a binding agreement, one that works quite well, I might add."

I kid you not! Here is the application Jeremy filled out for my father:

Application to Date <u>MY</u> Daughter

Name: *Knight*   *Jeremy*   *M.*   *17*
            Last   First   Middle Initial   Age

Address: *Eagle Grove*   *IA*   *Earth*
            City   State   Planet

Religion: *Christianity* Church: *Grace Evangelical Free Church*

# of times attended last year: *Every Sunday*

Your Family Information:

Father's Name: *Carl Knight*   # of marriages: *1*   # of years: *20*

Address: *909 NW 8th Street*   Aliases?: *none*

Mother's Name: *JoAnn Knight*   # of marriages: *1*   # of years: *20*

Address: *909 NW 8th Street*   Aliases?: *none*

1. Do you own or drive a van? Yes/<u>No</u> (If "yes" discontinue filling out form.)
2. What is my daughter's name? *Rachel.*
3. Who, besides God, should you fear most? *Mr. Mark Burres.*
4. Do you have medical coverage? <u>Yes</u>/No
5. Does your underwear have pictures or words on the outside? Yes/ <u>No</u>

Application to Date <u>MY</u> Daughter (continued)

6. Do you promise to take a shower, shave, use deodorant, comb your hair, brush your teeth and put on a clean shirt before you spend time with my daughter? <u>Yes</u>/No

7. In 20 words or less, explain what the word "NO!" means to you: *Something that should be stopped immediately.*

8. In 20 words or less, explain what the word "LATE" means to you: *Getting my date home past the time specified by her parents.*

9. Where would you least like to be shot? *In the butt.*

10. Which is the last bone you want broken? *My kneecaps.*

11. What do you want to be when you grow up? *Teacher or sports agent.*

12. Please complete this sentence: A woman's place is: *On a pedestal.*

13. Do you plan to be buried or cremated? <u>Buried</u>/Cremated

References from last three girls dated:

Father's Name:	Daughter's Name:	Phone:	Reason Relationship Ended:
1. *N/A*			
2. *N/A*			
3. *N/A*			

Rachel is the first girl that I've dated.

Special Notice: There will be a $50 deposit when you pick up my daughter. If you are more than 1 minute late, the deposit will be forfeited. If you are more than 30 minutes late, refer to question #13 above.

Of course, I was flabbergasted that my dad would go so far as to ask for written information, but I am the youngest of four children and I always heard him say, "When Rachel starts dating, I'm going to be more strict than I was with the other kids." I thought, *Oh, great! Just what I need.* Even so, the application turned out to be so much more than a first-date nightmare. What started out as a binding agreement, turned into a binding friendship—for Jeremy and my father and for Jeremy's family and my own.

Most important of all, it turned into a binding friendship for Jeremy and me!

Rachel Burres, 18

The Undertoad

Undaunted as a child was I,
   who had no fear of scary things,
   no gremlins, trolls, Grinches, moles,
   nor blackened leathery wings.
'Twas I who fought the bullies back
   and laughed away bad dreams,
'Twas I who stood and faced the night
   amidst the witches' screams.

Who else but I chased vicious dogs,
   with no fear of being bit,
and challenged all who dared to taunt
   with not more than guts and wit.
'Twas I who braved the blood and pain
   when came the time to lose a tooth,
Simply tied the string and pulled
   when ol' bicuspid grew too "looth."

Invincible, I bravely stood
   facing every dark and evil wind,
and all those slimy slithery things
   could not my courage bend.
'Twas I who spent my youth
   in this courageous, fearless place
Until that time when I met fear
   close up and face to face!

'Twas not the bully on the beach
   who pounded me with sand,
who tried to take away my breath
   and take me from this land.

Who pulled and sucked my flailing arms
    'til I thought that I might die,
And dunked my head beneath the surf
    and drowned my every cry.

So seductive was the lure—
    so gentle and sedate,
I never felt in jeopardy—
    until it was too late.
I was gone! Doomed! No return!
    I knew the end was near,
A watery grave would soon be mine—
    now this was *worse* than fear!

Then . . . strong arms reached out
    from a weathered, sunburned man,
Coughing, sputtering, I grabbed on for life
    to his strong and meaty hand.
He pulled me out and dragged me back,
    then warned me with forebode:
"If ever you should swim this place—
    BEWARE THE UNDERTOAD!"

The UNDERTOAD! "Oh no!" I cried,
    such horror I did have,
"Why has no one ever told me of this monster,
    so irate and fuming mad?"
I had felt his strength, had felt his will,
    'twas I he'd come to reap,
Had I but known of UNDERTOAD!
    "Save me!" I screamed, then began to weep.

But since that time I've learned the name
   of this gruesome, fearsome dread,
"Ha-ha! Foolish boy!" my friends all teased
   then sneered,
   "It's not undertoad but *undertow* instead!"
Still, late at night when ghoul things fright,
   and all dark things do bode,
I sometimes feel a freaky shiver thinking
   of that slimy slither sinister UNDERTOAD.

David Kirk, 15

The (Missing) Cotton Ball

Our school's Winter Ball was held this year at a local hotel. The hotel is really classy and the ball is always the most important social event of the school year. More than anything else in the world I wanted to go, *and* I was in love for the first time. I mean the run-into-the-door, forget-how-to-talk, drool-on-yourself love, and I wanted this first love to be my date for the ball. Her name is Marissa Benson and she is a very special girl, very quiet, very pretty, just really totally special. When I asked her to go with me and she said yes, I was over-the-moon ecstatic. Since I don't drive yet, we made plans to have our parents take us to the hotel, and we would meet there.

On the night of the dance, Marissa's parents brought her to the hotel where I was anxiously waiting in the lobby to escort her into the dance. When she came in, I took her coat and checked it, and then turned back around to look at her. She looked beautiful, dressed for the holiday in a red velvet dress with a Christmas-like design. It was hard for me to take my eyes off her face, because she just sparkled. Maybe she was wearing makeup for the first time—I don't know. I just know she was great to look at.

When we got inside, we met a few friends and were standing around talking, when the DJ played a song I really like. It was a slow song, too. Here was my chance to dance with Marissa Benson and hold her in my arms. My heart racing, I asked, "Would you like to dance?" And Marissa smiled and shyly answered, "Sure."

Out on the darkened dance floor, I took Marissa in my arms. It was heaven. Then, with my arms held gently on her back, we danced. As I pulled her closer, I felt something stuck to the back of her beautiful, red velvet dress. It felt like a cotton ball. Certain she'd be embarrassed if she knew she had a cotton ball stuck there that way—I know I'd be embarrassed if I had a ball of cotton stuck to the back of my jacket like I was the Easter Bunny or something—I tried to pull the cotton ball off. It was really stuck on tight. I decided it must be caught in her zipper, gave it a sly yank and it came off in my hand. Then I went back to enjoying holding Marissa. When the music ended and we made our way off the dance floor, I slipped the cotton ball into my pocket.

Halfway through the evening, Marissa and I walked out in the lobby to get some fresh air. As we stood talking, Candy Holden, a friend of Marissa's, came up to her and said, "Isn't your dress just adorable! Look at Santa!" That's when I realized the Christmas-like design I'd barely noticed earlier was a sequined appliqué of Santa Claus. His cap wrapped around the side of Marissa's dress. I fingered the cotton ball in my pocket and realized what it really was: I'd torn off the cotton puff at the end of Santa's cap on the back of her dress!

"Let's go back in," I suddenly coaxed, putting one hand on Marissa's back to cover the spot where the cotton ball should've been. The rest of the night was spent trying to think of a way to get the cotton ball to somehow reattach itself back on her dress (which it never did); it was difficult since it wasn't like it was Velcro or anything. So I did the next best thing: I danced with her to every single song, even the tunes I didn't like, even when I was so hot from dancing in my tux I thought I'd drop from heat exhaustion. Luckily, though, I managed to hide that empty spot from anyone who might report on the absence of the ball at the end of Santa's cap.

Well, I know it was wrong of me not to tell her what I'd done, but I just couldn't bring myself to do it (although I am still trying to figure out a way to get the puff ball back to her). While I did get my wish to dance every dance with my new love, I vow not to go ripping things off my dates' clothes, as well as to fess up when I mess up. It's simply way too stressful not to. Besides, as much as I like to dance, sometimes you do need a breather, most especially when you're dancing with a girl like Marissa— and wearing a three-piece tux!

Niles Lyton, 15

Sure, I Can Go Out with You . . .

My sister's very best friend, Katie, got engaged. I really like Katie. So when my sister, Renee, asked me if I wanted to attend the party Katie was having to celebrate her engagement, I immediately said, Yes! I'm up for almost any party—especially one my sister's going to. Renee is four years older than I am, and I've always looked up to her. Even though she moved out of the house two years ago, we're still really close. I've even gotten to be friends with a couple of her friends. We don't go places together or anything like that, but we always talk. I felt really cool to be going to one of "their" parties.

The night of the engagement party, I went all-out getting dressed. I wore my new long, floral skirt—which I bought just for the occasion. It had a slit on the sides of both legs that was stylish and sexy. To this I added a tank top that was just barely on the right side of not-too-revealing to get me out of the house without my parents telling me to go upstairs and put something else on. I spent more than a full hour styling my hair, and applying and reapplying my makeup so that I looked perfect—and a bit older, which was my goal. When Renee picked me up, she took one look at me, and with raised eyebrows, nodded and delivered the magic words: "You look *really* great!" Well, after that compliment from my big sister, I was feeling pretty great, too.

Between Katie's friends and family and her fiancé's friends and family, the engagement party was huge. It included all sorts of different people. A late-afternoon to early-evening affair, the catered event was in full swing when we arrived. The band playing on a side patio had a steady stream of couples dancing in the small open area in front of them. Other clusters of sophisticated-looking people stood around holding plates of food, which they nibbled on as they laughed and chatted. In the beginning, I pretty much just followed Renee around, and tried to look like I knew what I was doing. But in no time, Renee was busy with her friends, and I was beginning to feel a little uneasy—and alone.

I got a plate of food and then looked around the crowd hoping to spot my sister at a table so I could join her. She was nowhere to be found. So, I walked over to the pool area and sat down in one of the empty chairs. Checking just one more time for my sister, as I looked around, I saw the most gorgeous guy in the entire universe looking straight at me. I double-checked to make certain it was really me he was looking at. It was. And he was smiling at me too! I glanced his way again. This time I smiled back at him, at which point he made his way over and sat next to me there in a patio chair. He was even better looking up close. His dreamy hazel eyes, framed in thick black eyelashes, gazed straight into mine, and he said in an easy, friendly style, "Hi, my name is Mark Stevens." With cool self-assurance, he held out his hand. Trying to match his worldly manner, I reached up my own hand to shake his. Wondering whether I should say something or continue chewing the food in my mouth so that I could, I did both. "I'm Bridgette Bradley," I said with a mouth half-full of food—and a stomach exploding with butterflies from his warm hand touching—and lingering—on mine. I was very nervous, and desperately trying to imagine what my sister and Katie would do in this situation. Luckily, the man who looked to be straight from the pages of GQ took over. Poised and confident, he asked coolly, "So, how are you related to the couple, Bridgette?"

"I'm a friend of Katie's," I replied.

"Ah," he nodded, "I'm a friend of Jack's." He was quiet for a minute and seemed perfectly at ease with the silence. Then, pointing in the direction of the house he commented, "Great architecture, isn't it!"

"Yes," I replied. "I especially love the arches," I added, hoping that's what they were called.

"Yes, very powerful," he confirmed. "And elegant."

Bolstered by the seeming ease of our conversation, I chimed in with, "The lines are really commanding." I had no idea where these words came from, but you can bet I was pleased with myself, especially when he followed with, "That's for sure. Have you seen the foyer yet? It's *really* decorative."

"Yes, the marble is so cool . . ." I began and then quickly decided that didn't sound very sophisticated so I improvised, "It's probably *imported*." My remark seemed to impress him. (It certainly impressed me!)

"You're right. I wonder where it's from? It looks a little bit like the marble in my brother's house, and he had to special-order it from Italy." Now I was feeling a new surge of confidence at his approval of my fine eye and worldly sophistication. Luckily, there was no more discussion on the "architecture" of the house, and our conversation moved on to music. "Calypso isn't necessarily my favorite music, but this band is really good, isn't it?" he remarked. Until he mentioned it, I hadn't been certain "Calypso" was what the band was playing, but I didn't give that away. "Ummhmm," I agreed, "they're very good." Then, I coolly asked, "So what kind of music is your favorite?" I'm not ashamed to boast that Mark Stevens was hanging on my every word! This was the best party ever! "Oh, it varies," he responded, "I even like the mellow kind that's easy to relax to." Gaining more confidence by the minute, I now spoke with an easy flow and with a confidence I believed in. "I think schools should play music in the classroom so students can relax!" I quipped. With my words, a slow shadow of concern passed over the guy's face, and he asked, "How old are you?"

"I'm twenty," I replied, the lie slipping from my lips as easily and smoothly as when I announced my real name. Then, feeling a little guilty over my tall tale, I quickly asked, "How about you?" It was all my brain could come up with, while at the same time wondering if maybe I should've said I was twenty-one.

Mark looked relieved; I *felt* relieved! "I'm twenty-nine," he answered. "I'll be thirty next month." Still looking interested in talking with me, the man who was already fourteen years old when I was born then said, "I have to leave early to go to a ball game with a friend." As if to convince me this was really true, he explained, "We've had the tickets for months." Since this dream of a man looked really bummed about having to leave my ever-so-mesmerizing and magnetic company, I decided he was probably telling the truth and he believed that I was twenty. His next words confirmed it: "I'd love to go out sometime. Would you like to go to dinner and a movie next weekend?"

Though startled, I answered calmly, "Sure." Mark Stevens seemed very happy with my reply and then asked for my phone number. "Oh, I'm getting a new one," I blurted, "so if you give me yours, I'll call you with my new number in the next day or two." Again I impressed myself with my quick reply—even if I was digging myself into a hole that I didn't for the life of me know how I'd get out of. Mark wrote his phone number on a party napkin, handed it to me and after saying some good-byes as he passed through the crowd, left the party.

Just how I'd get a guy fourteen years older than me past my parents remained a mystery to me—one I was unprepared to ponder at the moment. But I was determined to go out on a date with Mark Stevens. I just needed to find a way to do that—something I managed to accomplish in my dreams all that night, where I saw the two of us going to dances, movies, dinners, the prom. By morning I was going steady with marvelous Mark Stevens!

Reality set in the next day. How exactly would I engineer going out on a date with a middle-aged man? My parents didn't let me date anyone older than eighteen.

I called my best friend, Allie, and told her all about my problem. We spent nearly all of Sunday afternoon formulating plots on how I could get away with going out with Mark. But after several hours, we still hadn't come up with a plan—or at least any that didn't involve deception and breaking any number of "grounds for serious grounding" rules. So when my parents told me it was time to get off the phone, Allie and I agreed to get to school a few minutes early on Monday so we could continue scheming how I could get together with handsome, hazel-eyed Mark Stevens.

The time Allie and I had before class was not enough to produce a satisfactory plan to get me out of the house on Saturday night. So my friend and I agreed we'd pick up where we left off during third period, a class we had together.

As I arrived for my third-hour class, I noticed everyone glancing at the note written on the blackboard. *I will be attending a conference today so you will have a substitute teacher. See you tomorrow, Mrs. Delancy.* "Wonderful," I thought. "Now Allie and I can do some serious note-passing and finally resolve my dilemma."

But it was not to be. I had no more than sat down when the substitute teacher came striding into the classroom. Going straight to the blackboard, he wrote his name on the board, underlining it twice: "Mr. Stevens." Well, I guess I don't have to tell you that my heart plummeted, and worse, like a deer frozen in headlights, I sat stock-still, horrified, staring at *"Mr.* Stevens." Turning to face the class, *Mr. Stevens*—the love of my life—announced, "I'm your substitute teacher for the day!"

As quickly as I could, I moved far to the right of my seat in an attempt to hide behind Tommy Kinder, the boy who sat in front of me. Slouching down in my chair, I reached into my backpack, fetched my sunglasses, slipped them on and tried to cover my face with my hair. Maybe, just maybe, I'd get lucky and my would-be Saturday-night date wouldn't notice me. How could anything be worse than this? I hadn't even formulated my plan, and already it had been slammed with bad timing!

Sitting there, with my heart racing and my cheeks burning, I got an almost immediate answer to how things could get worse: "Mr." Stevens picked up a pile of papers and announced, "Come get your paper as I call out your name. Mr. Uecker." Paul immediately jumped out of his seat and headed up to get his paper. "Ms. Edwards," he called next, handing Joanne Edwards her paper. The gorgeous substitute teacher was halfway through the stack when he hesitated, and enunciated slowly—so very slowly—"Ms. Bridgette Bradley." With these words he looked curiously up and down each row until finally—and probably because every kid in the class was by now looking in my direction—smiled coyly and directed, "Please come up and get your paper."

I cannot tell you how sickened I felt at having to walk toward him. My lovely *not-a-chance-date* looked at me, still with that smile and then said, "Please, take off your sunglasses, Ms. Bradley. While a lot of things have come to light, it's still not bright enough to require wearing sunglasses in the classroom. And you know, I think you had a good idea about schools playing music in the classroom for reducing stress."

Needless to say, there was no date with Mark Stevens.

This incident happened nearly one and a half years ago (I'm going to be eighteen in a few months). While it was anything but funny at the time, I do look back and laugh now. While telling a tale as tall as trying to pass yourself off for twenty when you are sixteen (and I was a young-looking sixteen!)—and knowingly accepting a date with someone who is nearly thirty—is probably more than a bad idea, I do look back and laugh at the odds of Mark Stevens showing up in my classroom that fateful Monday after Katie's engagement party. Of course, it was probably for the best. No telling how long I'd be grounded for conning my parents had I gotten caught—and Mark would have eventually found out that I was only sixteen and it's doubtful if he'd see it as anything other than dishonest, and I'm sure that would have ended his interest in me. So there was no way to pull this off really—though his showing up in my classroom did resolve my immediate problem of finding a way to go out with him!

It was all pretty humiliating at the time, though now every time Allie and I go back over the whole thing, we end up laughing. Every time we tell the story to someone, the story gets better and better, probably because we've embellished it so much! Every time the story gets jazzed up a bit, it's even funnier to tell my friends. As for my parents, I'm waiting until I'm out of the house to break it to them!

Bridgette Bradley, 18—almost

Bernie Couldn't Stand Snakes

A couple of months ago, Bernie Dawson, an older kid who lives next door to me, threw a cricket down the back of my shirt when we were sitting on the steps eating a sandwich. That night at dinner I told my big brother, Brent, about it. "We'll get him back for it!" he said. And then we came up with a plan to do just that!

We knew Bernie was scared of snakes (Brent and I had no problem with them). So Brent and I went to a canyon that isn't more than a mile away from our house and caught two small grass snakes (they're harmless little reptiles) and brought them back to our house. We knew we'd see Bernie the next day, Sunday, because we have a large-screen TV and Bernie likes to watch his favorite football team—the Dallas Cowboys—on the big screen.

Sure enough, the next day Bernie called and asked if he could come over and watch the Cowboys on our TV. "Sure," we told him, "c'mon over." Then, my brother Brent and I went to work putting our plan in place!

When Bernie got there, we just hung out and acted like everything was normal—although every once in a while Brent would look at me and we'd have to hold back our smiles. Bernie sat where he usually does, in the big overstuffed chair, the one with several big throw pillows. He liked to throw the pillows at the screen when one of his favorite players made a bad play—which happened this day, too. But this time, as Bernie grabbed one of the pillows, just as he was about to throw it, he noticed the snake now dangling from the pillow. And in that same instant, the little reptile dropped into his lap, where to his horror yet another little snake was making his way across his leg. Bernie let out a blood-curdling sound and jumped ten feet off the couch! He ran out of our house so fast! Brent and I nearly died laughing—as we still do whenever either of us brings it up.

That afternoon we took the sweet, harmless little creatures back to the canyon and let them go. Their work was done.

Marty LeBauer, 14

"Carl-Cool"

Last year when I was sixteen, getting my driver's license was my major goal in life. My parents had promised that when I got my license—and depending on my getting good grades—I could use the family car once a week and maybe, even more . . . *depending*. You know how parents are about it when they realize they've found something that will motivate you to do just about anything—most especially studying.

Needless to say, I was looking forward to using the car! After all, driving is a real status thing. It means you aren't a kid anymore, but even more than that, when you have a car, it's like instant friends. Everyone wants to hang around with you if you have a car! Especially girls. Nothing improves your popularity like having wheels.

"Carl, I need to go pick up your sister and little brother from school," my mother said to me one day. "Do you want to come along and drive?" Of course, I jumped at the chance. One thing hardly anybody thinks about is how much practice it takes to learn to drive, and I was absolutely intent on acing my behind-the-wheel driving test so I could get my license. I would go to any lengths to practice, including driving in public with my mom, my ten-year-old sister, Cheryl, and my six-year-old brother, Tommy—even in broad daylight.

Well, we had just picked up my sister and brother from their elementary school, which isn't all that far away from my high school. Pulling away from the school, I spotted Myra Mitchell, Kylie Litton and Natalie Andrews standing on the sidewalk near my next turn. (Myra, Kylie and Natalie are about the three most popular girls in my school, and I had been wanting to ask Myra out for months—and was just waiting until I had my license.) I was pretty sure the three girls hadn't seen me, but I couldn't take a chance. Even though I had my mom, my brother and sister in the car, I figured I could still salvage the moment by looking suave and confident—like I chauffeured the family around all the time, being that I was such a good guy and all. "Everyone just sit back and be cool," I warned. Then, riding low in my seat, head tossed back, looking slick and relaxed, I glided past Myra, Natalie and Kylie, casting a casual wave in their direction.

Looking over my shoulder to see if they had noticed me, I spotted my ratty little brother, his head out the window, one hand waving at the girls (probably because I had) and with the other hand merrily picking his nose. I was simply horrified! "Get your hand out of your nose and your head back in the window!" I warned, absolutely aghast, and reached behind me to pull him away from the window and back down in the seat. Now, you have to remember that I was just getting the hang of driving. I mean, it's not like I was all that experienced. Suddenly, I heard my mom's sudden sharp inhale! I glanced over at her bulging eyes, just as the car first knocked into, and then bounded up and over, the corner of the curb, before landing with a thud on the street again—causing me, my mother, my brother and my sister all to bounce up off our seats and toward the ceiling of the car before landing in our seats. Screams from my little sister filled the air, and my little brother was yelling, "Cool! Do it again, Carl! Do it again, Carl! Cool, waaaay cool!"

Realizing that at least we hadn't crashed into another motorist, I breathed a sigh of relief—until I heard the sound of both hubcaps on the passenger side clattering away. I looked in the side-view mirror in time to see them rolling down the street—and to see Myra, Natalie and Kylie watch their wild spinning escape! The girls were no longer on the curb: All three were scampering as fast as they could up to the shoulder of the hill, obviously scared out of their minds that the out-of-control hubcaps might jump the curb, bounce in their direction, and no doubt kill them!

I was humiliated beyond words—while my brother and sister

were laughing uncontrollably. My mother looked around and, after assessing the whole thing, joined in the laughter, too. So incredibly embarrassed, I put both hands on the wheel and peeled away, turning down the first street I could so as to leave this untimely and unfortunate scene. My life was ruined. For sure, Myra Mitchell would never, ever, ever want to go out with me. "Stop!" my mother shouted. "We have to get my hubcaps!"

"No way, Mom," I pleaded. "Do you know who those girls were? The most popular—and gabby—girls in the entire school, that's who. And they're sure to tell everyone about this. Oh, no. I'm not stopping. I'm getting out of here as quick as I can."

"I don't care who they were, I've got to get my hubcaps," my mother protested. "Besides being dangerous laying in the street, someone may steal them."

"Mom, *please*. You've got to understand," I implored. "I'll take the garbage to the curb for the next month if you just let me save face. Pleeeeease let me drive out of sight, and then I'll get out of the car and you can go and get your hubcaps and you can come back and pick me up. There's no way I can let Myra Mitchell see me. Please, Mom?" I begged.

"Okay," she laughed, "Pull over here and get out so I can go get the hubcaps. Stay put, and I'll be back to get you!"

Mom did find both of the hubcaps. I put them on for her later that night. The next morning when my mom went to get in her car, she found both the tires on the side that had hit the curb were flat! The impact had broken off their stem valves.

With only one spare tire, I had to walk to school.

As I was nearing the school—on foot—a car passed me, slowed, and then stopped and backed up to me. I might have known it was Myra, Natalie and Kylie! Natalie was driving. "Hey, Carl-Cool!" Myra taunted. "Want a ride? C'mon, get in, Carl-Cool." Teasing or not, I wanted to sit next to Myra Mitchell, so I got in. "We'd let you drive except that it's National

Save-a-Life week and the safest place for you is in the back seat, not in the driver's seat!" she teased.

"Speaking of Save-a-Life Week," Natalie said, "should we ask Carl-Cool if he wants to go with us to Greg's get-together on Sunday afternoon?"

"Oh yeah, come with us," Myra coaxed. "Bobby Rydel and Brad Elkin are coming along. We need another guy."

Just like that. Well, you could have bowled me over with a lot less than a runaway hubcap. There I was, sitting in the back seat with Myra Mitchell, and less than twelve hours after I'd made a spectacle of myself. "Sure," I said, hardly able to believe my good fortune of not only sitting next to Myra Mitchell but being asked to get together with her and her friends. "Good, but I'm driving," she laughed. "And speaking of driving, maybe I can give you a lesson or two about how to keep your wheels on the street, and off the curbs. Would you like that, Carl-Cool?"

"No problem," I replied, not even bothered by her teasing.

And that's how I got the name "Carl-Cool." But I also got the girl! Who cares if she calls me Carl-Cool for the rest of my life! Not only was I going to be with Myra, but she was going to teach me to drive. Even with my sixteenth birthday five months away, suddenly, I was in no hurry to learn to drive. Sitting this close to Myra Mitchell, I was quite sure it might even take longer than five months to learn!

Carl Joseph, 17

"Where's My Girl?"

I was at a restaurant sitting at a table fairly close to the hostess stand, when a hip and terrific-looking couple came in. The young man gestured to his girl that he wanted to take her coat. Slipping out of her coat, she handed it to him, so he could hang it on the coat rack behind him. Looking very happy, he turned around to do just that and, in that same instant, the girl, who obviously hadn't seen that there were steps in front of her, promptly fell down the stairwell. She grabbed for the railing, and hung on for dear life, but even so, she bounced and tumbled and slid down the stairs, crashing in a heap at the bottom. Oblivious to all this, the guy turned back around from hanging up the coat and looked startled by her absence.

Unaware that his lady now lay at the bottom of the stairs, he looked around, bewildered that she had "evaporated" so suddenly. He gazed to the right, and then to the left, eyeing the bar area. Looking self-conscious, he headed to the bar and sat down, perhaps thinking his girl went to the bathroom. Still searching the room, you could see that he was baffled, wondering how the girl got away so fast without his knowing it. In the meantime, the girl, now laying at the base of the stairwell, was wondering how she could get up gracefully in the long tight dress she was wearing, and how she'd retrieve her heels, one of which lay on the first step and the other on the third step. Meanwhile, the hostess was aghast that the woman had fallen. Rushing down the steps to help her, she glared in the direction of the unwitting man when she saw that he had nonchalantly "left the scene of the accident."

Between the man's confusion, the slapstick sight of the woman's completely unexpected tumble, and the hostess's misplaced indignation, it would've been impossible not to laugh. The scene unfolded in such split-second timing, it was hilarious—even though it wouldn't have been so funny if the woman had really been hurt.

But it didn't end there. While I started out trying to stifle a giggle, the woman on my right, because she was trying to control her laughter, "snorted." I mean, it was a weird and totally strange sound. Because of it, the more I tried not to laugh, the harder I laughed. Pretty soon, I was laughing so hard that tears were streaming down my face, and the water I had just swallowed was fizzing out of my nose. Of course, the snorting woman—as well as my own laughter—drew the attention of everyone around us. You know how it is when you see one person dying of laughter and then you just can't help laughing, too? Well, it was like that. Now my date was laughing, too; then a person at the next table started laughing at me laughing, then another person at his table joined in. Before you knew it almost everyone around me was laughing—even though some of them didn't even know what I was laughing at in the first place!

Then, much like the girl's unsuspecting date, the waiter showed up with no clue what he was walking into. In the midst of all our gales of laughter, he stood somber in the middle of the room with all the tables around him and decided everyone must be laughing at him. Baffled, he immediately checked to see if his fly was zipped, then scurried out of the room. Knowing we'd all had a hand in his sudden flight, a whole new round of laughter broke out. Apparently the waiter sent the chef out. The chef looked every bit as confused by the laughter as the waiter had been and went to get the manager. Hustling into the room with the chef behind him, the manager searched all our laughing faces with suspicion, then leaned down and asked one of the customers what was going on. The woman tried to explain—but quickly realized she really didn't know how to. As she giggled between stammered phrases, the manager, breaking into a smile, just shook his head, threw up his hands as though he had been let in on a joke too funny to share, and broke out in laughter, too.

Luckily, the woman who had fallen was helped, and reunited with her date. Now I know exactly why they say about laughter being contagious. There was a major breakout of it that night.

Jennifer Leigh Youngs

Yes, Oh, Yes! Brandy Smith . . .

After school everyone walks down to our school's parking lot where parents pick up their kids and where most upper-classmen gather around their cars to talk and hang out. This is always the best time to be seen looking cool. And, of course, if you have a car, you stand outside the car, polishing its hood or whatever. I mean to tell you, it's a real deal to have a car!

Having a car was my goal since the first day of seventh grade, because I saw how all the kids gravitate to those who had wheels—especially the girls. Planning ahead, I had saved my money since that very day for the sole reason of owning a car. And every single birthday or Christmas or any other time I had a gift coming, I asked for money to put into what I referred to as "have money/have college" account—but secretly called "have car/have girls" account.

And that precious day arrived. I was the co-owner (the bank was also co-owner) of a 1992 Mustang with only 124,203 miles on it. The first day I saw that car—September 18th, to be exact—I promised myself I was going to make it mine. If a person could have a soul-car, this car would be mine. Shiny, sleek, and other than needing a new fan belt and a new muffler and an oil and lube job, four newer tires . . . and a new engine, it was in perfect condition from front fender to back bumper. This was the car of my dreams. Me and my beautiful cherry-red "have car/have girls" dream! I was stylin'!

So there I stood, on Wednesday, October 1, polishing a spot on the hood that looked like it just might've been smudged since the last time I'd polished the car (just that morning). It had been only the first day I'd driven it to school, but the word about another car in the parking lot was out. Standing there as the proud new owner, I was quite sure everyone's eyes had to be drawn to me and my gleaming new wheels. Best of all, Brandy Smith took notice! We'd known each other ever since we had

English together in our freshman year, but this was the first time her interest seemed more than just casual. "So, do you think he'd give me a ride?" she cooed, as she and a group of about a zillion girls were about to pass me while I was spit-shining a side-mirror on my car. She sidled up to the car and, glancing in the window, noted, "Oh, and you've got a great stereo system, too!" By now, practically all the kids were on their way out of school, and you should have seen the look on their faces when they saw Brandy Smith looking over my car. Talk about a stamp of approval! Thinking, "It doesn't get better than this," I replied as loud as I felt I could get away with, "I'd love to give you a ride, Brandy. Where to?"

"Sure," she agreed, acting cool like it was her idea. "I'd like to be chauffeured to the library."

"No problem!" I said, and then, acting like the cool guy I am, I took my time while opening the door for her, in case any of the kids just coming out of the school building hadn't noticed Brandy Smith standing next to me and my car. Pausing to make sure everyone could see me, I took my time letting her get in. Then, just to make sure everyone who hadn't already noticed *would*, I triggered the car alarm, and then quickly turned it off so as not to look like I didn't know what I was doing. Then, with everyone watching, I slammed the car door extra hard with a snappy flair! Jazzed, I then went around to my side of the door and, noticing Teddy Laird, a guy in my English class, I tried to waste a little more time by asking for his phone number so I could call him and compare notes on our English assignment. Like I would! Then, smiling with contentment, I opened my car door and got in. I was about to put the key in the ignition when I decided to drink in the sight of my Brandy's beautiful face one more time before we started out for our "cruise" around town. There she was, a look of stunned shock on her white-as-a-ghost face, big tears trickling down her porcelain cheeks.

She couldn't even speak. Yet though she didn't so much as mouth a word, the look in her large green eyes screamed of pain.

Her movements stiff and shaky, she raised her left hand and pointed to the passenger door—the door I had slammed shut extra hard with a snappy flair. Following her unspoken instructions, I looked in the direction she indicated. My mouth dropped open in horror as I saw what I had done. One of her graceful little fingers was caught in the car door! In a flash, I leaped from the car and ran around to open the passenger door and free her finger.

As it turned out, Brandy did get a spin in my new car that day—all the way to the emergency room. Slamming the door on Brandy's finger had not only bruised it, but broken it as well!

While there was absolutely nothing funny about Brandy's broken finger, my friends got a laugh out of me doing such a thing when I was trying to look so suave and cool. Even funnier than that, it was Brandy's middle finger. Those weeks her finger was in a splint, she looked like she was flipping everyone off any time she was holding anything in her hands—like her books, tennis racket, even a fork or spoon. The guys really thought that was funny. And of course, from time to time, the gesture was aimed at me. The good news is that Brandy saw the humor in it, too—at least she did after the bruises went away and the bone healed!

But the even better news is that we've been dating for over six months now! Brandy doesn't credit her attraction to me as being caused by the humor of that situation, nor does she say it's because I co-own a really cool car. Brandy said she decided I was a great guy when I rushed her to the hospital, full of apologies, and stayed by her side as they x-rayed and splinted her broken finger. She said if that hadn't already cinched it, my being there to open her locker, carry her books, take her to the doctor and do everything I could to help her when her finger was healing would've convinced her. As if anyone could have stopped me!

Christopher Collins, 18

D. Rodman—the Creature

Ms. Wiesman teaches math, and it's a really dull class. I'm not saying that to be mean. You can ask anyone in the school, and they will tell you that math is dull, dull, dull. Well, finally one day last March something happened to liven it up!

Ms. Wiesman was in the middle of taking apart an equation when Lisa Johnson, her eyes practically bugging out of her head and her mouth twisted like she was going to drop down and writhe with the creeps any minute, suddenly let out this blood-curdling scream.

"What?" shrieked Darcy Miller, who sits next to Lisa, no doubt scared out of her wits by Lisa's sudden outburst—as well as by the severity of her shrill. Whatever it was that caused Lisa's fear, it scared the "b'geezus" out of everyone in the classroom. You have to keep in mind that Lisa is a no-nonsense sort of girl, and known for her athletic prowess, so nothing much scares her. This made her screaming all the more out of character—and precisely why it now frightened everyone in the class. "Wha'd ya see? Wha'd ya see?" Karla Munce quizzed at the top of her voice.

"It's a reptile of some sort," screeched Alana Medlin. This was followed by, "There it is!" from Jessica Schultz who was reporting a supposed creature-sighting. "Over there!" Billy Minks yelled, all eyes turned to where he pointed. "No, over here," taunted Bobby Skeets, and as he wanted, all eyes instantly darted in the direction he pointed. "Where? What?" squealed Alesha Denton, now thrashing her way to the top of her chair. Panic began rippling throughout the entire classroom.

"I saw it! Omigosh! It's positively *huge!*" shouted Teresa Amos, at the top of her lungs. "Positively prehistoric!" Sheila Sams, the brain in the class, yelled. Well, that confirmed it and sealed the fate of the scare as being one of epidemic proportions.

The classroom was now in the midst of full-blown pandemonium. It was great!

Then, Penny Perkins—who had a clear view of the trash can—shouted, "It's heading to the trash can." And that's when the thrashing end of a scaly reptile's body fighting to madly slither behind the trash can came into full view. Well, that *really* did it! The classroom was even more alive and positively exploding with roaring excitement. At least half the girls in the class scurried up on their desks, and most all of the guys charged all at once toward the trash can, colliding in clumsy, laughing attempts to be the hero.

Chuck Halgrem, proving he was a real guy, hulked up to the trash can, and with his foot swaddled in high-top boots, edged the trash can a little, where the "huge reptile"—a six-inch alligator lizard—came into view. Desperate to get away, the little creature dashed frantically across the tiled floor of the classroom, looking for a place to hide. The girls who were already on their desks continued to scream in alarm, while a throng of other girls lifted their feet, all the while letting out high-pitched squeals of terror. Some of the guys lifted their feet, also, and, too macho to scream, they laughed instead, but for the most part they were as scared as the girls.

In a matter of mere seconds the dull math room flourished with first-class excitement. It was thrilling. But the funniest sight had to be in the front of the classroom. There, Ms. Wiesman was perched precariously in her heels on her desk chair with its roller wheels! One of her hands reached out to the blackboard to ensure her chair didn't roll away on her, and the other hand was held up to cover her mouth—perhaps to hold in her own screams. Being an adult and all, it seemed hilarious that she was as petrified as the kids were, especially by a lizard less than six inches long! All this took place lickety-split, just like the lizard's pace careening around the room, trailed by all the would-be heroes, who were now near hysterics.

After trying to outrun the swarm of aspiring captors, the poor, terrified lizard slowed momentarily to try and wriggle under a cupboard near my desk. Having sat quietly through all this myself, I calmly reached down and picked it up. "Don't you worry about a thing, Ms. Wiesman," I reassured the frightened teacher and my peers. "I'll take this life-threatening creature out of the classroom." From her four-legged wooden pedestal, Ms. Wiesman nodded without saying a word, and waved me on my way—without so much as a pass to give me Wilson-High legalized permission to go wherever it was I was supposed to be going.

Once out of the classroom, I stroked the little alligator lizard's head to calm him. My little pet, D. Rodman—who I'd taken to school to carry out this very scenario—had livened up an otherwise-dull class. (I'd named D. Rodman after Dennis, for his ability to add excitement to almost any situation.) I put D. Rodman back in my locker from whence he came and went back to the classroom. Though still full of murmurs and giggles, everyone had climbed off their desks, including Ms. Wiesman. As I took my seat, I stifled my own laughter and instead sighed with satisfaction. There's nothing more fun than livening up a boring classroom.

Jack Holmes, 15

Member of the Gang

"What a 'fraidy-cat," my sister, Judy, taunted. "All you have to do is run over there, pick it up and run back. How difficult can this be, for goodness sakes! I've shown you how to do it ten times now. It's simple, there's nothing to it, and besides, you know it's your turn. I've taken my turn four weeks in a row now, and since your birthday comes after mine, you have to go next. Besides," she added, resorting to scare tactics, "if you don't go, we are going to vote you out of the Gang!" Four younger club members looked first at their leader and then at me, no doubt thanking God that my birth had preceded theirs.

Being voted out of the club was definitely a legitimate threat! When you were on the outs with my older sister, you were in for some bad times. Judy had a knack for doling out stiff penalties; she was extraordinarily gifted at making alienation seem like a prison sentence. Besides that, I had just been granted some good-ies I didn't want taken away, so I was really at risk here. Hadn't she let me sit with her and her crowd this past Friday at school during lunch? Hadn't she let me read the note bad-girl Marilyn Johnson had written describing her date with Stuart Stockdale? And when Marilyn became upset because Judy showed me the letter, hadn't my sister admirably defended her actions by saying it was okay because I was her sister? Judy had even come to my rescue when Tommy James told everyone I had kissed him, an embarrassing and reputation-ruining lie. And she had sided with me against that smart-aleck Dennis Christiansen's brutal verbal assaults on the bus. This big arrogant bruiser had a pen-chant for teasing and name-calling. No doubt because he was a handsome guy with cool clothes, pumped-up muscles and a fast mouth, everyone at school both idolized and feared him. Except for my sister. It didn't matter that Dennis was older than my sis-ter; whatever Dennis alleged, Judy would dish back worse than what he offered up. My sister did not fear anyone!

No, I simply could not gamble with losing my sister's approval, no matter how scared I was at taking my turn in the activity at hand. I would do what I had to do. I was not about to chance being voted out of the club.

And so like any other young kid allowing herself to be coerced into subversive activity, the following Saturday I darted to the delivery truck some three hundred meters away. The goal was simple: Get to the van, grab one or more items, then dash back to the Gang's headquarters without getting caught! Some "grabbables" were more desirable than others, and most especially if Judy had a preference for them. Brach's butterscotch candies, for example, were worth two points, while just any bag of candy was worth one. And, the points varied between flavors. For instance, chocolate ice cream was worth three points, strawberry was worth two points and vanilla, only one point. For sugar-wafer cookies, the three-color flavor was worth five points, chocolate rated three points and vanilla was worth a lowly one point.

This game, the latest of many, was invented by my sister herself. "The objective," she would say, "is to show that you are worthy of being members." Judy hadn't yet learned about participatory management; her rule was somewhere between Eva Perón and Attila the Hun, her leadership style somewhere between dictatorship and sole proprietorship. She elected herself leader and appointed us members. Our motto, "We're not a club, we're a gang!" was made up by Judy and presented to us for a vote. That's just the way things worked. Judy decided on the activity we were going to get involved in and presented it to us for a vote. Of course, no alternatives were ever presented. We met every Sunday immediately following the ritual of Sunday school and the family noon feast and cleanup. Judy liked to keep these meetings short, so we dispensed with time-consuming things like asking questions and having discussions.

Judy's dictates were final. We five siblings were loyal subjects to our older sister.

Too frightened to actually step foot inside the truck (Judy was a very discriminating thief and would go inside and carefully select the goods that would qualify for her heist), and scared to death of getting caught red-handed, I stood outside the opened sliding door of the van, and with my eyes peeled in the direction of Great Auntie's house, grabbed the first thing that my hand touched. Feeling successful in my robbery, I ran back to the hideout where the rest of the posse awaited my return.

"Bread! No way! You dumb kid, you got a loaf of white bread," Judy laughed, holding it up for all to see. Her laughter stopped abruptly and with great scorn on her face she yelled, "What are we going to do with a loaf of bread?" Mocking my catch in front of the other members was definitely not very good for building self-esteem, but she wasn't into that sort of thing. I secretly wished I had been born first and then I could say these things to her and she would have to put up with it. Better yet, I wished I had been born an only child and I wouldn't have to play this nerve-wracking, heart-stopping game. As though I had not already been berated enough, she added, "Can't you do anything right? Get out there and do it right this time, you stupid fool." With that she opened the door to the pump shed, our sacred little hiding spot, and pushed me into the wide open yard. For added effect, she grabbed the door and slammed it shut behind me. She really had a way with drama.

Without questioning her authority, I darted back to the truck to make another hit. I had been both coached and warned that this had better be "successful." Knowing that the delivery man would be leaving Great Auntie's house at any minute, and even more fearful of getting caught, I once again kept my eyes peeled on the screen door to Great Auntie's house, still too frightened to actually enter the truck. I reached my hand into the truck, and flopping it around until I felt something that wasn't breadlike, grabbed it. Panting and with heart pounding, I ran with my new acquisition back to the hideout. Once more, I lay my catch before the gang's Queen.

"Good Lord!" my sister roared as she looked at what my heist had reaped. "Look what that idiot brought us this time!" She held up a plastic bag that contained a pair of yellow rubber gloves, the kind that, when I was a child, was mostly worn by fancy ladies on television when they were doing dishes. Like a good manager keeping track of our progress, Judy graphed and plotted the results of the trips to the delivery van on the badly worn sheet of paper tacked to the wall of the shed. In the column under my name she wrote, "dumb bread, stupid gloves."

"You are one dumb kid and useless to the club," she said, going for maximum embarrassment. She was a master at ridicule, too. Pausing just long enough to build suspense, she announced, "I say you're out!" She grabbed the bag of rubber gloves and flicked them over her shoulder, hitting Shep, the family dog and Gang's mascot, in the head. Shep had been lying in the corner, observing our every move, but always kept a trained eye on Judy. He, too, knew that whatever the next action was, it would be initiated by her.

"Hey, wait a minute!" I countered. "How was I supposed to know that truck carried something other than food? And didn't I prove that I took my turn? It's not fair that I'm out of the club. Let's vote on it." I looked to the other members, all younger than I, for support. Watching Judy's domination over me had given them a pretty good theoretical understanding of hierarchy, pecking order and other forms of oppression—at least enough to know they had little to no clout with this dominant force. Their eyes instantly turned from me to Judy. Perhaps swayed by the ballot of pity and distress on their faces, she voted on behalf of all of us and said, "Okay, you can stay in the club under one condition. You have to take another turn for the next two weeks, but you better do better. If you don't, you will be out for good!" My sentence had been levied; I had been found only *half* guilty.

And so began my membership in the Gang made up of six kids, all of us brothers and sisters. My older sister Judy had crowned herself Queen and King, all in one. Bold, gutsy and colorful, this budding teenager could and would take on many a challenge, from standing up to my father—the ultimate sign of omnipotence and machismo, to outfoxing old Mr. Samuels, the driver of the vending truck, whose fate it was on every Saturday to become an innocent victim to our Gang's holdup.

Great Auntie Hilda was another matter. She was my father's aunt. Her house sat about twenty rods from our home, both places nestled deep within forty acres of picturesque homestead. Hers was a majestic old mansion built in the mid-1800s, a house with nine bedrooms. Great Auntie had outlived her numerous brothers and sisters, her childhood friends and a great many of her relatives, for that matter. Still in good health at ninety-two, she was vigorous and as sharp as a tack. A grand old dame and wealthy, too, Great Auntie took pride in the fact that she could afford to have groceries delivered to her house by way of the traveling vendor. She justified this extravagant measure by saying she didn't want to inconvenience others by asking them to take her into town.

Frankly, I think the delivery truck was a premeditated scheme, a strategy to manipulate us kids. When you live on the same farm as your nephew, his wife and six children, you need to carve out a role for yourself and assign it the status you need. Great Auntie did this by fashioning herself a grandmother of sorts to my brothers and sisters and me. She assigned herself the duty of ordering us around. But first she spoiled us. She was one savvy old lady—but at ninety-two, she also needed bargaining power. A supply of ice cream and cookies became easy bribes for kids when she wanted us to mow the lawn, fetch the mail down the long lane, weed her garden or other jobs and errands that needed doing. We hated doing these things, of course, but given her talent for stockpiling cookies, candies and sodas, Great Auntie Hilda could hold her own with the six of us. In fact, the odds were in her favor!

The delivery truck arrived without fail every Saturday, right around noon, and coincided with the rise of Great Auntie's popularity with us. From about noon on Saturday and for the rest of the day, we could be bought, bribed or enslaved. No doubt Great Auntie was aware of her transitory popularity, too, since it was on Saturday that she presented each of us with a list of things she wanted us to do for her. When we had completed these chores, Great Auntie rewarded us with generous amounts of sweets. Unfortunately for Great Auntie, though, there was one drawback to using this approach with us. Should she need errands done on any other day, we children feigned having mounds of homework to do instead, and given her concern about our getting good grades, she would tell us to go work on our homework; the errands could wait—until Saturday! "Shouldn't we go help?" one of us would ask our sister Judy. Ever so unsympathetic, my sister would cajole, "She has no ice cream or cookies left. Hold out until Saturday, and it'll be well worth our time!" And then to ensure that none of us would break rank, she would taunt, "If anyone betrays the rules, then that person is out of the Gang!"

This heist-without-getting-caught game went on for nearly three months. On one particularly beautiful spring Saturday, Great Auntie gathered us all around. She informed us that today's To-Do list was not like other Saturdays; this was going to be an extra big spring cleanup day. Judy would be needed for five hours; I would be needed for three-and-a-half hours; Mark and Kevin would be needed for three hours. Tim could help anyone he wanted, although his real responsibility was to watch Laurie who, at just three years old, was more hindrance than help. It was decided that she could hang around anyway, as could Shep, the canine member of the family. Great Auntie knew kids and dog were inseparable, so why fight it. Shep was right there in the lineup along with the rest of us.

We greeted the announcement of our work schedule like a child with an excruciating toothache agrees to go to the dentist: groaning, but grateful, too. While the amount of work seemed enormous, we were also anticipating enormous rewards. After all, we were used to being well-rewarded for our Saturday work.

Great Auntie, no novice when it came to motivating others (having been the oldest of nine children herself and chiefly responsible for caring for them), began by stating the wonderful outcomes for accomplishing all these tasks. These included the possibility of finding some old toy or keepsake in the attic cleanup, enjoying the sight and smell of the roses we would be planting when they bloomed in the not-too-distant future, and feeling proud when others—the bus driver and kids on the bus, for instance—miraculously remarked how nicely groomed the yards looked. When we rolled our eyes on that one, she glanced over at the dish of chocolate chip cookies sitting on the tabletop nearby. Having enlisted our support once again, Great Auntie told us where each body would be stationed for his or her assigned work. And finally, to set the stage for this production, this wise old manager added a final gesture to lure our full participation. She had choreographed the whole thing by setting four paper sacks on the table.

And so kids undertook a most arduous half-day of work, with great anticipation of the big payoff. Finally, after what seemed like the longest day of our lives, the work was done. Great Auntie led us dirty and tired children into her huge kitchen, where we awaited our promised rewards.

Great Auntie knew how to milk the situation. She slowly walked to the refrigerator, then stood there for a second. She turned and smiled at us, no doubt sensing our excitement. Great Auntie opened the door, pulled out something with both hands and shut the refrigerator door with her foot. She put her hands behind her back; it was obvious she had one treat in each hand. She walked toward the two youngest kids and, smiling, told each child to choose the hand they wanted. When they did, each was handed a Popsicle—a complete Popsicle, mind you, a two-part one, not just the half-a-Popsicle we were accustomed to. The older children exchanged glances, almost drooling in anticipation.

With four other children watching in obvious expectancy of what awaited them, Great Auntie methodically told these two younger children what a wonderful job they had done. Too young and unworldly to know this lowly payoff was below minimum wage, they were ecstatic with their treats.

Next Great Auntie singled out Mark, the oldest boy, leaving Kevin, the middle boy, to wait his turn at being praised. Mark was praised, given a bag of chocolate chip cookies and dismissed. Accustomed to rewards and punishments given out in order of hierarchy, he seemed a bit confounded that he should have his turn before Kevin, but gladly accepted his treat and praise. He went outside and sat on the step waiting for the rest of his gang.

The three remaining children sat in total silence, now perplexed and quite unsure of Great Auntie's incentive plan. Finally she walked over to the table and handed both Kevin and me one sack, and two sacks to Judy. We were directed to open them. With great anticipation, we tore open the bags. Inside my bag were the following:

> a dilapidated empty strawberry ice cream box
> three empty packages of sugar wafer cookies
> two empty jars of marshmallow creme
> an empty bag of white bread
> a package of yellow rubber gloves

Just when I thought there was nothing more, I noticed a wrinkled, dirty piece of paper. It was Judy's itemized list of things I had personally been responsible for taking from the delivery van over the past three months! (You can only imagine what was in Judy's bag.) In Great Auntie's neat printing down the side of the list was a tally of the dollar amount of the goods. Though I wasn't quite sure what was happening, I knew it couldn't be good. I looked up at Great Auntie. Her face no longer smiled. Slowly she handed me one more piece of paper. It was a list of how many hours of work it would take for me to pay off the debt. She then pulled a small chiseled pencil she had stuck behind her ear and, as three children watched in shock, she wrote, "Paid in Full" on each of our lists.

We sat there, too horrified to speak, now all too willing to be subjected to the obligatory lectures that we knew we were about to receive.

"We promise never to do this again," stammered my sister Judy.

"Oh, please don't tell Mom and Dad," Kevin stuttered.

I was still in shock, and so said nothing.

Great Auntie looked at three very scared and sincerely sorry children. "I'm happy that you have learned a lesson," she said. "I trust this sort of thing will never happen again."

"Oh, Great Auntie," Judy said, with the proper amount of remorse in her voice. "We promise never to do it again." And then, glancing at the piece of paper she was clutching in her hands, she hastily added, "And we promise to do all the errands you want done from now until we die."

Knowing that we were all truly remorseful, Great Auntie said, "That will be very nice." And then she quietly added, "You may go."

And we did.

Bettie B. Youngs
Excerpted from Values from the Heartland

Part 2

Friends—Pizza for Life!

Friends leave footprints in your heart.

—Jennifer Leigh Youngs

A Word
from the Authors

Does anyone ever forget his or her first kiss? Of course not, and the many memories you create with friends are unforgettable as well. Being with others makes our world sizzle: We are a part of something, accepted, wanted, needed, maybe even loved. To be accepted by others, and to feel as if we belong, supports our natural instincts for self-acceptance—making us feel whole and complete. Belonging is a powerful contribution to how secure, happy and content we are within our own lives.

Being happy with yourself is the starting point for being a successful human being and experiencing success in the world around you. But as the old saying goes, "No man is an island." We live in a world with others, and just about everything we do is done in concert with them. We live in families and within communities; we go to school and work with others. We communicate with people on a daily basis. As we learn the best ways to live in tandem with others, we find that moving from "me" to "you" adds yet another dimension to our inner contentment. It makes us happy. Pure and simple, being on friendly terms with others is a good feeling.

"Mom, imagine what it's like going to school in the morning and not having anyone save you a place on the bus, or in the cafeteria or at the assembly. Imagine not having a friend to hang out with when you want to 'check out' the guys (or for the guys, check out the girls)! A big part of the experience of being a teenager is exploring the world, a world spent away from your home and parents, even your own neighborhood. You're out there in school and in life doing things for the first time and learning to do things in your own way. It just wouldn't be fun, much less comfortable, to do those things all alone. So, having someone to do them with is important, and having someone you like, a good friend, makes the experience more than just fun, it adds to it in just about every way."

"I understand what you mean, Jennifer, and that's what the teens we worked with on this book said: 'Friends are a huge part of what makes the teen years both fun and *bearable*.' Teens need people their own age to help them go through these years, helping them realize that others their own age see the world as they do—or not. It's confirmation, validation, a baseline by which to gauge how you are doing and faring."

"This is so true, Mom. When I was a teen (and even today), while you and Dad tried your best to help me with things, it was my friends who best helped me understand the situation at hand, and to dissect the experience I was trying to come to terms with. Friends *share in the experience*. For example, take preparing for SATs. A teen's parents can provide encouragement, saying things like, 'Let's get you some tutoring.' 'You'll do just great.' 'Don't worry, just do the best you can.' But your friends will say, 'Let's cram together Saturday, okay? You can help me with algebra; I'll help you with science.' And your friends are apt to confess, 'My stomach's been in knots for days just thinking about it!' Or offer real words of comfort such as 'I failed for sure. How do you think you did?' It's the 'I know you know what I'm going through because you are, too,' the 'I'm just as scared (or confident) as you are,' and so their feedback is real, it's authentic— because they're there right on the line, too. They have the same kind of 'real life' as you, so you can trust their words have merit. They're going through the same problems, so each knows how the other feels inside. While parents offer love, protection and direction, they simply can't relate to what a teen is going through in the same way your friends do."

"I think that can be a loving message of important information for teens and parents, Jennifer. Teenagers don't need and love their parents *less* than they do their friends, it's just a *different* kind of need and love. If parents are the cookies and milk of life, then good friends are, as teens told us, 'like having pizza for life!'"

We all know that pizza is a staple in the diet of teens, and friends are too. Acceptance and belonging are powerful feelings within our hearts—necessities that, for better or for worse, shape our lives. We humans love to have a little time for ourselves and some private moments alone, yet we will always seek the company of others: This drive is simply within our natures.

As we learn and grow, we discover that life with others is not just about how to navigate the waters of getting along with a wide array of personalities. Almost as if by design, friendships are about lessons, teaching us so much about ourselves—as expressed in the beautiful and eloquent words of Anaïs Nin: "Each friend represents a world in us, a world possibly not born until they arrive." People enter our lives and change it in some way, whether they do so by giving you the chance to walk into the crowded cafeteria—but not alone—or by having someone to chat with on the phone late at night, someone so personable and trustworthy as to lead you to believe you can safely share your innermost thoughts. The point is that each new person represents a new possibility to see ourselves and our lives in a whole new way.

That a special friend can open our eyes to a new idea, changing the way we see the world and ourselves, is one of the reasons we guard our friendships and treat each friend as a unique and special person, one who, until he or she proves otherwise, holds a special place in our hearts.

As so many of the teens we worked with found out, friends can be the very best mirrors we have. Not only are they willing to honestly assess how we're looking—physically or otherwise—they also view us with hopeful eyes. Never is this a greater gift than when we're being hard on ourselves. A friend offers understanding and acceptance during times when we struggle to understand and accept ourselves. Perhaps, most important, in a world that can seem so big and overwhelming, friends offer us the comfort of connection—with friends we're not in it alone! Knowing you have friends you can trust makes the whole world seem like a safer place. As so many of the teens we worked with said friends "help you have a *real* life."

When it comes to discussing the importance of friends, you teens threw open the doors to your hearts to share not only what you learned about the friends in your life, but what you've learned about yourself in relation to them. Good friends can help us grow into the sort of person we wish to be, to put our best foot forward, to strive toward goals that may seem too lofty to tell others for fear they will not support us in going toward our dream.

In the following stories you'll read of friendships made, friendships changed and friendships lost, and ways friends, as Jennifer says, create those *footprints in your heart.*

Stars in Your Eyes

You say that I'm the prettiest girl you've ever seen,
That my eyes glisten like diamonds
That my hair smells of gardenias
That my skin is soft to the touch
That my smile lights up the room
That my nose is "perfectly cute"
That I am a wonderful person.
Funny, because when I look into the mirror,
I don't see any of that.
I only know I don't feel
    as pretty and perfect as I would like to be,
And I wonder what keeps you with me.
And then you reassure me.
That's when I look away from the mirror and instead
Enjoy you gazing at me with stars in your eyes.
And I know then, that what you say is true:
I'm the prettiest girl you've ever seen,
My eyes glisten like diamonds
My hair smells of gardenias
My skin is soft to the touch
My smile lights up the room
My nose is "perfectly cute"
I am a wonderful person.
Amazing isn't it, how seeing one's own worth and beauty
    comes easier when you see it reflected
    in the stars in another's eyes.

Kayleigh Minutella, 14

Intense About Pokémon

I baby-sit for a little seven-year-old named Stephen James Whitney Jr. who just loves Pokémon. It seems to be the most important thing in his life: Pokémon cards, toys, dolls, videos, backpack—you name it, he has it. Or wants it. Pokémon. Pokémon. Pokémon. Everything is Pokémon! Stephen has got to be the biggest Pokémon lover I have ever met. The moment I come over, he drags out all his Pokémon paraphernalia and shows them to me, explaining what's new. I am hired to care for him, so of course, I listen carefully to his serious interest in the Pokémon hero—and his plans for acquiring even more Pokémon stuff.

When the Pokémon movie came out, Stephen nearly drove his parents crazy about wanting to see it. Finally, his parents said okay and told him he could take a friend with him. Stephen said he wanted to take me. "Meghan?" they asked, surprised. "Don't you want to ask a friend from your class?"

"No," the little boy insisted. "I want Meghan to go. She loves Pokémon even more than I do, even more than any of my friends at school, and I want to make sure she can see the Pokémon movie. She's intense about Pokémon."

When I heard this, I thought it was so cute. But it also made me realize how much my simple gesture of listening and paying attention to the young boy had meant to him. Stephen was adamant that I *needed* to see this movie. My listening to his interest in Pokémon convinced him that I must be as big a Pokémon fan as he was, and so he wanted to make very certain I didn't miss out on it.

Now that's a friend—always looking out for you, always making sure that *your* needs are met, too.

Meghan Sauerheber, 16

The Illegal U-Turn

I live one mile from my school. That's not a long way, really, but still, I absolutely detest having to walk to school, especially in the mornings. My parents argue that walking to and from school is "good for my health," so unless I'm running late or have something special going on before or after school, they're not likely to give me a ride. So, as often as I can, I mooch rides from friends who drive, especially from my friend Kenny, who has a monstrously rad Ford truck. "Can I catch a ride home with you after sixth period?" I asked him one day last year. "No problem," my newest best friend assured me.

Just like the other kids who have wheels, Kenny has a lot of friends eager to catch a ride somewhere. So if you get lucky and he's still got space, you need to get to his truck early if you want a good seat—like a window seat or, best of all, the front seat. Sitting there is on a first-come, first-served basis.

I prefer the front seat, so as soon as the bell rang, I sprinted from my class to Kenny's truck in hopes of getting the front seat. Even though I hurried, when I got to his truck, his sister, Cyndi, had already claimed the front seat. "You always get the front seat. How about giving it up just this once?" I coaxed. "If you let me sit here today, I promise I won't ask you for it again for a whole month." It worked. She scooted in the back seat, and I climbed in and buckled up. I wasn't about to give up my "real estate" to anyone else who had also been promised a ride. There were five of us total. Kenny counted heads, and off we went.

Taking his usual route, Kenny headed down the street and made a left turn at the stop sign. Soaring along, Kenny drove right past the turn he needed to make to drop off his first passenger. Realizing his mistake, Kenny decided right then and there to turn around! The problem is, rather than going to the end of the street to make a proper turn, Kenny looked over his shoulder to check on the oncoming traffic, and then proceeded to make an illegal U-turn. Surprised—and feeling ill at ease—I, too, glanced over my shoulder, and noticed a dark-blue Ford Bronco coming right at us at a very high speed! Then, in the very next moment, about the same time I yelled to Kenny about the oncoming truck, the Bronco was on us. There was the incredible sound of the two automobiles crashing and sliding, and Cyndi screaming. The Bronco smashed into Kenny's truck on the driver's side, pushing our car into a wild slide, while the impact caused the Bronco to go airborne. The Bronco then landed with a thud, bounced, rolled and landed on its hood, skidding twenty-some feet, then flipping once again on its side and sliding into the nearby curb—which caused it to flip once again before it finally skidded to a dead halt, facing the opposite direction. Talk about scary!

After a quick panicked search to see if the passengers in our truck were okay (they were), I knew I'd better get over to the Bronco to see if anyone needed emergency help. Though Kenny's truck had been brutally hit, it was now upright. Even so, the impact had jammed the car door on my side, so I rolled down the window, climbed out and ran over to the Bronco. Thankfully, everyone was alive, but two of its three passengers needed emergency medical care. I ran across the street to the closest professional building and was told that help had already been called and was on the way. I raced back to the scene of the accident.

Within minutes, police and paramedics arrived and one of the passengers was life-flighted by helicopter to the nearest hospital. As for the passengers in our car, Cyndi didn't have her seat belt on and was thrown into the front seat. Thankfully, she was okay. Like the others, I had my seat belt on, so while I was a little sore from being yanked by the force of my seat belt holding me in place, I was okay. The driver's side of Kenny's truck sustained the direct hit of the Bronco, but incredibly, Kenny didn't have any injuries whatsoever. The two other friends in the car were both okay also.

After the immediate commotion of the car crash was over, Kenny and I sat on the grass, waiting for our parents to come and get us, just staring at his badly damaged truck and what was left of the Bronco. Still scared from our ordeal, Kenny and I talked about what had happened and what we were feeling. We recounted every detail of the crash, and admitted how scared it made us—we even described the rusty taste of adrenaline we felt when we saw the Bronco was right on us. Then we talked about the consequences of what had just happened, like the illegal U-turn, and how if Cyndi had been wearing her seat belt, it might have prevented her from being thrown into the front seat. She was lucky she wasn't injured. And we talked about what was going to happen next. I wasn't exactly forbidden to get a ride home from school, but my parents made it clear they preferred that I walked home. As a licensed driver, Kenny was at fault in the accident and had totaled his truck as well. For sure Kenny would have some explaining to do to his parents!

It was a good talk. We both were still so frightened and so concerned for everyone, including facing the consequences of all this, that we didn't hesitate to be honest about how we were feeling. In fact, it was one of the most "real" conversations I remember having with another guy friend—one that made us feel close to each other. It also established us as *real* friends. For the rest of the school year, Kenny and I found ourselves drawn together out of a certain commonality. Whenever we found ourselves in the same activity or study group at school, we instantly clicked, as if we had been lifelong buddies. We became such good friends that, right now, I'd say he's my closest friend.

It was the discussion that made all the difference. I think the main reason we got so close is not just because we went through a very frightening ordeal together, but because we opened up and talked about it with total honesty. It was our frank and open discussion—on a level that classmates don't ordinarily have—that cemented a friendship that's deeper than most of my other friendships.

From this incident, I've learned an important ingredient in friendships: "Real" conversations make friendships stronger and your importance to each other greater.

Curt Lindholm, 17

Needed: Body Parts

A friend:
A brain to pick
A shoulder to cry on
Ears to hear all
An arm to rely on
Eyes to reflect hope
A voice to give cheer
A hand to hold
A heart that's sincere
Someone who cares
A soul you can share.
A friend.

Jennifer Leigh Youngs

Sticks and Stones . . .

Do you believe the saying: "Sticks and stones can break my bones, but words can never hurt me"? I don't.

I think words are very powerful, and while they may not break your bones, they can break your heart. Consider the words, "I love you." Just these three short words can change your life when someone says them to you. Just like the words "I hate you." They definitely have the power to hurt you. So I think words can sometimes be as forceful and have as much effect on a person as actions. I should know; I experienced this firsthand.

My friend Brenda Hall couldn't seem to accept that her boyfriend and I could be platonic friends. But we were. Tom and I had been friends even longer than Brenda and I had—and we'd all been friends since grade school. But when she and Tom broke up, for some weird reason, she thought it was because of me, but it wasn't because of me. I didn't do one thing to cause them to break up, nor did I want Tom for a boyfriend—as Brenda must have thought. In fact, once Brenda and Tom weren't together, he started dating another girl at our school, Leeza Nero.

You would think that would be the end of Brenda's being upset with me, and I wouldn't be blamed as the reason for the breakup after that. But for some reason, Tom's liking another girl made Brenda even more furious at *me*. So the very next day after she saw Tom and Leeza together, she started a rumor that she'd seen me making out with a guy at school (a guy with the most sleazy reputation—reportedly for having sex with someone). Of course, this slimeball was more than happy to say that the rumor was true. I thought I would die.

Even though I knew my close friends didn't believe such terrible gossip, my life was still ruined. I was sure the rumor would travel very quickly throughout the entire school. Luckily, I learned about the rumor during the last period of the day, and after that I could just go home. But how would I make it through the next day . . . and the next? I hardly slept at all that night. All I could do was think about having such a dreadful scandal circulating throughout the school about me—and started by a "friend"! Some friend. I woke up sure that words could hurt as much as "sticks and stones," and I was certain my broken heart hurt every bit as much as any broken bone could.

The next day I went to school miserable, knowing that all day long everyone was going to be hearing the disgraceful lie. In my first-period homeroom, I settled in my desk and stared down at my notebook, so I wouldn't have to meet either the looks of pity from classmates who didn't believe the rumor, or the smirks and leers of those who did. I could hardly wait for this day to end. I was even considering going to the nurse's office and saying I was sick—which, given how I felt, wouldn't be such a big stretch. I had an enormous headache, and my stomach was positively turned upside down. I decided that just as soon as morning announcements were over, I'd head to the nurse's office. But then something unexpected happened.

Each morning, right after the principal greets the students and announces what, if anything, is urgent for us kids to know, there is an "inspirational" message read by a student. This always follows the announcements. One by one, everyone in the school has to read one, and we were now up to the H's; it was Brian Holt's turn to read something today. Yet, surprisingly enough, Brian Holt didn't read the message. Instead, Gina Issacks (who would normally follow Brian Holt) read it. "Hi," she began. "I'm Gina Issacks and this morning I'd like to read a message that I think relates to a lot of things going on around school. I think you'll get my drift. Here goes: A man came to a rabbi and said, 'Oh, Rabbi, I have done wrong. I have slandered a friend. I have told lies about him. I have spread rumors. But now I am sorry for what I have done and what I have said. How can I be forgiven?' The rabbi looked thoughtfully at the man and then said, 'Take this feather pillow and go to the town square. Cut the pillow open and let the feathers fly to the wind. That will be your punishment for the ill words you have spoken.' Though quite puzzled by the rabbi's instructions, the man did as he was told. Then he returned to the rabbi and said, 'I have done what you told me. Now am I forgiven for slandering my friend?'

"'No, you are not forgiven yet,' the rabbi replied. 'You have fulfilled only half of your task. First you let the feathers fly to the wind. Now go and collect every single feather.'

"I think it's a great parable. When you think about how important it is to be a good friend and to be considerate of the feelings of our friends, then you shouldn't start rumors that aren't true, or say things that are hurtful." Gina paused a moment, as if giving her words time to sink in, then finished by saying, "Enough said."

This warm feeling of relief just seeped through my heart. I had to fight back tears, I was so touched that someone cared enough to stick up for me. Gina isn't one of my close friends, but she's considered a nice girl throughout the school. I'm sure she read this piece either for Brenda's benefit, or because the rumor about me was by now going around like wildfire, and reading the parable was an attempt to quash it. Whatever the intent, I was thankful. Even better news is that right after homeroom, Brenda met me at my locker and apologized for being mad at me over her and Tom breaking up, as well as for starting the rumor. Though she didn't say if her change of heart had anything to do with Gina's reading, she did promise to make sure everyone knew that what she said wasn't true.

So I forgave her and said we could still be friends. And speaking of friends, real friends, I knew I'd always be grateful to Gina who used the power of her words to help friends be *real* friends. That's why Gina is now one of my best friends!

Audrianne Adams, 16

Do You Miss Me?

Hello Grandpa!
I just wanted to say,
I love you and miss you
And wish you had stayed.

You were my best friend,
A friend pure as gold
My most favorite best friend,
If the whole truth be told.

Do you miss me?
Can you feel the pain in my heart?
I'd like to believe
We're not really apart.

I'm playing my music,
It always brings me to tears
If only we'd been together,
For a couple more years.

I love how you listened,
How we'd sing you and I.
As you now sing with angels,
Do you see how I cry?

Know that I miss you,
And I need you still
Even if you're in heaven,
Know that I always will.

So keep watch over me Grandpa,
My very best friend,
And know that I'll always love you,
You're the truest of friends.

Jenna King, 12

Spring Fling

At my school, attendance at the Spring Fling is a big deal. Everyone goes, especially since all the junior and senior guys play "host." Spring Fling is more of a have-a-date event than a singles thing. The day of the big event was fast approaching, and I still didn't have a date. I was hoping that Ben Tripp, a really cool senior, would ask me to go with him. Sometimes when Ben passes me in the halls, he'll give me a certain look, so I know he's interested in me. But Ben Tripp had done nothing but give me that look; there was still no invitation to be his date at Spring Fling. So on Wednesday, two days before the dance, when Larry Welch asked me to be his date, I said I'd go with him.

Now, Larry is a nice guy and all, but he's someone that fits the "he has a nice personality" category. And you know what that means. He's not your "to-die-for" date, or at least he wasn't mine. Still, I really wanted to go to Spring Fling. It was unthinkable to show up alone. Going with a group of girls was a dead giveaway that you couldn't get a date, so that was a no-no, too. So, I accepted Larry Welch's invitation.

But by the end of the next day, I wished I hadn't. I mean, what if Larry Welch expected me to dance with him, and only him, the entire evening? And what if Larry got the idea that because I went to the dance with him, he and I were "dating"? What if Ben thought that because I was with Larry, that Larry and I were dating? As you can see, I simply had to get out of the date with Larry Welch. The problem was, I really didn't have a good reason to break the date, other than that I shouldn't have accepted it in the first place. An even bigger problem was that I didn't know how to tell Larry. I didn't have the nerve to tell him face-to-face.

"So, what are you going to do?" my good friend Brad asked me when I told him about my predicament.

"I'm just going to pretend I'm not at home when he comes to pick me up!" I answered.

"Speaking from experience," Brad replied, "that's a pretty cruel way to learn you no longer have a date! And besides, there's a better way to undo a date."

I was sure I knew what he was going to say, so I argued, "Brad, I'm afraid that if I call him up, I'll back down from telling him I've changed my mind—and then I'll be stuck!"

"You don't really know what Larry's going to say," my friend responded.

"What do you mean?" I asked innocently enough.

Boy did I get an answer. "I'll show you. Pretend I'm Larry and you're phoning me. Go ahead." Even though I felt silly, I put an imaginary phone to my ear and said, "Hi, Larry."

"Hi, Julie!" Brad said in return. "Now say something like, 'I'm calling about the dance tomorrow night.'" So I said, "I'm calling about the dance tomorrow night."

Taking on Larry's persona, Brad responded, "I can hardly wait! My dad said I could borrow his car instead of using my old beat-up one. And guess what, Julie? I'm taking us to dinner before the dance. It's going to be so much fun. I'm really looking forward to it. I'll pick you up at 6:30."

"You see, Brad," I shouted. "That's exactly why I don't want to call Larry. Because I wouldn't want to disappoint him—at least while I was on the phone with him—I'm sure I'll say, 'Oh, okay,' and then I'll still be stuck going out with him. I'm not going to take that chance, and that's that. I'm sticking with my plan to leave my house before Larry arrives!"

"Not so fast," Brad told me. "That's one possible scenario, but there are others. Come on, one more time, pretend you're phoning me." And so I did. "Hello, Larry," I said once again. "I'm calling about our date for Spring Fling."

"Oh, Julie," my friend Brad replied. "I'm glad you called. I'm really sick. I won't be able to go. I'm really sorry to back out at such a late date, but I have strep throat; I'm running a fever and taking medication." Well, you can imagine how surprised I was at Brad's words, because it presented a different view. I mean, maybe Larry would get sick or would want to back out of going—which would be okay with me!

"Hey, that went pretty well," I told my friend Brad. "Now, how do I make sure Larry gets strep throat?"

"Very funny," said Brad. "But there are still a lot of other ways that things could play out. C'mon. Let's try it one more time."

"Okay," I agreed. "Hello, Larry. I'm calling about our date for Spring Fling."

"Yes, what about it?" Brad asked, then paused, obviously forcing me to say something first this time. "Well, I can't go with you," I blurted, "and I was hoping you might make other plans."

"Oh, I'm sorry to hear that, Julie," my friend Brad replied. "I was really looking forward to going. Are you sure I can't change your mind?"

"Yes, I'm sure," I said. "I really have to say no. I'm sorry." Sounding disappointed but accepting it, Brad said for Larry, "Okay, Julie. Well, since we won't be going to the dance together, would you be okay with my asking Karen Hood to go with me? I know she's a friend of yours, but I really would like to go out with Karen. I've been too shy to ask her, but just yesterday her sister told me that Karen was hoping I'd ask her to the dance. It all sounds very complicated, but if you wouldn't be upset, I'd love to ask Karen."

In short, I was surprised at the possibility that Larry could respond to my backing out in a number of ways.

I found the little exercise with Brad helpful because it gave me the confidence to handle a situation that I not only knew would be hard to deal with, but also knew I could easily mess up. Then Brad said, "If you want a real eye-opener, Julie, we could reverse roles. You play the part of Larry, and I play you." That's when I realized that if I were to put the shoe on the other foot—put myself in Larry's place—I wouldn't want him to stand me up. So I decided to treat Larry exactly the way I'd want to be treated if the same situation were reversed. I'd want someone to give me time to make other plans, and to be honest, I wouldn't want someone to go out with me if they really didn't want to.

I called Larry; he took it much better than I had first imagined. He was disappointed, but he didn't act totally devastated or anything like that. I was kind about it—and we stayed friends.

Brad really helped me learn to say what's on my mind without hurting someone else in the process. In my case, Larry had done nothing wrong. I was the one who wanted to back out of something I'd committed to. As Brad said, standing Larry up would have made him feel rejected and humiliated. That's not a very nice thing to do. The approach I thought I was going to use gave him no time or chance to make other plans. And so it was my friend Brad who taught me one of the most important things ever about being a friend. Not only does the way you communicate make a difference in how good your friendships are, it can also make you a taste-berry friend—which was what Brad was to me, and ultimately, what I was to Larry. I'm happy to say that Larry and I are not only friends, but we're now good friends, too.

Brenda Walters, 16

"It'll Never Get to Us"

It started out like a typical day, but turned out to be anything but typical. As usual, I went to school and sat through my eighth-grade classes, then came home with mounds of homework. And, as usual, I prepared to put off doing it for as long as possible. Little did I know, I would soon have every excuse to put off getting it done.

The neighborhood was stirring with talk of a fire burning in our direction. Filled with curiosity—and alarm—my mom, brother and I walked to the top of the street to survey the situation and get a better idea of whether or not there was any possible danger. Looking out to the hills behind my house, we saw a wall of orange flames, set against a background of ominous, thick, black smoke. My mother and the other adults that had gathered there tried to reassure us kids, as well as each other. "It's so far away," someone offered, while another one said, "It'll never get to us." But I could tell that they were only trying to reassure us and convince themselves. We kids grew worried—because we could see our parents were. Everyone fretted over the flames growing closer, as if being annoyed and upset might somehow hold back this fiery mower that was eating its way through the brush towards us.

"You know, maybe we should pack up our things . . . just in case," someone soon ventured. I looked up at my mother, and she nodded kind of stiffly and agreed, "Yes, better to be safe than sorry. . . ." So we went back to our house to pack up our belongings . . . "just in case"—to be "safe" rather than "sorry." In the next split-second everyone left, like all they needed was someone to give them permission to be downright scared of the fire coming in our direction.

"Just take the basic necessities and valuables!" my mother instructed. Rushing into my room, I looked around in a panic, trying to decide what to take. Other than one bulletin board I'd trashed and wanted to replace, everything there was "basic necessities and valuables" to me. It was so hard to pick and choose what I would save and what I wouldn't.

Soon my dad got home from work and joined in the packing frenzy. In no time we had both cars loaded to the brim with picture albums, journals, family keepsakes and, of course, our dog. By now police cars were driving down our street, telling us on their loudspeakers to evacuate our houses. My dad stood with a hose on the roof of our house, trying to water it down, as the wall of fire seemed to march like a deadly infantry of flames down the hills in our direction. My mom kept yelling up at my dad to get down off the roof so we could leave. "Take the kids and go! I'll meet you somewhere!" he hollered back at her. "No! I'm not leaving you!" she shouted in reply. Finally, my dad could see that she meant it—we wouldn't leave without him. So, he gave in and got down from the roof. As we drove away from the house, we were all somber and silent. It was the strangest feeling, because I didn't know if I would have a house to come back to.

After a strained dinner at a local restaurant with some of our neighbors and several other evacuated families, we spent the night at a friend's house. For once in my life, I wanted to do my homework. . . . I wanted everything to be normal again. But we just stayed awake and watched the news coverage of the fire. For someone who doesn't like to get up in the morning, I was awake at 5:30—and then discovered that everyone else was already in the process of getting dressed. We all wanted to return home—to see if we still had one.

Lucky for us, our house was untouched by the fire. As happy as we were that our home was okay, we were saddened to see that our friends at the end of the street weren't as fortunate. Their home was burned to the ground. Standing there assessing the neighborhood, emotions from gratitude to sorrow flooded my mind. I was thankful that I had my home and all my things to come home to, and thankful that no one was hurt from this disastrous fire. And I considered how terrible it must feel for those who lost everything they owned. And I was filled with a deep, overall appreciation for life—for being alive, and for just everything.

The idea that fire could claim lives just as it had homes made me especially grateful for having both a home and a family. Having watched each member of my family grab the things that were valuable to them—things that were basic, and the little mementos that were so precious to each person—filled me with a special appreciation for each of them. We were a family—a real family. And now, a safe one. Right then and there I made a pact with myself never to take for granted the things that can be swept away in an instant, like your home and possessions—and the life of family members.

The experience left me with a new sense of the importance of *family*, and for sure, a new sense of meaning behind my mother's words, "the basic necessities and valuables." My parents and my brother, and the close relationships we share as a family, are definitely basic necessities and my most treasured valuables in life. My family members are also among the closest and most precious friends I have.

Carrie Hague, 17

New—and Late

There's someone who is different
As different as she can be
She's walking into my classroom
I pray she'll sit by me.

Like me, she is wearing braces
Her hair is black and straight
Dark eyes look at our faces
She knows she's new—and late.

Our curious eyes are on her
Most staring blank and grim
But my eyes are open and hopeful
My heart invites her in.

And in that aching moment
When throats feel dry and tight
I'll volunteer to help her
And make her first day right.

Leslie Hendrickson

Destined to Be Friends

Do you think it's possible for friends to be soul mates? My mom always says that the very day she met my dad she knew they were meant to be together for life. And my grandmother has called me her "little soul mate." She says we "connect" in a way that goes beyond even flesh-and-blood ties. So what about friends? Can they be your soul mates—people you were simply destined to be connected to? Are some friendships just meant to be? I think they are. I'll tell you why.

When I was in grade school, I had a best friend named Beth. We lived three houses away from each other. We did everything together: We walked to and from school each day together, laughing and sharing "big" secrets along the way. We played on the same soccer team, did our homework together, and often stayed overnight at each other's houses. We had so much in common, and we just liked each other so much. We were the *best* of friends. Even our parents thought of us as "sisters." Then, when we were in the sixth grade, Beth and her parents moved to a different city.

Our parents allowed us to talk by phone every once in a while during the first year we were apart; and at first we wrote to each other often and let one another know how much we missed each other. But with starting junior high and all the new people and classes and demands on our time, we each got busy with our own activities and things. Later that year my parents and I moved away, and before I knew it, Beth and I lost touch with each other. But I never forgot her and always missed her.

Almost two years later, when I was in eighth grade, something happened that was a big surprise! I had been accepted to a National Summer Soccer Institute program, one that had three different sessions throughout the summer. My parents and I had decided that I would attend the first of the three sessions. My registration and payment for the session had been sent in and everything was set to go. But at the last minute, I got a really bad case of the flu and couldn't attend. Since the camp needs to put together the teams and hire coaches and camp counselors in advance, they have a very strict policy on cancellations. In my case, they made an exception and allowed me to attend the third session. The Institute was held in Denver, Colorado, and I live in Sacramento, California.

I arrived for the third session at the soccer camp, picked up all my registration stuff, and took my things to my dormitory. Guess who turned up as my bunk mate? Beth! I was totally surprised! It was so great to be back together! It felt like old times.

Once again two years passed, and each of us got into the friends we had at our own schools and neighborhoods. But we had vowed to keep in touch by mail this time. Then one day, after not having talked with her for nearly five months, I got a card from Beth telling me that she intended to attend Texas A&M! I couldn't believe what I was reading: Without even knowing it, Beth and I are both going to attend the same university! But that's not all! We have since learned that of the two different dormitories for women on the campus, we had both chosen the same one!

Since learning this, we are now planning to room together! It's nice to have a friend who knows and understands how you feel so well that even time and distance can't change it. But when you add to that connection the kind of coincidences that seem to all but shout that it's fate, there just has to be something even greater going on—and that's why I think that it's possible that some people can just be destined to be friends! Like Beth and me.

Darla Henderson, 17

The Mystery Letter

My little brother was diagnosed as having an inoperable brain tumor. There was nothing anyone could do except enjoy every second Stevie had left to live. It was a sad time, but it was a special time, too.

Stevie believed in God and told everyone he wasn't afraid because he knew he was going to heaven. He even wrote letters to God expecting God to write back. Well of course, no one wanted to tell a sick little boy that God didn't write letters, so no one did. Then one day, a letter from God did come for Stevie. My mother gave it to Stevie, and he read it to us: God said he was reading every one of Stevie's letters and was watching over our family. Stevie kept writing. And God kept answering! Stevie found great comfort from these letters.

Stevie died six months later. Though it seemed like he had been ill forever, it was only ten months from the time he learned he had the brain tumor until the time he died. But during those ten months, our family was closer and more loving than it had ever been.

The day after Stevie's funeral the mailman knocked on our door and handed my mother a shoebox filled with the letters Stevie had written to God. Seeing Stevie's devotion in writing so many letters to God, the mailman had taken it upon himself to bring comfort, encouragement and hope to my little brother by answering his letters to God. I guess some people would say it takes a lot of nerve to play God—but in this case, I think it took a lot of heart. I think it's a cool thing for the mailman to have done—he befriended a little boy going through the roughest time imaginable. I can't help but think how happy all of us in the world could make each other if we were the kind of friends the mailman was to Stevie—and if we would encourage and comfort each other.

Bill Lempke, 15

Bonham

When I was twelve, my mother and father divorced. It seemed like after that, my life just fell apart. My mother and I moved into a smaller house in a different neighborhood. Because of the move, I had to go to a new school. Leaving my friends was the pits. At first, I didn't know anybody and felt really out of place. Since my mother doesn't get home from work until around 7:00, and because I hadn't made any new friends at school yet, I didn't have anyone to hang out with, so I just went home. With only me there, the house seemed really spooky. I'd put the TV on and play my music, but then I started going to the nearby arcade just to hang around. It wasn't too long before I began hanging out with a couple of kids who were always there. Unfortunately, the two who were the most friendly had dropped out of school. But they were fun guys, and I looked forward to seeing them after school. As soon as the last bell rang, I'd head straight to the arcade. Sometimes I stayed there later than my mother allowed, and we began to get into arguments about it. She said if I continued to hang out with them, they'd get me into trouble.

My new friends and I did get into a lot of trouble, mostly because we were looking for things to do. Like the day we threw rocks at every single window in the old abandoned warehouse down the road—even though it was an area I had been told I was not allowed to go to. This was also the same warehouse we later spray-painted all over—"tagging" the whole building. Nobody found out about it or anything, but I was getting pretty wild, and I knew what I was doing wasn't right. I'd never acted like that before. Then, one weekend when I was staying with my father, out of the blue, he gave me a dog, a golden retriever, one who already had a name, "Bonham." Dad let me take Bonham home to my mother's with me and bring him on the weekends when I visited him. Obviously he had talked this over with my mother, because she welcomed the dog without complaining about having Bonham in our house. That really surprised me, because Mom didn't necessarily like animals, especially living in the house. I'd wanted a hamster and she said it was too messy; I'd asked for a bunny and she said it was too smelly. But she seemed to welcome Bonham. She even put up the little knickknacks from the coffee table because Bonham would be so happy all the time, he would swish his big tail and all the little figurines would go flying. One of my mother's favorite ones, a little glass kangaroo my father had given her, broke in a gazillion pieces. She was upset, but then, when Bonham saw her huddled on the floor gathering up the little pieces, he ran over and licked her face, and she couldn't help laughing. And she wasn't upset after that.

But it's more than just that Bonham is fun to have around and is a great friend. He's really changed how I feel about coming home after school. It may sound dumb for me to call Bonham my friend, but he really is. You may not believe that a dog can have such a big effect on a person's life, but Bonham has on mine. He needs me and depends on me. When I get home from school, he's waiting right there for me. He knows exactly when to expect me. He's really cute about it too. He'll stand on his hind legs and put his paws on the window sill, and when he sees me coming into view, he starts barking. Then he runs to greet me at the door. It's a great feeling. Bonham jumps on my bed when I put my stuff away; he sits on the couch with me when I watch television; and when I fix dinner, he's right there. I'm really important to him.

And he's really important to me, too. I take him with me for walks. I know it sounds silly but I really think he knows what I'm saying, because if I ask him a question, he looks at me, cocks his head and barks! Bonham is the reason I come home immediately after school instead of hanging out with the kids I used to get into trouble with. Bonham depends on me to take him outdoors. He depends on me for food and water, and for companionship, too. Right now I'd say that he is just about the best friend I have. He's probably the best friend I've ever had. I love him very much. I am so happy my father gave him to me.

Bonham taught me that it isn't so bad being responsible; it actually brings out the best in you. Because of what Bonham taught me about the importance of being a friend who can be counted on, I've also learned to make friends who I can count on. Today my friends can count on me not to get them in trouble, and I can count on the same from them. So, I'd have to say my friendship with Bonham taught me how to be a better friend to everyone—to my parents, to my new friends and even to myself.

Randy Candenwell, 14

Perfect in My Mind

Ethan and I met at church over a plate of oatmeal cookies. We were both ten. We talked about everything from sports to what the teacher did that was stupid in class that week. Always he had a big smile on his face. Through the good and bad, I was there for him and he was there for me. Whenever you saw one of us, you saw the other. He was like a protective older brother. All the guys knew if they messed with me, they would mess with Ethan. He wasn't a bully, he just looked out for me. We had the perfect friendship.

At the end of eighth grade I moved to Germany. Both of my parents are in the military and so we move every five or six years, sometimes more often. When you move such a great distance, you can't always take everything with you, even some of the personal things. You have to either sell them, give them away or put them in storage. But I can take some things. For instance, I can't take something as large my bicycle, but I can always take my photo albums. And, of course, I can't take my friends, but I can always take my memories of them.

Sometimes, you don't have any choice, you just have to move. My family thought we would be in Germany longer than we were, but soon after the move to Germany, we moved to Korea. After almost a year and a half, Ethan moved somewhere new, too, and he and I lost touch. I heard through the grapevine that Ethan changed, that he's now a troublemaker and a bully. That's hard to believe.

Earlier this week, I sat on the floor with old pictures piled up around me. I was halfway through one stack when I came across one of my favorite pictures, even though it brings tears to my eyes every time I see it. I was playing hand bells for the last time and there was my best friend beside me being the funny guy he is—the Ethan I want to remember—playing hand bells, too.

I once heard it said that "memories are life's second chance at happiness." Boy, is that true when it comes to my memories of Ethan, memories that will always remain perfect in my mind.

McKenna Jagger, 15

Free Speech

I was throwing a tantrum, the kind that's typical when you've been told "no" by a parent and understand fully that the no means no!

"But I'll die if I can't go. . . ." "Somebody else will dance with the boy I like. . . ." "All my friends are going. . . ." "All the kids will think. . . ." "I . . . I . . . I . . ."

I had tried every possible angle of persuasion on my father, but his answer was still a resounding "No!" Realizing that pleading my case with him was useless, I decided to take my case to the president of second chances—Mom. Surely she would see that Dad had been an ogre in his decision and get him to see how unfair he had been to me. She had all the clout in the world with him; when their discussion was over, I would be going to the dance! "And Dad said no, that stupid jerk. . . ."

I didn't get a chance to finish my sentence. "Don't you *ever*, ever say that about your father," my mother warned.

I couldn't believe she was defending him. Dad had said "No!" to my going to the most important school function of the century. I had expected her to understand and to be on my side. Mom knew how important it was to me that I be allowed to attend the school dance. I wanted her to say, "I'll talk to your father and see if I can get him to change his mind." After all, Mom was used to intervening for her children, and pretty successfully, too. Instead, she said, "I want you to understand that you will not speak like that about your father. Speaking that way about your dad is disrespectful. Do you understand?" I nodded in agreement. Softly now and very respectfully, I begged, "But Mom, you have to get him to say yes."

"That's another issue," Mom said. "Right now I want you to understand that you are accountable for what comes out of your mouth." She looked at me for a long moment; the silence was painful. Finally she asked, "Who do you consider your best friend among all the girls you know?" I could see I was in for a lecture; at this point I wanted to make sure that was all I got, so I decided to be as compliant as possible. "Karla," I answered.

"How do you feel when someone puts down your friend?" she countered.

"Pretty awful," I said honestly. "It makes me feel bad, sometimes mad."

"Yes," Mom responded, still looking at me intently. "Your dad is my best friend. No one will be permitted to put him down in my presence. Being disrespectful to your father is also being disrespectful to me."

It had not occurred to me that respect encompassed the boundaries of the listener as well as the person being talked about. I had violated my mother's loyalty and respect for her friend, her husband.

When Mother realized that I finally understood, she pulled me close to her and said, "I love you very much. That you learn to treat others with respect is important to me. I want it to be important to you, too." With one hand she stroked my hair, and with the other hand she wiped away tears now trickling down my cheeks. "I'm sorry, Mom," I said, crying softly.

We stood with our arms around each other for a moment longer. I resigned myself to the idea that I would be at home on the night all my friends were at the school dance. "I guess this means I won't be going the school dance, huh?" I said with a big sigh. She moved me away from her so that she could look into my eyes. "Maybe. But maybe not," she said lovingly.

It was a sweet victory. And the best school dance I ever attended!

Bettie B. Youngs
Excerpted from Values from the Heartland

Part 3

Being Friends with the Face in the Mirror

*The big question is whether you're going to give a
big hearty YES! to your adventure.*

—Joseph Campbell

A Word from the Authors

As teens everywhere told us they discovered, it's important to get to know, understand and make friends with the face in the mirror. It's a big task that's filled with hurdles along the way. Maybe that's why so many teens loved Leslie Hendrickson's poem, *Mirror Mirror*, our first selection in this unit.

"I loved it too, Mom. Reading it reminded me of a cartoon I saw recently in which a teen catches a glimpse of herself in the mirror, and wishing she were taller, imagines herself that way. Then, next to it was a second frame, this one of a very tall girl— who obviously didn't like how tall she was. In her mirror is a reflection of herself as a shorter girl. Both girls wished for some-thing other than what they were. Hope against hope, of course: Unless the tall girl is likely to shrink four inches, and the shorter girl is going to grow four inches any time soon, they are going to have to get comfortable with themselves as they are."

"Of course, it isn't just physical looks that teens sometimes don't like when faced with the mirror, Jennifer. Some teens admitted they didn't like the *person* staring back from the mirror."

While many teens like who they see and are quite comfortable being themselves, some teens are still working on it. One of the things that makes having a wonderful relationship with yourself challenging is that assessing yourself as you go about life is not just done in private. The world is watching you! The way you communicate—your choice of words, your tone and style of relating, how well you listen—as well as how you present yourself—your appearance, your manners—are just a few of the many telltale signs of how much you value, honor and respect yourself. It's all about a *self* picture, one that becomes a price tag of sorts—hence, the old saying, "Don't sell yourself short."

"Mom, when I'm doing a workshop for teens, invariably someone tells me about someone he or she is dating, and asks for advice on how to help that person see himself or herself in a better, more positive light. Someone that comes to mind right away is Gianna, who complained that her boyfriend always acted so, 'Poor me.' It made Gianna wonder how someone as bright and terrific as her boyfriend, Robbie, could be so down on himself. 'I still can't believe you're my girlfriend,' he had said to her. But instead of taking the comment to mean, 'I'm so lucky to have you as my girlfriend,' Gianna didn't see it that way at all. 'I'd like to think that I'm going out with someone who thinks of himself as more worthy,' she informed him. 'If you don't think of yourself as very special, *I* must not be all that special either.'

"'Why on earth would you think that?' he asked, completely surprised at her words. 'Because,' Gianna replied, 'if you don't think very much of you, how could you possibly be going out with a really great girl? I'd like to think of myself that way—as a really special person.' It's an interesting point. Obviously Robbie's girlfriend thought he was *special* enough to be dating him. It was a put-down to Gianna for Robbie to think poorly of himself."

It's a valuable idea. Just as you think positively about others, so must you hold yourself in a positive light. Doing so not only makes you more pleasant to be around, but how you feel about yourself is also crucial in how you interpret what others say to you. For example, when you feel good about yourself, you're less likely to feel angered or hurt by good-natured teasing or constructive criticism.

Luckily, we can improve our sense of self. Raising the bar on the image we hold of ourselves begins with questioning not only *what* we think but *why*. Though self-image begins in your own mind's eye, it shows up in your self-confidence, in how you care for your health and well-being, how meticulous you are in your grooming, the friends you choose, and the goals you set and achieve. It also makes a major difference in how happy you are!

As teens everywhere found out, a good sense of self derives from some basic goals set in motion:

- Treat yourself with respect. Don't put yourself down with sarcasm or hurtful words. (Others will take your lead and treat you as you treat yourself. Remember, *you* are the one setting this standard.)
- Recognize your own worth and achievements; if you do, you won't need constant approval from others.
- Don't compare yourself with others. Make your measuring stick for judging yourself *within*.
- Take time out regularly to be alone with yourself, so you can listen to yourself and ponder your inner thoughts and feelings. The goal is to become your very best friend, to truly enjoy your own company.
- Reach out to others to talk about how things are going for you. You will find others know what you are talking about; they've been there.
- Fess up when you mess up. It's only natural that sometimes you'll mess up. When this happens, admit it, talk about it, apologize for your shortcomings, and then vow to do better. This shows maturity. And you'll feel better about yourself and more confident in getting through the next "crisis"—and there will be many. That's just the way life is when you're a teen.

- Think about what you want out of life. The more ambitious you are in going after your goals, the more likely you will be to achieve them.
- Take responsibility for your own actions. When you're off course, self-correct. Stop going in a negative direction and begin anew.
- Hang in there, even when the going gets tough. When you persist, your chances for experiencing success are greater. The more success you experience, the less likely it is that you will feel devastated or deflated by periodic setbacks.

In this unit, you'll meet teens who, like teens everywhere, are coming to terms with lessons in life that may involve others and seem like they are about "somebody else," but nonetheless, teach the importance of becoming and being your own best friend.

Mirror, Mirror

My imagination
Awful me
The mirror reflects
Catastrophe

My private thoughts
Vogue magazine
Human perfection
Imperfect teen

Unsaid truth
Homecoming scene
Everyone envies
The Beauty Queen

Silent secrets
My heart's a stone
If I'm not beautiful
I'll be alone

My thoughts feel ugly
I say good-bye
If I can't be perfect
I'll surely die

Until I learn
a truth more pure:
Within is where true
beauty does endure

I'm looking up
There is no storm
I'll trust my heart
To keep me warm

Mirror, mirror
Show me how
To love myself
Starting now.

Leslie Hendrickson

Jenni—with an "i"

I stood before the mirror in my bedroom, studying myself in my new letterman's jacket. In the corner of my mirror I had placed a hand-painted sign that read "Jenni"—it was my mirror—and I liked my name spelled with my own unique twist. That day, I gazed at both "Jenni's" with approval.

In high school, I spent a lot of time playing sports. I played soccer, tennis and was proudly voted "Most Inspirational" player by my softball team. The letterman's jacket I wore was very impressive: besides having my school's mascot—the eagle—emblazoned and embroidered on the back, it was riddled with an assortment of pins—my trophies—neatly arranged on the large *S.F.* letters (for my school, Santa Fe).

In accordance with my school colors, my jacket was red with white leather sleeves. It was very cool! It didn't have the sissy hood in the back, which was the girls' standard letterman's jacket. It was "the guys'" style—and it was all mine. Wearing the jacket was an announcement of who I was and of affiliation—I "belonged." It was the sound of trumpets hailing all to look and take notice that Jenni was approaching, so they could make room at the lunch table!

My jacket had other perks of prestige, too. On each arm of my jacket were symbolic patches. The right arm declared my rank— a numerical "92" for the year I was to graduate—the other displayed a shield, encompassing a soaring eagle with a burning torch behind it. It represented athletic achievement in our school, and because of the three consecutive years I competed in varsity sports, I was awarded one. Very few students at my school had one of these shields, and I was the only female to boast such "jock-hood." Just looking at it made me feel as though I could accomplish anything I put my mind to.

Above my adorned *S.F.* letter was my name, embroidered and

slightly angled to the right. In beautiful white letters it spelled "Jenni." I was always referred to as "Jen" or "Jenni" by my teachers and friends. Sometimes during practice I was affectionately called "J. J.," short for "Jen-Jen." I always liked nicknames, but J. J. was as close as I ever got to having one of my own.

I learned a thing or two about identity in high school—your name being one of them. You have to know yourself and see if your name *is* you. When I stood in the mirror back in high school, and looked from my face to my name there on the sign I'd made and placed in the corner of the mirror, and then turned to the right angle to get a glimpse of my name on my jacket—*Jenni*—it was definitely me. And in those moments, I was very happy with the unique me whom I saw.

I seemed to be alone in identifying with the face smiling back at me in my mirror. My mother never spelled my name like I did, and it made me feel like a child in pigtails when she added her own touch to my spelling. My brown lunch sack flamboyantly claimed ownership to "Jennie." No matter how many times I told her the correct way to spell my name, she insisted it was "more fun" to spell it *her* way. When she realized I was very serious in spelling my name *Jenni*, she resorted to my birth name, Jennifer. I had some thoughts on that name, too. All through high school, I remember thinking to myself, "Jennifer is the most boring, average name in the entire world!" So I never used it in its full length. I reinvented the spelling from the traditional "Jenny" as my father spelled it and the ordinary "Jennie" as my mother spelled it and replaced the "y" and "ie" with an entirely unique "i."

My grandmother gave me a bookmark that had *"Jennifer . . . Gentle Spirit"* stitched on it in pink letters. I never used that bookmark because I didn't like pink, though I did save it. I don't mind looking at the sissy pink letters while reminiscing about my grandmother. I really love my grandmother; she is so dear to me that even that pink "Jennifer" bookmark has earned a right to be displayed on my dressing mirror.

All this got me to thinking, wouldn't it be nice if we could choose our names instead of having others choose one for us? But since we acquire our names at birth and have little say in the matter, each of us must decide how we can make our names our own. Either that or ask our parents if we can have our name legally changed—which probably won't go over very well with them.

Since a name is who you are, who you *feel* you are, you have to find a way to claim it for yourself. I've done that. What was surprising to me is how the identity I had of me has changed over the years. Perhaps it has to do with making friends, new friends, with the face I see in my mirror. What I've discovered is that my friendship with me has evolved since high school—and that was only a few years ago! This came as a complete surprise to me. Amazingly, now I prefer being called by both my first and middle names, Jennifer Leigh, as opposed to going by just my first name only. I feel that my middle name has more pizzazz than my first name, because of its unique spelling: *Leigh* as opposed to *Lee*. Not only do I like the spelling, but I find the letter *L* to be poetic and graphically beautiful: $\mathcal{L}$.

Jennifer Leigh Youngs. It's not so bad after all! In fact, I now feel I know much more about Jennifer Leigh Youngs than Jenni—though I liked her a lot, too. But that was then; this is now. Now, when I look in the mirror, Jennifer Leigh Youngs is who I see smiling back at me. And so, I smile back at her, too, and know that all the distorted spellings of my name are woven into a tapestry of fond memories—each one representing a very special friendship with others (who probably went through similar metamorphoses in growing into their own names, as well).

Now I understand and accept that each person who spelled my name differently knew me differently, just as I know me differently—then . . . and now.

Jennifer Leigh Youngs

My On-Line Love Affair

I'm in a messy situation, and I'm trying to figure it out. And straighten it out. Here's my dilemma: I met a girl, Nicole Black, when she began attending my church and Sunday school class.

From the moment I saw her, I thought she was great, and I wanted to have her as my girlfriend. I've never had a girlfriend before. Nicole doesn't attend my school, so I only see her on Sunday at church. After learning her name, I started to call her occasionally and invited her to small get-togethers, with some of my friends. She didn't come and hang out with me and my friends, nor did she really want to spend time talking with me on the phone that much. Even though I took that to be a sign Nicole may not want to think of me as a boyfriend, I couldn't be sure. I didn't know if she was just shy, or if she really didn't like me. But I knew I liked her—regardless of what she thought of me.

And that caused a part of the problem I now have. Because I wanted to know what Nicole really thought of me, I wrote her a letter telling her how I felt about her—only I was too insecure to sign my own name to the letter, so I just used the name "George." The next Sunday at church, to no one in particular, Nicole announced that if anyone had something to say to her, they shouldn't hide their feelings—and they could email her. Then, she blurted out her email address. Well, I memorized it immediately and the moment I got home, I emailed her, asking if she knew who "George" was, and would she like to discuss what "George" had to say. I was still afraid to let her know who I was, so once again I just used a phony name, this time calling myself "Adrianna." I also gave Nicole my email address.

Nicole emailed back asking, "Adrianna who?" Not knowing what else to do, I told her that I was a "friend of Teddy's" (that's me)—and wondered what she thought of Teddy. I thought that though Nicole might not want to come right out and share how she felt about me, she just might share what she thought about "Teddy" with another girl—and that way I'd at least know how she felt. I asked if she liked Teddy more than a friend. Nicole did not answer that question.

But my problem is bigger than the web of deceit I've been spinning with Nicole. I've been emailing everyone, and now it's really gotten out of hand. Though I'm now talking to friends from school on-line, I still use other names, never my own. The result is both good and bad: I am learning what other kids think about me. I get mixed reviews. I receive good comments, such as, "He's such a nice guy," which make me feel good, and receive bad comments like, "He's sort of geeky." That makes me feel bad, even though I've opened myself up to the comments because, after all, I did ask the question. I'm pretty sure they would never say this to my face.

But not only have I gotten myself in a position where I can't just be who I am with Nicole, I've told so many stories to so many different people, I've forgotten what I told each person. Now everything is really convoluted; I have the stories all mixed up.

In trying to get myself out of this mess, I went to my priest for advice and confession. He suggested I stop the "whole charade." I have stopped writing on-line as my "fake self" to my friends from school, but I continue writing to Nicole without identifying my true self.

There's yet another problem: I have a bad feeling that my friends from school may know that I am the one who wrote all these emails to them. I also think Nicole knows that I am emailing her.

Nicole is my first love, but it's not working out the way I hoped it would. Nicole never answered my question about liking me as more than a friend, so I still don't know if she does. We don't spend any time together outside of the time I see her at church and Sunday school. We don't talk to each other unless I go up and start a conversation, so I still don't know how to get her to like me as much as I do her. I think that if I tell her what I've done, it will mean she may never like me. And, how could I tell all my friends at school about this whole email situation? I'm sure they'd think I was weird.

My three-year-old brother sometimes puts his hands over his eyes and shouts, "Now you can't see me!" I'm afraid that's what *I've* been doing from the very beginning with this whole situation. I'd like to get myself out of this mess and have everything return to normal! I'll never make the mistake of pretending to be someone else again.

Teddy Bonaducci, 18

Is This the Way It Must Be?

When I am nice and sweet
I'm taken for granted.

When I am compliant and give in
I'm discounted.

When I give up or give in
I'm taken advantage of.

When I am a doormat
I get stepped on.

When I am difficult
I am taken into account.

When I won't compromise
I am respected.

When I am demanding and angry
Others defer to me.

When I am most tough
Others listen up.

Is this the way it must be?
Must I become what I don't want
To get what I want, to have what I need
To be?

Jennifer Leigh Youngs

Hello, World!

Hello world! Do you see me? I see you!

I'm watching the sun go down and rocked by its beauty!

I'm watching the mystery of waves crashing to shore, totally in awe as they return to sea.

I'm feeling the wind, curious as to where it begins and ends and why.

I'm watching the birds fly free without a care, wanting to know what their sweet little melodious chirps mean.

I'm watching tiny flowers: How do they know when to produce such gorgeous, colorful blooms?

Oh, it's a beautiful world, and I'm so happy to be alive!

World, I belong here!

Hello, world! I totally love being here!

Sadie M. Eckhart, 14

Rocker Randy Roe

Last year, I thought I was really cool. The truth is, I was a real nerd!

The good news is, I'm not the same person I was last year! Everything about me has changed. For one, I no longer wear my hair in the dorky style I used to. And I no longer dress in the clothes that I found so "rad." But perhaps the biggest sign of my leaving "Nerdville" behind is that I no longer have larger-than-life-size posters of rock star "Rocker Randy Roe" on—get this, not just one, but all four of my bedroom walls! And it wasn't just my bedroom that I had decorated as a shrine to Randy Roe. I was so infatuated with him that I had yet another picture of his sappy face stuck on my mirror—complete with a larger-than-life-size lipstick-kiss (mine) on top of it!

I cringe to think of how cool I thought he was. Being a kid at the time, I actually thought his music was not just awesome, but also inspired. I was totally devoted to his music. Because of it, I baby-sat that spoiled little brat Shaun McCallen so I'd have the money to buy Randy Roe's next and latest album. I could lip-sync all the words to every one of his songs. But my adoration of him didn't just stop there. I actually wrote in and joined his fan club! And, of course, that's where I sent the many love letters I wrote him.

Yes, rock star Randy Roe was the coolest of dudes—and because I thought so, I was cool, too. No one could persuade me differently—even though my brother and sister tried to convince me otherwise. My brother would swoon, clutching his heart and crooning Randy Roe's name, and ask, "So, has your precious Randy Roe proposed marriage yet?" Glancing in my room, my older sister would shake her head, give me a look of condescending pity and warn, "You're going to look back at this and feel really stupid."

I hate it when she's right.

Ah well, that was last year. I'm long over teen idol, Rocker Randy Roe. Now, I have better taste. Rocker Randy Roe's posters have been stripped from my walls. In their place hangs a beautiful poster of Leonardo DiCaprio. Gazing at the beautiful life-size picture of him, his eyes, his sly smile, I now know what true magnificence is. I've seen all of the movies he's been in; one of them, *Titanic*, I've seen nine times.

This year, I really am cool. And when I think that just one year ago I was attracted to a teen idol who is only going on his fourteenth birthday, and think of my humiliating attraction to Rocker Randy Roe, it hardly seems like it was me at all—seems more like it was just some nerd I once knew.

Mom said this reminded her of her own brief infatuation with some group called The Monkees, that ended with her new love of The Beatles, then The Stones and then Kenny G (who I think sounds like elevator music). "You always end up wishing you knew *then* what you know *now*," she told me. "And probably you will say that about every passing year."

So I've decided not to worry about how next year I might think I was a nerd this year. Instead, I'm just going to enjoy who I am this year—and enjoy my love for Leonardo, too—even though I'll probably have a new Rocker Randy Roe next year! In fact, I sort of have my eye on Ben Affleck.

Denise Platt, 15

Stranded on a Desert Island . . .

"She's the one person I wouldn't mind being stranded on a desert island with," Kelsey Cramer wrote about *me*—and Kelsey's not a nerd. When I read his words, I checked to see if I had the right paper! How could he possibly say such a positive thing about me?

Everyone was always telling me to look for the positive in myself, to believe in myself. It's a nice line but can be a very hard thing to do. I mean, there are lots of things about myself that are not that nice, things I'm not all that proud of. I've done my share of stretching the truth, even lying. And, worse, I even started a rumor about Sheree Holt when she was eyeing my boyfriend— a guy she knew I'd secretly liked all year long. I had asked Sheree to deliver a note to him and I guess she thought that if she could get that close to him, she would see if she could get him interested in her instead of me. Even so, starting the rumor wasn't the right way to handle the situation. I've also taken a few dollars from my mother's wallet without asking, as recently as last week. And that probably qualifies as stealing. So you see, I have plenty of reasons to be down on myself.

Feeling this way, you can imagine how surprised I was when I learned in addition to all the bad stuff, there are some things about me that are great! I discovered this several weeks ago when our teacher in Life Skills had each student take a seat in front of the whole class, one-by-one. She asked each one of us to talk for a couple of minutes about our family, pets, hobbies and our goals now and for the future—those things that were most important to us. Then, while each student sat there before every-one, all the other kids in the class were to write down a thing or two that he or she felt was a really nice trait of the student speak-ing. (We had to do this for ourselves, as well.) Well, when I sat there, it was sheer terror for me. I mean, even Sheree Holt, whom

I'd started the rumor about, was in the class; to say nothing of my friend Lauren Lucas, who'd asked me last week where I got the money for the breakfast I was buying at McDonald's on the way to school. Being that I'm so honest (ha ha), I told her the truth—I'd taken it from my mom's purse. So you can see, some of the kids in this class knew the *real* me. Naturally, I was really squirming, wishing I didn't have to be on the hot seat.

Then, the teacher went around and collected the individual "good things" and put them aside. One by one, this went on for all the kids in the class. Then we were allowed to read what each of the other kids had written about us.

Talk about being in shock! Here are all the things the other students said about me:

One said I am "cute and have great eyes."

One said I have pretty hair.

Three said I'm a good listener.

Two said I have a great sense of humor.

Three said I'm one of the nicest people they know.

Three said I was really confident and sure of myself (one of them was Sheree Holt!).

One (Lauren Lucas) said I'm trustworthy. (I could hardly believe it.)

Three said I'm a loyal and good friend.

Three said I'm really smart and a good student.

One said I was one of the school's *best* athletes.

Two said I love my dog.

One said I'm a really good sister to my two brothers.

Four said I'm really capable and a good problem-solver; and then, there was Kelsey Cramer, who, as I mentioned before, said that I am the one person he wouldn't mind being stranded on a desert island with. (I never knew he liked me, so this was something new and nice to know. If Bobby Schmits doesn't ask me to be his girlfriend soon, I just might consider chatting up Kelsey.)

These were a lot of really good things to hear about myself, but then I came to my own list. Remember how I was supposed to write one or two good things? Well, I wrote three things: "I'd be pretty if I lost five pounds; I'm a good student when I try—which I usually don't; I'm not always honest." It struck me that even though the assignment had asked us to write *positive* things, I hadn't. It made me wonder if I'm in the habit of seeing only the negative, or canceling out a positive with a negative comeback. I thought about this habit just this morning when my math teacher said, "Jeanie, that's a pretty smile you're wearing. You must be having a good day." I replied "Me? A good day? I doubt it!" My statement just sort of made his own smile wilt.

My retort wasn't a positive one. And it not only made the teacher feel bad, it made *me* feel bad. Why wasn't I a better friend to others? To myself?

Reading all the good things that were said about me was a definite high! It made me realize that looking at the positive things about myself is an important view, because focusing on the good helps me raise my own expectations to be that positive, good—and happy—person. The better I feel about myself, the more I want to live up to being a positive and happy person in return. What an important discovery! It's just great to have your friends think you're wonderful, but I've learned that I need to be my own best friend, too. After all, if I'm stranded on a desert island, I'm going to be there with myself, whether or not Kelsey Cramer is there, too!

Jeanie Metcalf, 15

Especially by Me

In the midst of work or play,
I sometimes fade,
And think of the time when I couldn't laugh,
When nothing good was noticed,
Especially by me.

I was a girl who cared too much
and lived through others' tangled lives,
Weaving their crosses through my heart,
But nothing made a difference,
Especially for me.

Now I look at all I've done
to find my happiness in others,
Singing songs that weren't mine,
But somehow left impressions,
Especially on me.

I don't need others' joy or pain
to make my life whole or complete,
I laugh or cry, and it's all mine,
As is all the love which I'm now sharing
Especially with me.

Jennifer Leigh Youngs

Confidence, Dedication, Pride and Desire

Confidence: an ingredient that helps makes you whole;
An attribute that forms from within your soul.
Confidence comes from goals completed with pride,
And results in a good feeling which stirs around inside.

Pride: an ingredient that brings out the best of who you are;
And makes you keep on reaching for your highest star.
Pride comes with mentoring, coaching and good teaching,
And results in attaining goals that are worth reaching.

Dedication: an ingredient that helps you persevere when things
    get rough;
But with it you'll finish first, so hang in there and be tough.
Dedication leads the way in these goals—called excellence,
And results in your arriving at that place—known as success.

Desire: an ingredient we call motivation,
Going for the gold, being a sensation.
It's doing a lot and wanting it all,
It's seeing a challenge and answering its call.

So when you are tired, feeling as if you can't take it,
Tell yourself that you can do it, and know you can make it.
You're a teenager now, climbing higher and higher,
Just hold on to confidence, dedication, pride and desire.

All of these are signs that you are your own friend,
That you care for who you are and will do so to the end,
A friend with desire, dedication, confidence and pride,
One who knows that all these things begin on the inside!

Peggy Nunziata, 17

Negru Voda

Last year, I was on a study tour with a group traveling throughout Europe. On our way to the Black Sea, we stayed in Negru Voda, a remote and very beautiful (and impoverished) town located on the southeast corner of Bucharest. On the night we arrived, we immediately checked into the hotel—a most awful hotel! The room I stayed in challenged my every source of comfort: It was not heated; the sheets were soiled; and the frigid, leaking shower overflowed onto the floor where a rubber grate separated our feet from saturation, centipedes, millipedes and who knows what else. Leaving on my jeans, jacket and high-top boots, I climbed between the unlaundered sheets and prayed for warmth, comfort and stick-to-itiveness to see the night through, no less the week it would take until I would once again return to the warmth and softness of my bed and home. This was definitely deprivation—at its worst.

I woke up to blue skies, sunshine and the smell of breakfast. I hurried to the outside veranda to eat. Within moments of sitting down with my group, a young boy in dirty tattered clothes appeared—a sewer boy who called himself Odie. Without prompting, he began to serenade our group with a repertoire of songs he hoped to exchange for coins or candy. Gradually, his "choral backup" appeared—an ensemble of young teens respirating into plastic bags lined with glue. The "glue" they breathe isn't that of the Western world drug users intended to produce a high, but rather the glue of sewer children, used to suppress hunger. Odie literally lived in the sewer, taking refuge and finding shelter therein. I found this scene disturbing; I felt really sorry for this boy's—and his friends'—circumstances.

That night as I once again crawled into bed in a hotel room I considered far below standards of sanitation, my thoughts turned to Odie: I wondered where he was spending the night.

The night before it was all about me—comfort for me, warmth for me, escape for me. But what about Odie, the little choirboy from the sewer who didn't have the comfort of a bed, a blanket, or even a shower? The few insects that crawled around my bathroom floor were nothing compared to the community of rodents that shared Odie's "bedroom." The reality was, at the end of a week of enduring antiquated hardships and miscellaneous discomforts, I would be returning to a warm home, a soft bed—and a safe community. And when Odie's week was over, where would he be?

Maybe he wouldn't be at all. . . . The very thing that I was praying to survive and escape was the same thing he was dreaming and praying would some day come true for him.

I returned home a week later, different. Less self-centered. Less selfish. My trip to Negru Voda touched my heart and changed my life. Though I never saw the young boy again, he has never left my mind. All the time, most especially as darkness nears, I think about how, although miles apart, the two of us lay our heads down for the night—my head resting on a pillow, and his on a sewer pipe. He has no blanket to draw over his hungry body at the end of his hours of begging.

The haunting memory of Odie, no matter how many countries away from him I have traveled, has made me understand how important it is that we make each other's lives a little more comfortable. Probably I will never see Odie again—in person—but I see him in the faces of other children and other people in need. His memory even comes to mind when I see a stray dog or cat in need of food and a safe place to sleep. And always I am reminded that we must never doubt that others need us, and that we must each do our part to make their lives more comfortable. I, for one, have written it upon my heart to always think of others and to never take things for granted.

Thinking of others is one of the most important things I've ever done for me. I'm more in touch with my heart and who I am than I ever was before. My life is in focus: I live in a world where people need each other. I think seeing life from this view, while certainly about others, is also how you see yourself and your own importance. After my experience in Negru Voda, a part of my self-worth will always be in relation to how I reach within myself and share myself with others. And all because of a little boy named Odie.

Colleen Morey, 20

A Change of Heart

I always saw myself as shy and reserved, like my dad. Lately I've had a change of heart.

My mother is gregarious—I mean *really* gregarious. She'll start a conversation with a total stranger. I could never understand how she could just talk to someone she had never even met before, but this is exactly what she did everywhere she went—in the supermarket, in restaurants, and always when she came to my sports activities. I couldn't imagine myself just walking up to someone I didn't even know at the mall or at school and just starting a conversation—but my mom did this all the time. I used to even be embarrassed by her openness and say, "Geez, Mom, why do you have to talk to everyone?" Mom would smile and reply with total certainty, "We're all here traveling through life together—why shouldn't we talk to each other? Besides making the journey more fun, you make new friends and maybe even help make someone feel less alone." Mom was just so good-hearted and I thought it was a very nice way to look at things, even though I just couldn't picture myself being so outgoing.

After school the other day, I answered a call from a lady in Virginia. "Can I please speak to Jan?" she asked. "I'm sorry," I answered sadly, feeling a squeeze around my heart, "my mother passed away three months ago."

Obviously shocked that my mother had died, the lady told me how sorry she was and asked what had happened. I told her how my mother had cancer for a year and went through all sorts of treatments, but finally her body just got too weak. Then the woman told me she and my mom were only friends over the phone and had never actually met in person. She explained that one day, while she was doing volunteer work, soliciting donations for a local charity's thrift store, she got my mother on the phone. They exchanged home phone numbers and stayed in touch. The lady said my mom was such a good-hearted person and so easy to talk to, sometimes they talked for hours. Then, she said, "Your mother's kindness just radiated from her, even over the telephone. She just loved people, and it showed."

I agree with everything the lady from Virginia said about my mom. Even the last weeks of my mother's life, when she was in the hospital, she was still smiling and chatting with the nurses, asking them about their families, reminding them not to work too hard—and telling each person who took care of her how she was going to take them all to dinner when she got better.

After talking to the lady on the phone (to this day, I don't know her name), I realized that while sharing and talking with your friends is great, it's important to reach out to others, too. Sometimes even a conversation with someone you hardly know can help both of you feel less alone. I've learned even small talk is powerful. It took me a while to work myself up to being less reserved, but gradually I've gotten more comfortable with reaching out and being a lot more outgoing.

Now that I'm more open, I understand why my mom was able to stay so happy, because I understand what a gratifying feeling it is to talk to a completely new person.

A lot of my close friends tell me that they like my *new and improved*, friendly and open personality. I love this compliment. But the best compliment I've ever received came from my dad, when he said recently, "You remind me a lot of your mom; you're so outgoing like she was. I loved that about her."

Tsinsue Chen, 16

The White Lie

It's not been easy being a Chinese girl in a "white" community. Especially since my family moves to a different region of the world about every two to three years. In each new place I try my best to "fit in" with the crowd, but it's a struggle to make new friends.

The most difficult change was the move three years ago from Hong Kong to the United States. Maybe it was because I was a teenager and not just a young kid anymore, so fitting in seemed even more important than it did all the other times when I was a new kid at yet another school. What fun is it when everyone else is going off and doing things—being invited to birthday parties or getting together to go to the movies and then out for pizza—everyone, that is, except you? You aren't invited if you aren't seen as one of the group. Or, maybe this move was the hardest because I was just finally tired of never having really close friends, friends who would be in my life for a long time.

Once I came to the United States, though, I was determined to have really close friends. I decided to act like everyone else—surely this was the key to having friends. Well, I didn't exactly get it right.

Knowing how important it was to be "one of them," I was careful to buy only what everyone else was wearing, and I'd try to find a radio station that played the songs everyone else was listening to. The music I used to listen to was much different than the music the kids listen to here, and I really liked my old music much better. But I don't ever play it anymore, because I want to learn to like the music all the other kids like. I try to fit in other ways, too. At school, though I am usually an A student, when someone asks me what I have gotten on a test or project, especially if I know she doesn't do as well in that class as I do, I lower my grade to make it seem like I am not doing so well. I don't want anyone to think I'm too smart to be their friend.

There are also times I've told little white lies to *impress* others. This happened just recently. I started being friends with a guy I met in one of my classes. We talked a lot, and I could tell we were starting to like each other. Maybe because I felt like I had to impress him, when he asked me whether I had two phone lines at my house, I said, "Of course, we have a couple"—even though my family only has one line. I assumed that he had two lines himself and thought it would make me look better if we had something in common. But to my surprise, he said, "Oh, we only have one line." Then, I felt really stupid. A few days later, he told one of my good friends that he used to think I was really nice, but now he's changed his mind because I'm "arrogant." The little white lie didn't help me get any closer to him at all; it actually did the opposite.

Unfortunately, I exaggerate stories to other friends, too. For example, when some girls asked me if there is someone in the school I like, I said, "Oh, no. I'm dating a boy who goes to another school." But the truth is, I don't even know any other boys, and I couldn't tell you the name of even one other school.

It can be tiring always trying to say the right things, dress the right way, like the right things and wear my hair the right way. I want to be someone all the other kids want for a friend, but going as far as I have, I can see that I'm losing the truth about myself. Almost nothing about me seems real anymore. And it's not even getting me anywhere. In fact, it's hurting my reputation with others, not helping me make friends. Worst of all, I don't like the way those lies make me feel about myself. Now, I can see that stretching the truth has caused me more trouble than it is worth. Sometimes I wish my parents would move just one more time, or at the very least that I could go to a different school, so I could start over again. This time, I would just be me. Since I'm obviously failing at being who I feel the other kids would want for a friend, it's time for me to try being a friend to me.

But it doesn't look like my parents have any plans to move any time soon, so I'll have to stop lying to others—and to myself. One good thing about all the moving I've done, at least it's taught me a little about how to start over. Now, I need to start over while living in the same place—like here.

Rae Cheng, 15

Sheila Garcia

Natalie, my best friend, told me that she'd seen my boyfriend, Chad, with another girl in his car after school. I asked Natalie if she knew who the other girl was. She told me it was Sheila Garcia.

Sheila is a really pretty girl with long brown hair. She transferred to our school just two weeks ago. She seems to have made a lot of new friends really fast, so she must be pretty nice, and wouldn't you know, she's smart, too—the rumor is, she practically got straight As last year.

I went straight to Chad and confronted him about being with Sheila Garcia. Chad denied it—and even sounded pretty convincing. Although a part of me truly believed him, on the other hand I just *knew* that Natalie wouldn't lie to me about something that serious. All my friends encouraged me to do something and not to just let him "get away with it." So even though I wanted to trust him enough to take him at his word and give him another chance, I called Chad a liar and broke up with him. Though I didn't know her, I was mad at Sheila Garcia, too. I mean, Sheila Garcia wasn't at our school more than a couple of weeks and already she was after our guys! Who did she think she was?

"It would serve her right if nobody ever even spoke to her!" my friend Kylie said. "We can do better than that!" my friend Patrice dared. My friends are all very loyal to me, especially when it comes to something this serious, and so we all agreed that it was only right to let everyone in school know that Sheila Garcia wasn't beneath taking away another girl's guy. Everyone should beware of Sheila Garcia!

Part of carrying out our plot to let Sheila Garcia know she had started a war was that whenever she walked by, in unison, we friends all glared, whispered or smirked at her. Our whole aim was to make Sheila Garcia as miserable as we could. This went on for several days. To be honest, I felt for her, especially because Sheila really didn't seem overly bold or arrogant or anything, so I began to feel less sure about the way we were treating her—but I couldn't call off the battle now. What would all my friends think? They had joined in my cause, and it was up to me to take my place among them on the front lines. Then, a week later, something totally unexpected happened.

A friend and I were walking to the bus after school, when we passed by Sheila—also on her way to the bus line. In that same instant, we spotted Chad driving out of the lot with Sheila in his car, her long dark hair spilling over her shoulders. But I knew it couldn't be Sheila—I had just passed her. "Who is that with Chad?" I asked my friend. "Oh," she said casually, "that's Chad's sister, the one who was going to that language arts magnet school, but goes to our school now."

Then it all came together: I'd made such an awful mistake. Not only had I been mean to Sheila for something she hadn't even done, I had broken up with Chad over something that wasn't true! I'd gone against my own conscience and better judgment and been so unfair to both Chad and Sheila. I felt so bad my stomach was actually upset. I had some serious apologies to make.

First, I apologized to Chad. He accepted my apology and said we could be friends. But he made it pretty clear there wasn't any way to get him back as my boyfriend. Then, I apologized to Sheila, even though I couldn't undo all of the things I had said. As it turned out, she was a pretty sweet person and graciously accepted my apology. Finally, I apologized to the friend whose face I had to look at in the mirror. I'd gone against my own integrity, intuition and values, and I felt just awful.

It was a lesson to be sure. I've learned not to be so quick to believe something just because I hear it from someone, even if it looks like it might be true. It's my new promise to myself.

Angie Maringa, 16

Sneak Preview: Romeo and Juliet

During my sophomore year in high school, I got sick with the flu and had to miss a few days of school. When I returned, I was greeted with two essays due, three days of math and history homework, an honors biology lab to make up, plus several tests to take. Even though I went home from school that day exhausted, I still had to stay up really late to accomplish it all.

I thought I had it all finished, but the next day at school, I got a rude awakening: I'd totally forgotten to study for the test on *Romeo and Juliet*, which I had promised I'd take over my lunch hour. I couldn't believe I'd forgotten about this test! It wasn't like I could just sail in and wing it: Because I was absent, I had missed out on the last two scenes of the play in class, which the rest of the class read together. I had also missed out on the in-class discussion, as well as all the notes and dialogue translations they went over! And though I'd seen the movie, who knew if the film version was like Shakespeare's? Worse, because there was so much going on in my morning classes, I had no time to talk with anyone about the play, or even study for it. When lunch came, I went to the English room to face my certain doom. All I could do now was try to remember as much as I could, and guess on the questions I didn't know.

As it turned out, I didn't know a majority of the questions. I was just about to give in and turn in my paper, knowing I'd bombed the test, when I snapped the lead on my pencil. I quickly walked to the front of the room to the pencil sharpener at the edge of the blackboard near the teacher's desk. Standing there sharpening my pencil, I looked down and there in full view lay the answer sheet for the test on the teacher's desk. My first thought was, *What good fortune! I can kiss good-bye all my worries of failing the test!* My heart started thumping, and my brain whispered a joyous, *Yes! Do it! Read over the answers—quickly!*

This was quickly followed by my conscience yelling, *No! You'll get caught!* Of course my heart was thumping faster and faster; my mind flip-flopping back and forth, *Yes! No! Yes! No! Yes! No! Yes! No!* This went on for ten of the longest seconds in my entire life.

Finally, I decided to finish the test on my own, without cheating! Why? Because I knew I would feel completely guilty if I copied the answers. So I finished the test and handed it in, satisfied with my decision—even though I was pretty certain I had failed the test.

When I walked into the English room the next day, my elation of having been an honest soul changed to a wave of doom as I saw my test laying face down on my desk. I knew what awaited me. I stared at it a few seconds before I got up the nerve to turn it over, facing the inevitable F.

You can only imagine my shock when I learned that I had passed the test! I have never in my whole life been so happy to see my grade, a D-.

My mom says the victories that take the most courage are won within. Now I know exactly what she means. Sometimes it can take *a lot* of courage to do the right thing. It certainly did for me. It may have been a "star-crossed" fate for the answers to be left right there before me, but thankfully I was able to find the courage to do the right thing. Now not only can my conscience rest easy, but I don't have to worry about getting caught and meeting a tragic end like Romeo and Juliet (because, believe me, if my parents had discovered I'd cheated, I'd have been as doomed as those star-crossed lovers).

Jenny King, 15

Opinion, Anyone?

We each have an opinion
Of course, we're pretty sure it's right,
But when an opposing view is spoken
We might see things in a different light.

Everyone has an opinion
So don't be afraid to change and grow,
Listen with an open mind
Free to learn what others know.

People have different opinions
We're not required to be alike,
Just respect human differences
And see their opinion as their right.

Sometimes what others think
Can change your point of view,
Yet another's opinion,
Needn't change your sense of you.

Jennifer Leigh Youngs

Involved

Want to do something really special for yourself? Here are ten ways to get involved in activities that help others—and give you a glimpse of your personal best.

Youth Volunteer Corps of America
6310 Lamar Avenue, Suite 125
Overland Park, KS 66202-4247
913-432-YVCA
www.yvca.org

Earth Force
1908 Mt. Vernon Avenue, Second Floor
Alexandria, VA 22301
703-299-9400
www.earthforce.org

Habitat for Humanity International
Youth Volunteer Programs
121 Habitat Street
Americus, GA 31709
912-924-6935
www.habitat.org

National Crime Prevention Council
Teen Crime in the Community, Youth as Resources
1700 K Street, NW, Second Floor
Washington, DC 20006-3817
202-466-6272
www.ncpc.org

Boys & Girls Clubs of America
1230 West Peachtree Street, NW
Atlanta, GA 30309
800-854-CLUB
www.bgca.org

Points of Light Foundation
1737 H Street, NW
Washington, DC 20006
202-223-9186
www.pointsoflight.org

National 4-H Council
7100 Connecticut Avenue
Chevy Chase, MD 20815
301-961-2973
www.fourhcouncil.edu

YMCA of the USA
101 North Wacker Drive
Chicago, IL 60606
312-977-0031
www.ymca.net

America's Charities
12701 Fair Lakes Circle, Suite 370
Fairfax, VA 22033
800-458-9505
www.charities.org

American National Red Cross
National Office of Volunteers
8111 Gatehouse Road
Falls Church, VA 22042
703-206-7410
www.redcross.org

Bettie B. Youngs and Jennifer Leigh Youngs

The Pheasant

One afternoon, as my father mowed the alfalfa, the large sickle of the mower clipped the legs of a pheasant as she sat on the eggs in her nest carefully hidden in the hayfield. Because she had been so wounded, my father killed the pheasant to spare her from suffering, and from being attacked by a fox or dog that would prey upon a helpless pheasant. My father then gathered up the three orphaned eggs from the pheasant's nest, which now lay in disarray, and took them home.

My brothers and sisters and I were very upset by this incident, and had many questions for my father. At the table that evening, my father talked to us about how mankind and nature are inter-related. He also spoke about the nature of Mother Nature and our role in protecting and comforting all her creatures.

"But, Dad," my sister Judy inquired, "why didn't we let the pheasant live? She could still sit on her eggs and hatch them, even without legs."

"Without legs," Dad answered, "the mother pheasant wouldn't be able to teach her chicks to hunt after they hatched. And worse, without legs, she couldn't protect herself against predators like the fox, or gather the food she needed to live. No, I'm afraid she wouldn't make it out there without legs." Always the humanitarian, my brother Mark chided, "Dad, no one, not even a hungry old fox, would hurt a poor pheasant who didn't have legs."

"Legs or no legs," my father responded, "a fox will eat a pheasant any day, any time."

"That's not very nice," cried my littlest brother.

"Why?" I questioned. "Why would a fox want a wounded bird?"

"Because," replied my father, "it's in his nature."

We all looked curious and confounded. Sensing that he had

not been completely understood, our father leaned forward, rested both elbows on the table and, with his best storytelling voice and most animated face, began his yarn.

Once upon a time, there was a pheasant who, while out forag-ing for food, broke both her wings. And since her wings were bro-ken, she couldn't fly. Now this was a real big problem because her home was on the other side of the lake, and she wanted to get there. She stood by the edge of the lake thinking of what to do. She flapped and flapped her wings, but it was no use; she was too injured to fly.

Along came a fox who, seeing the pheasant's problem, said, "Looks like you have a problem. What's the matter?"

"Oh," said the pheasant, "I live on the other side of the lake and I've broken my wings and now I can't fly home."

"What a coincidence!" said the fox. "I live on the other side of the lake, too, and I'm on my way home. Why don't you hop on my back and I'll give you a ride?"

"But you're a fox and you will eat me," said the pheasant.

"No, no," said the fox. "Don't be afraid. Hop on. I'll take you home."

So the pheasant, anxious to get home, hopped on the fox's back, and he began the swim home. But just before they reached the shore on the other side of the lake, the fox shook the pheasant from his back, causing her to fall into the water. Frightened, the pheas-ant cried out, "Oh, please don't eat me."

"I'm afraid I have to," said the fox.

"But why?" pleaded the pheasant.

"Because," grinned the fox, "it's in my nature."

With differing degrees of understanding—and deep in thought—we kids quietly absorbed the visions of the story we had just heard. It left us with no doubt of our father's under-standing and respect of Mother Nature and all her creatures. But we also understood that our father was talking about an even bigger lesson here—*character*. Certainly, we never questioned our father's character; it was impeccable. Unlike the fox, there were no inconsistencies in his life, no hidden agendas, no false pretense, no lies. My dad, a strikingly handsome, strong, charismatic and energetic man, walked his talk in every way.

To this day he is an honorable man, very principled. Farming, his chosen work, is a passion. He's at home raising and caring for animals. He feels at one with the earth and takes great pride in planting and harvesting the crops. He refuses to hunt out of season, even though deer, pheasants, quail and other game roam our farmlands in abundance. He refuses to use soil additives or feed the animals anything other than natural grains. A most conscientious man, he taught us why he did this, and why we must embrace the same ideals. He is still a model teacher—always focusing on the whys, the reasons for doing. He taught us the concept of being and becoming, and not just having and getting, and in his words, "Never sell out on your heart." He told us about gut instincts and how to decipher between those and emotional sells, and how to avoid being fooled by others. "Always listen to your instincts, and know that all the answers you'll ever need are within you. Your goals should be aligned with your values, and then your work will radiate your heart's desire. Care about people," he says, "and always respect Mother Earth; wherever you shall live, be sure you have full view of trees, the sky and land."

My father. He loves and values his children. Knowing him as I do, I'm genuinely sorry for the young people who will never know their fathers in this way, or will never feel the power of character, ethics, drive and sensitivity all in one person—as I do in mine. I knew he felt me worthy, and he wanted me to see that worth. And I know my father as a man of character because never have I seen any conflict in the way he lives his life.

In accordance with his protective nature and his caretaking ways, the pheasant's three eggs were given to a plump old goose, who dutifully sat on the eggs around the clock, getting up from the nest only briefly to turn the eggs and to eat. Within weeks, three pheasant chicks emerged. After several weeks of caretaking, we released them into the wild, making the cycle complete: My father had taken from Mother Nature and given back to her as well. In making the exchange, he taught us a bit more about Mother Nature and our role in protecting and comforting those in our world. And he also taught us to hold Mother Nature in the highest regard—with the same regard we hold for him.

While the fox may not have been such a good friend to the pheasant that day, my father's friendship to all his children, as well as to everyone and everything around him—nature's creatures included—never wavered. Friendship, pure, simple and uncomplicated, is a gift, and one we can all give to each other. It begins with self-love. For my father, his friendship with others started with himself, a relationship he never, ever compromised.

Bettie B. Youngs
Excerpted from Values from the Heartland

Part 4

Love in Our Lives!

If only we could love deeply enough and sustain love long enough, we could become the source of our own miracles.

—Jennifer Leigh Youngs

A Word from the Authors

"Mom, I heard somewhere that you need at least one hug a day to survive, two to be healthy, three to be a happy person and four to feel loved."

"Count me in, Jennifer. I'll have five a day, please!"

"I know giving hugs sounds simplistic, especially as it relates to *survival*. Certainly love is more than just hugs—but the point is everyone needs love. Maybe the need to feel loved and to give love is even built into our genes, you know. Maybe as teen Amanda Mossor said, we're 'coded' for love. Maybe that's why we seek love: We need it to be happy and healthy—to live."

"Good point, Jennifer. It's been said that love is the most potent force in all the world—as the teens we heard from confirm. They were amazed, and thrilled, at the awesome energies of love and its ability to influence their feelings as powerfully as it does. Certainly its supremacy of power is what prompted the great philosopher Teilhard de Chardin to remark: *'Someday, after we master the winds, the waves, the tides and gravity, we shall harness the energies of love. Then, for the second time in the history of the world, man will have discovered fire.'* What greater force for good, what greater depth of emotion exists, what greater gift could one give or receive, for what gift is more priceless than love? Perhaps none. Some believe that love is our sole reason for being: that our earthly mission is to expand our capacity to love along the way. One of the major tasks we are charged with in our lifetimes is to learn to love—to come from our hearts, to lead with our hearts."

When it comes to matters of love, you teens certainly led with your hearts. "Love and the human heart just go together," you said. How appropriate! The heart represents love, and in turn, the symbol for love is the shape of a heart. The very image of a heart conjures up feelings of tenderness, affection and caretaking. Love—feelings and actions motivated by giving and receiving *from the heart*—bestows an essential ingredient necessary to the well-being of our lives.

"Jennifer, I think it can be good to chronicle the importance of love in our lives, especially since without love we cannot grow and develop in healthy ways. With love our lives sprint into full bloom, causing us to see more clearly the beauty and potential within ourselves—and others."

"You know, Mom, I remember a child development class I once took that helped me realize the power of love and its importance in our lives. We were taught about a study that was done with twenty children from an orphanage. The children were divided into two groups of ten. One group of children was taken every day to a nearby home for developmentally disabled teenage girls. Each of these ten children was assigned to one of the teenage girls to be taken care of. The girls would feed the child, play with the child, hug and kiss the child. Then, at the end of the day, the girl would sometimes even cry, as she waved good-bye while the child went off on the bus, back to the orphanage. Each of those girls truly loved the child she cared for. The other group of children was left at the understaffed orphanage.

"Researchers followed both groups of children all the way into adulthood. The results were amazing and worth noting: All of the children who were given the love of the teenage girl while growing up had finished high school, married, had jobs and families. Only one of the ten ever divorced. But the ten children who were left at the orphanage and not given that special love hadn't fared as well. In fact, the difference was striking. Not only had none of them finished school, all ten of them were either in institutions for the emotionally disturbed or the developmentally disabled or in prison. The power of being loved by one disabled teenage girl affected the entire lifetime of the orphan she cared for—it could even be said that it transformed that child's future."

"Jennifer, fortunately we all have the ability to bring the transforming power of love into our lives: It can be as simple as giving love. We found this out in our first *Taste Berries for Teens* book in the *Making a Difference* unit. As we profiled there how teens were actively involved in doing things for others—such as you do in your work with Airline Ambassadors delivering humanitarian aid to children in orphanages around the world—we witnessed that giving love in this way creates miracles for others. And as you say, creating miracles for others is the way to become the source of miracles in our own lives. My heart so opens to your quote, *'Giving love when we are without it becomes the potent form of peace.'* Love is a powerful catalyst for transforming our homes and communities into places where peace and a sense of community is the standard for how we share our lives—and earth home—with each other."

Such are the miracles born of taste berries of love.

That we can *give* love speaks to the miraculous determination of the human heart to seek what it needs—time and time again. Even in cases where the heart loses a love—or rejects one because it isn't right for us—it begins a new search. Our hearts, it seems, are on an endless search and quest for such love. As they say, love makes the world go 'round!

No one needs to remind teens that love is the essence of life! As you awaken to feelings of love beyond that of self, family, pets and best friends, you are convinced that love is the point of life! As the teen years prove, there is no shortage of things to learn on the subject. Learning what love means to you—and to others—and finding the boundaries that make love a healthy two-way street for those involved, are only a few of the lessons found in the exploration of love. Which is why love cannot only make the world go 'round, but in some cases, it can make your life seem as though it's spinning out of control! Alas, Henry David Thoreau was right, "The heart is forever inexperienced" when it comes to matters of love!

Making the world go 'round, or spinning out of control, either way, love changes things. Teens across the country shared stories of love's transforming power, and how it changed or touched their lives, and the lives of others too. May their stories touch your heart and life, as well.

Coded for Love

It wasn't until recently that I realized there is more than one kind of love. I used to drive myself crazy trying to figure out how I could be in love with my boyfriend, but then be instantly attracted to a new guy I saw at the mall. Well, I've finally gotten it figured out. You see, there are different kinds of love. For example, there is love, as in family; love, as in best friends; love, as in first love; love, as in being excited about something; love, as in crush; and love, as in infatuation, to name just a few.

As I see it, these different kinds of love are divided into three categories:

Category 1: Obligatory Love

Love for family: This sounds simple enough, but it's really very complicated. Everybody in your family is different, and they each want individual things. And, as I'm sure you've learned by now, their motivation for getting them varies. You have to figure out each person in your family if you're going to make the most of family love or else these people will get on your nerves. I've also discovered that you never really know how much you love each of the members of your family—especially your mom and dad—until you are away for a long trip and get a chance to be lonely. That's when you realize you love them and need their love way more than you think you do.

Love for best friends: You have to really step out on the line and go the distance for your friends. Being on the outs with your best friend hurts about as much as breaking up with a boyfriend. So you really have to learn how to be fair, listen a lot and be willing to let this person in on things you normally wouldn't tell someone else. I could never have made it this long without my *best* friend; I could not even imagine my life without her! She's the one person who helps me survive from Monday through

Friday, lets me know what others are thinking about me; covers my back and clues me in on things—should I happen to miss something. Best of all, she is the person who opens her heart to me whenever I need it. (Love for regular friends is not the same as love for best friends—whether they are the same sex as you or not.) **Note:** It's important not to accidentally fall in love with one of your guy friends (or if you're a guy, then your female friends), because why waste a good friendship? In the end, while every now and then you hear where the relationship turns into true love, mostly you'll find that you were only meant to love this person as a good friend.

Love, as in being excited about something: Everyone's most likely been in love with something. For instance, I *love* to dance. I dream of dancing right in front of the stage at the next Backstreet Boys concert—because I *love* the Backstreet Boys' music. I'll be dancing in my new platforms, because I *love* them too. (You get the idea.)

Category 2: Definitely Love (or Sure Feels Like It)

Childish love: Who can ever forget that? In fifth grade, it's being in love with every boy in your elementary school class (at least once) and sobbing when the pick of the week checks "no" on the note you pass him. In sixth grade, it's being in love with every boy in your class, and knowing if one checks "no" you can always give your note to your second, third or fourth choice.

First love: Now this is the most unforgettable love there is. You could fall in love a hundred-plus times, and yet never, ever experience that wonderful feeling of a *first* love. When you've experienced love for the first time, you've been irrevocably changed! From that moment on, "love" is never an option—it's a must, an absolute necessity—like air or water. First love is the one you spend countless hours on the phone with even when there is nothing to say. This is the person you are absolutely, positively forever sure that your life will never be the same without. This is also the one who leaves you with a horrible empty feeling when he breaks things off with you (or vice versa).

Love, as in crush: Tell me you have never had a crush on someone! A glance, a fleeting smile and suddenly: *He's the one!* Now you look forward to going to school, and when he's even in the nearby vicinity, you giggle, laugh and basically act like the girls who profess to be in love—even though you once promised yourself you'd never act so dumb. And, of course, you now have to keep tabs on all the girls around, in case they decide they have a crush on your Mr. Potential-for-a-First-Kiss. You spend hours drooling over that person, doodling his initials next to yours on paper, and you spend your nights dreaming about him. But eventually you learn it was and always will be just a crush. Nothing more.

Love, as in "geographically undesirable" (GU): Will he ever be mine? You try not to fall for him because he lives so far away, goes to a rival school or is pierced in the wrong places, but you can't help it. In your eyes, what's keeping you two from being the next Romeo and Juliet is only a matter of time, space and perspective. (Not that this can demolish the hopes of your being together some day.) All and all, this love is pretty much ill-fated and never becomes anything more than just a prolonged crush. Except it's easier on your heart when you realize it's over.

Love, as in infatuation: Ohmygosh! He's so hot! It's that one with the trendy hair, great eyes, a killer smile, the guy that finally gets your digits. The star football player asks you, YES YOU, out. Then you realize you've spent all this time admiring "the football star" and never taken time out to meet the real him. Unfortunately, he is hardly ever the guy you thought he would be. For such a winner on the football field, he doesn't score many points when it comes to loving you as much as he loves himself—nor for spending as much time with you as he does with football and his friends. But you are so in love with his exterior that it's not until your best friend smacks you upside the head and makes you realize he's no good for you, that you grudgingly dump him. (After all, being seen with him has its perks.) **Note:** Another warning, while on this subject, it's also important to be aware that you will probably stay a little longer with a guy in this category than you should.

Category 3: True Love

Love, as in true love: True love is the one you live for, the one you thank your lucky stars for. It is what almost every person in the world seeks in life. I've been told that true love makes an already complete person even more complete. Poets write poems about it, musicians write songs about it, artists are moved to create masterpieces because of it. True love is destined, fated, meant to be. **Note:** A few of the other loves might also inspire such artistic tributes, so you can't count on this alone to prove that you have found true love.

So you see, love truly is a complicated feeling, no matter which category or what kind it is. The thing is, we humans are probably just coded for love. And that's why if you don't get it right the first time, you just keep trying until you find the category that's best for you at the time. You just keep working your way through the list. So if you don't get it right, you need to just decide to overcome your heartaches and give love another chance somewhere else, with someone else. Really, there's enough love to go around. There isn't a person alive who isn't feeling love somewhere, somehow, with someone—and, of course, hopefully it begins with feeling love for themselves.

Amanda Mossor, 17

In Love, What I've Become

Wow, yesterday he smiled at me! That's never happened before.
Or maybe he was laughing at the sweatshirt that I wore.

I can't believe I change my clothes a hundred times a day,
And when I think I've found what's right, I still run the other
  way.

Who is this weirdo person I've suddenly become?
Each day I have to ask myself why I've grown so dumb.

I think up all those witty things that I intend to say.
Then when he comes up to me, I just blush and walk away.

That seems to be the easy part, this zombie who can't speak.
I fall apart when he comes near, and my knees get weak!

Why can't I just go up to him and tell him how I feel?
Instead, I simply tell my friends—it's bizarre and so unreal.

I've made a list of all the things that won't work when he's
  around!
Can't breathe, can't talk, can't walk—and what's with those
  goofy sounds?

Now I'm bumping into things; I stutter when I speak.
I sometimes use too much perfume—surely I must reek!

My smile is no longer good enough, and I really hate my hair.
My eyes! My ears! My nose—all wrong; my shape is like a pear!

My clothes: completely out of style. My makeup: really drab.
My laughter: all but disappeared. My shoes: they need rehab.

My heart is but an empty shell and aches throughout the night.
My stomach churns, my heart deflates, my pulse rate isn't right.

My teachers just don't understand—once sweet, now Grinch
   instead.
My parents just gave up on me. My cat does not get fed.

It's all because of this one boy my life is such a mess,
A boy I cannot hold or touch, can't kiss and can't caress!

I know that I should tell him, and let him understand,
My love for him is very real, but his interest seems so bland.

I know I can't go on this way—I'm not even on his "list."
Why has fate bestowed on me a plot with such a twist?

How come it is he doesn't see the sorry state that I am in,
And want to make it up to me, to see my suffering end?

Just how long can he ignore the way my heart does yearn?
Or maybe fate has chosen him, for me to live and learn.

There must be many lessons here on which I have to work,
And then one day I'll understand, why he (or is it me) is such a
   jerk.

Alynn Kirk, 16

Puppy Love

A really mean-looking man leaned against a wall, his large tattooed arms crossed over his massive chest, waiting. Just waiting. Meanwhile, a plump ball of fur, its tail wagging so hard it literally shook his whole body, innocently romped down the corridor outside the room. Looking this way and that, the puppy seemed to know just where he wanted to go and so continued his bouncy stride. A blank look on his face, the surly tough guy stood motionless, waiting. Waiting.

Suddenly, there was the clanging of keys unlocking the door on the other side of the room where he waited. The tough guy's stony face broke into a gigantic smile and he called out, "Zolie?" It was all the puppy needed to confirm he was in the right spot. "Zolie" wiggled right up to his newfound pal. Leaning down, the man, Jesse, picked up the soft little puppy and crooned, "Zolie! Zolie! How's my Zolie?" Patting, stroking and snuggling the dog, Jesse pulled Zolie even closer, buried his head in the puppy's little round belly, and blew on it, like a parent does on a baby's stomach. It was love. True love.

As Zolie licked the man's face in appreciation, Jesse was moved with adoration. Perhaps for the first time in his life he melted with love. You see, Jesse is a prisoner, a "hardened convict" at a federal penitentiary. Zolie, a mere pup, has been placed in Jesse's care—for a reason.

Jesse and Zolie are part of an experimental program where prison inmates are given a puppy to care for and to train, a job that will last anywhere from twelve to fourteen months—depending on how the training goes and how the program itself works out. It puts the transforming power of love to the test: Can such a loveless and hardened man give love—and teach it to a puppy?

The experimental program is set up so, after their training, these puppies are given to people who are looking for a "mature" dog for companionship, like an elderly person who isn't able to care for a young, energetic and untrained puppy, but would really love to have a dog. Some of the puppies go on to get even more training, and then they're placed with handicapped people, where the dogs help them with specialized needs by doing things like alerting them to doorbells, buzzers or special beepers, or signaling when it's time to take medications.

The most important thing is for the inmate to give the puppy enough love and attention to make sure it'll grow up to be a friendly, loving dog. They call it "socialization." The inmate also "house trains" and grooms the puppy, but his biggest role is just giving the puppy love, attention and affection.

It's a role Jesse takes to heart. The first day I watched them, Jesse played with Zolie every single minute for the entire time they were together. Jesse threw Zolie his ball and watched as Zolie lunged towards it, pouncing into it, so the ball shot away and Zolie had to race after it. Laughing, Jesse called, "Get it, Zolie! You can do it! That's it, boy!" Later, Zolie squirmed as Jesse gave him a bath, then wrapped him in a towel and dried him. After waiting for Zolie's coat to dry, Jesse gently and tenderly brushed the puppy. For this Zolie stood still, leaning into the strokes of the brush—eyes filled with gratitude that the indignity of the bath was over.

This went on month after month, until Zolie grew into a gentle, loving animal. But he wasn't the only one that had become "socialized." In the process of giving love and care, Jesse had changed, too. He seemed less mean, less hard and less uptight; there just seemed to be something more gentle and vibrant about him.

Perhaps the biggest change was seen the evening before the day Zolie was to leave the program—and leave Jesse. The puppy was ready for the next phase of his training. On this last night, the puppy was allowed to stay the night with the inmate. Though he knew this day was coming—and in fact, it was the goal—Jesse's eyes were red with tears, as he laid awake all night with the doggie cuddled on his cot, stroking and talking to him.

All too soon, the next day arrived, and it was time for Zolie to leave. Jesse's massive arms wrapped around his not-so-little Zolie's neck; he buried his face in the dog's fur and proceeded to give the dog "the pep talk." Holding the now-stately dog's head between his hands, Jesse looked at the proud animal and, choking back sobs, told him, "I know you'll do good—because you're a great dog. You be good now and remember me. I sure do love you—don't you forget that." As if he understood Jesse's words—and sadness—Zolie lapped at Jesse's face. And then, the "socialized" and well-trained nearly grown dog was taken away, ready to begin his new role—loving someone new. But this moment was heart-wrenching. Watching the dog walk away, Jesse put his hands to his face and simply wept.

I learned of Zolie, Jesse and the experimental program they were part of while watching a television program that covered their story. After watching the whole program, I'd not only fallen in love with Zolie, but I had a soft spot for Jesse, too.

Once they'd taken Zolie away, the camera just lingered, waiting for Jesse to say something. For a few seconds—though it seemed like an eternity—Jesse, his head buried in his hands, was unable to say anything. Then, removing his hands, he confessed, "This is the first time I've ever loved anything so much. This is the first time I've ever felt loved so much. I'm definitely hoping for another puppy. And soon. Real soon."

It was one of the most touching shows I've seen—and one of the most remarkable turnarounds. Love can really make a difference in someone's life. Luckily, because the program has been a success, hundreds of puppies are finding love, and hundreds of inmates are being loved—some for the first time. The power of love: simply remarkable!

Trisha Gerald, 18

Anatomy of First Love: Nine Kisses

I was sitting in the school cafeteria having lunch with my friends, Amanda and Rachel, when a really cute boy, who I'd never seen before, walked by. "Amanda!" he called out, just to get her attention. We all looked up and Amanda waved at him, and then, as though he was no big deal, she turned her attention back to the discussion the three of us were having. "Wow!" I whispered so that only Amanda and Rachel could hear. "He's so cute. Who is he?"

"Paul Turkell," Amanda said, adding, "Ninth-grader."

Our school is in the shape of the letter H, as in Herbert Hoover, the thirty-fourth president. Grades six to nine attend classes at our school and each grade has classes in a different part of the H. So we hardly ever run into kids in other grades. Even though the cafeteria is in the center of the building and everyone eats in the same place, for the most part we all go to lunch at different times, so we usually don't run into students in different grades there either. That's probably why I hadn't noticed Paul Turkell. He was a "freshman," and I was only in the seventh grade.

It was already April fifteenth, and for the rest of the school year, I saw freshman Paul Turkell only six more times: April twenty-fourth, twenty-sixth, May seventh, sixteenth, twenty-sixth and June second (which was also the last day of school). On those times, Paul and I would wave to each other. That's as far as our friendship went until summer vacation, when we ran into each other four times in Walgreen's. Each time we did, we were both with our mothers. When we saw each other, he and I would stand together and talk about school stuff and friends until our mothers were ready to leave the store. Towards the end of the summer, we traded phone numbers. That's when we began calling each other just to talk, to catch up and to pass the time of summer vacation. I had never had a boy as a friend before, and it was fun having a boy be this good of a friend.

When the next school year began, Paul James Turkell was now a sophomore and went to the high school, which was in a different part of town. So, for the first three months of school, I never saw him. But almost every night, Paul would call me or I would call him. We'd chat about our day and other general things—like when his dog had to spend the night at the animal hospital because he had eaten through an electrical wire while digging in the yard, or the huge scene at my house when my nineteen-year-old sister got her nose pierced.

It wasn't long before Paul and I were not only talking about what was going on in school, but what was going on in our family life. Then we started sharing some of our most sacred secrets with each other—like how much he liked a certain girl at school (even if she didn't like him) and how much I was looking forward to having a boyfriend. We even talked about how many kids we'd each like to have when we grew up and got married. And then, right at the start of the second nine-week school term, Paul and I discovered we shared many of the same interests. We both love to sing, and we both had a couple of years of dance lessons, so we knew the steps to almost all the different kinds of dances. So we decided to audition at our local community playhouse for *Grease*, a production that was advertising for teens who could sing and dance to star in its upcoming season of plays. Of course, this meant Paul and I would have to practice dance routines—together. So for two weeks we met at the community playhouse, where the staff of the production had set aside a practice room for those intending to try out for the play.

The more Paul and I practiced, the more I started having feelings for him—as a boyfriend. But I wasn't too sure if I should tell him. From some of our many talks, I had the feeling that in addition to Natalie Parker, a girl in his class at school that he liked, he also liked my best friend, Amanda—even though I didn't exactly know how much. And even though Amanda acted like she didn't have time for him, I know she liked him because she was constantly talking about him. Then one afternoon when Paul and I were at a rehearsal, he said: "I like you."

I was completely shocked. Now I really wanted him for a boyfriend. So I told him I liked him too. "I know," he said, smiling. That was all he said. But his words changed everything!

And so my first guy friend became my first boyfriend. I was on top of the world. I went to school the next day in the best mood I have ever been in my life. Things got even better when, just two days later, Paul called me and asked me to the sophomore semi-formal, telling me that I was to dance with no one else, only him. I was really sure he would be the only guy with whom I even wanted to dance. For the rest of my entire life. Throughout all of human history. Forever. And ever.

I did only dance with him. And it was incredible, another "something" I had never experienced. Then on our third dance, Paul pulled me close and sang the entire song to me. It was awesome, and right then and there I knew for sure I was totally in love with him. And I was sure he must feel the same way, because he and I danced to every single song at the dance. And with each and every slow song, he pulled me closer and closer. Eventually, there was no space between us at all. During the very last song, "End of the Road," I looked into his eyes and told him I'd love him forever. On the way home, Paul left his arm around me and held my hand. As we sadly said good night, he kissed my cheek and gave me a hug.

Six days later, Paul asked me to go with him after school to pick up his paycheck at a place he works part-time. The entire way there and back, we held hands. On the way back, he left his arm around me the entire time. And when he dropped me off at my house, he rubbed his cheek across my forehead, and then kissed my forehead a total of nine times. Nine times! My friends, Amanda and Rachel, have both been kissed. Rachel twice by Ben

Henry. Amanda's had a lot of kisses, too—six—once by Raymond Lux, once by Clay Lloyd, and four times by Joey Edwards. But I've been kissed nine times. Nine! And all nine by Paul James Turkell, my true love!

Then, just two weeks later, the day after my birthday to be exact, Paul said he thought we should be "just friends." That was it. Just like that. Not my boyfriend, just back to being my "friend."

I cried myself to sleep that night. And every night for two weeks. But then it didn't feel as bad, so I figured I had successfully fallen out of love. Then, two weeks and one day later, I was at a party at his friend's place and Paul was there with a girl from school, Krissy. The two of them started kissing and I started crying, because I knew I'd never again do that with Paul. When Paul saw me crying, he came over and asked what was wrong. Though I didn't tell him how I was feeling, it felt so good to have him care. At that point, I didn't know what I missed more, our friendship before we started being boyfriend/girlfriend, or being with him as his girlfriend. I finally knew what it felt like to have a boyfriend. "Let's dance," he said, and then we danced to two slow songs—the same way we did at the sophomore semiformal. I fell in love all over again and told him so. "You're a good friend," he said in return.

While at the party he met a girl named Liz, and the two of them fell in love. And before the party was over, she was wearing his bracelet. So, that means they are really in love. So now I have to start the whole process of feeling hurt again, so I can go back to being just friends.

After that party, Paul and I didn't talk to each other for nearly two weeks. But then he called me and said, "Let's be friends so we can talk about things." So I thought about how good it felt to talk with him and decided that having Paul as a friend was better than not being able to talk with someone about all the things that he and I were able to talk about. So now Paul and I are back to calling each other every night again.

I know he'll never be my boyfriend again, because he told me he should be with girls who are at least as old as he is. So, that's that. But I've decided that it's okay. It's kind of like not making it for the final cut of *Grease*—it was a disappointment, but the practice and the anticipation were a lot of fun. Besides, Paul *is* a good friend, one who I can talk with about almost anything. And I really love him as a friend. But, I will always remember how he was my first boyfriend, and all the things I felt *because* of him. Especially those nine kisses. For a first boyfriend, I think that's a good record!

Nicole Syngajewski, 15

The "Side Effects" of Love

I'm in love, and it sure brings out the best in me! Just ask anyone who knows me! Now that I have a boyfriend, I'm so much more together. Love is very motivating.

"Are you making the honor roll this quarter?" I asked Kyle Wilson one day in the cafeteria, just to strike up a conversation.

"Sure, aren't you?" he replied.

"Hope so," I said, knowing there was probably a better chance of me winning the lottery—and I'm too young to play. But hearing the expectation in his voice that I would be on the honor roll with him, I was determined that "yes" I would be on the honor roll—even if I'd only made it one other time in the last two years. Then, in the next breath, Kyle asked me if I'd like for him to "swing by my house" to go to the library with him later that evening. From that very "first date," I've taken every single one of my books home, because I decided then and there, I was going to study harder than ever! I mean, since Kyle really cares about getting good grades, and his goal is to be on the honor roll (and his last girlfriend was Debbie Corso, the smartest girl in our class), it made me think about my own grades. When I started going out with him, my grades were just average. I did what I needed to do to get by. But knowing good grades are important to him, now I work harder on keeping my own grades up.

I've even enlisted my good friends Melinda and Morgan. We always get together after school, just to hang out. We listen to music, talk, laugh and just mess around—but we don't do homework. Until now! Now, sometimes we get together and really study, especially if one of us is having a difficult time in a subject that the other one is good in. It's made our grades better—and our friendship too.

"Where do you keep the vacuum bags, Mom?" I asked one Saturday last month. "Why do you want to know?" my mother questioned, looking honestly puzzled. Well, she almost fell over when I said I wanted to vacuum the carpets.

"Kyle is picking me up, and I've been to his house—it's perfectly spotless, so I think I'll vacuum, especially the TV room where we ate popcorn last night." After the initial shock, my mother walked around looking like she was the one who had won the lottery. Making her that happy actually felt good. Now I'm in the habit of doing my part to help keep the house picked up and neat.

With Kyle in my life, I'm really getting my act together. And I've discovered it has some really good "side effects." For example, now that I'm getting my homework done each weekday—rather than procrastinating and letting it go until the weekend—I can spend time with Kyle on the weekends. Since my homework is done on time, my parents don't have to constantly remind me to get on it, so we talk more and argue less. It's really cool how once I started acting more responsible, my parents started to give me more respect. All these things that they used to have to nag me about, I now find myself doing because of Kyle. He just brings out the best in me. Not only does it make all my relationships better, but I'm real sure I'll be on the honor roll next quarter. About that time, I may even be wearing Kyle's class ring around my neck!

Like I said, love is very motivating!

Erin Conley, 17

A Little Fight Never Hurts . . .

When Joel and I decided to go with each other, I knew right away I wanted to fall in love with him.

We'd been going together for one week when we got into our first argument. I have no idea what we disagreed about, but I do remember everything about the fight. It happened when we were sitting together at a basketball game for my school. He just got up and stormed out of the gym. Like I said, I don't remember what was said, or why he left, but he did.

After he left, I sat there, not knowing what to do. At first I was just confused over what happened, but the next moment my heart ached at the thought of being on the outs with him. I wanted to tell him that I was so sorry, that I didn't mean whatever it was I did, or whatever it was I said. So I ran after him to tell him. He kept walking away. So I wrapped my arm around his stomach and told him I was sorry. But he pretended I wasn't even there, too cool to notice that I was even living on the same planet—much less had my arms wrapped around him.

Finally, I just gave up, let go and let him walk away. Besides, I didn't know what to do or say to him to get him to forgive me. I slowly walked back into the gym not wanting to talk to anyone. Staring at the ground, so my hair would hide the tears trailing down my face, I made my way back to the spot where he and I had been sitting right before our argument. Within minutes, he came back in too, and stood with his friends, not far away. I felt like running over and giving him a big hug to tell him I loved him and how sorry I was. But I just sat down where it had all started, wiping my eyes and peeking up at him. I really didn't know what else to do.

He walked over and sat down next to me, then he grabbed my hand and just held it. We didn't say anything for a while, then he said, "I'm sorry. It was all my fault." Well, he was so sweet, I couldn't just let him take all the blame, so I said, "No, I'm sorry. It was my fault—a misunderstanding."

That was our first argument, our first fight. It was also the night of our first kiss. A kiss I will always cherish.

Joel and I have been going out for more than four months now and we've had many arguments. As I've gotten to know Joel better, it seems like I've also gotten to know myself better, too. I've also learned what to say when we're having an argument—the truth. Sometimes the truth calls for an apology, but then again, sometimes the truth means not taking the blame for something that isn't my fault. I guess now that our relationship isn't brand-new, I'm secure enough not to feel like I have to do that anymore. Just a few days ago Joel told me, "We may fight a lot, but we sure make up beautifully." I have to agree with him on both points.

Melissa Hamil, 15

Always, Someone Is Happy

My friends Trevor and Samantha were in love. Then they broke up. Now Trevor and Leanna are in love, and Cody and Samantha are in love.

> LOVE . . .
> It comes and goes as it pleases
> Never failing to make someone happy.

Kayleigh Minutella, 14

Venus, Goddess of Love

From the moment I first laid eyes on her, I thought of her as someone mystical and magical. I've been under her spell ever since.

I'd stopped over at my friend Dave's house one day after school to return a CD he'd loaned me. As I was getting out of my truck, I saw him standing outside his house, talking to a goddess. I was instantly attracted. *Who is this girl? I want to know everything there is to know about her!* I thought. Then I wondered if this was whom Dave had been referring to when he said that he'd just met a new girl. They seemed pretty deep in conversation, so to draw attention to myself, I flipped on my car alarm. Of course they both turned in my direction and then came over.

I handed Dave the CD I'd borrowed and he and I started talking about it, and she just stood by his side, smiling, but saying nothing. She and I exchanged hello's but that was it; I was nervous and tongue-tied just from being in her presence. Since he didn't introduce me to her, I took it to mean he was interested in her, so of course, I didn't press it. I didn't want Dave to think I was interested in her until I knew for sure how he felt about this incredible girl and how she felt about him. I mean, just because Dave had a girlfriend didn't necessarily mean she was *this* girl. *She* was so cool—way too cool for Dave, that's for sure. Besides, if this angel really was his girl, maybe she was thinking of breaking up with him. After all, they just met!

I let several days go by and then, trying to hold in my excitement, I nonchalantly asked Dave who the girl with him that day I'd come to his house was. "Venus," he said. "The Goddess of Love." But he didn't say anything else, and given he'd said she was "the goddess of love" I felt maybe this was his girl. Still, I was left wondering just what he meant to her. It was easy to see why anyone would be interested in a creature as *fine* as her. But that sort of a girl interested in my friend, Dave? I don't think so. Even with this limited—but highly intriguing—information, I was in love, and just had to see her again even if I didn't know when, or how. I mean, I didn't even know her last name, let alone her real first name. Of course, I didn't know anything else about her, either. But fate was on my side!

A few weeks later I was back at Dave's house, just kicking back, playing his Nintendo. The doorbell rang, which was odd because we weren't expecting anyone to drop by. "Get the door, would you?" Dave called.

"Sure," I said, opening the door. There she stood, Venus, the Love Goddess! It was an awkward moment. My palms were sweating, and I was trying to remember how I'd always managed to stay cool with so many other girls and play like they didn't impress me. Guys know this is always the best strategy when you're interested in a girl, especially if deep down inside something about the girl makes you nervous. I've always been nervous around pretty girls, so you can imagine what was going on with Venus, the Goddess of Love, standing in front of me. While I was searching for something to say other than "Hi," she decided it was the best opener.

"Hi," she said, "My name is Jennifer." Then, cool as a cucumber, she breezed past me, tossed her purse on the nearby counter, and started talking to me like we were old friends. Just like that. Within seconds I learned she was only a friend of Dave's, and within the next ten minutes, I knew where she went to school, where she had grown up, what she liked to do for fun—you know, the basic stuff. Then we got into talking about horoscopes and found that we both had an interest in learning more about astrology and each had purchased a couple of different books on the subject.

When it was time for her to go, she nonchalantly asked for my phone number. I asked her why she wanted it, stalling since I didn't want her to go at all. Ever. Of course, I gave it to her. "Oh, just in case I want to call," she answered.

She didn't call.

Every day for more than two weeks, I hoped that she would, but she didn't. I finally confronted Dave; I had to know everything about this girl. "Too late," he told me. "She was just visiting from Iowa for the summer." Now she was gone. Like an angel dropping in for a brief earthly visit, she appeared, reappeared, then disappeared from my life.

The next time I see someone I really want to meet, the heck with acting cool and uninterested. I plan on being honest with my feelings and saying something. I learned a very important lesson about love—and no wonder. Venus, the Goddess of Love, taught it to me.

Orevilo Nahte, 17

A Different Kind of Party

My life changed the day I met a special girl . . . the day I met Tonya Damron. Meeting her made my life as different as night and day, like I had once been living in a torrid rainstorm with ominous dark clouds looming overheard, and then suddenly, there were blue skies, the sun was shining and birds were singing. At least, that's how my heart felt. What did she do to make such a difference? Well, you know, I think it had to do with who I was, and how I had strayed from being myself.

Growing up in the small town of Pike County, Kentucky, there were a lot of things to do for fun that kept me and my friends busy and out of trouble when I was a kid. But by junior high, many of my friends began to drink alcohol and use different drugs. I didn't do drugs, but I did get into drinking—a lot. My friends and I would try to find (or make) a party every single weekend. We got pretty wild. We went from being friends who would get together to play basketball, to believing that we were only having a good time if we were drinking and going to parties where there were drugs. I'm not saying it wasn't fun; it's just that everything began to get more involved—like some of the really serious fighting and brawling that went on at the parties. That may sound exciting, but it's not very fun at all. And, the truth is, I wanted to break away from the group.

Meeting Tonya was the perfect way out for me. She was a terrific girl with high standards for herself—ones she expected to meet, too. We started going out. Having her in my life gave me somebody important whom I really wanted to impress, and we started spending a lot of time together. Still, many of my old friends came over and wanted to hang out. I found it tough to say no to them, even though I wanted to. Tonya had no qualms letting me know that it's cool—and intelligent—to think about what you want, and then make choices accordingly. She certainly did that with me! She didn't just accept my opinion without thinking about it herself. If she didn't agree with me, or if she thought I wasn't seeing the other side of some issue, she'd say so. And, she told me that if I was still interested in hanging out with some members of the group who were always getting into trouble, then she wasn't interested in being with me. It was nice to be with someone who was so certain about what she stood for—and acted accordingly. I loved that about her. She helped me "step up a notch" in terms of my expectations for what I want out of life. Having a friend to help you realize this is a very special thing.

Recently, I moved to Knoxville, Tennessee, over three hours away from the place I used to call home. Even though I am so far away from Tonya, we still keep in touch by email. Tonya is someone I will love forever—no matter how many miles are between us. My memories of her are of a girl who knew herself, was sure of herself and was principled. After Tonya, the friends I hang out with and the girls I date will definitely have a standard to live up to. So I'd like to say to Tonya: "Thanks for bringing out the best in me. You are the reason my life is no longer headed in the wrong direction."

Larry Epling, 19

What Are You Saying About My "Ex"?

Josh and I broke up after we'd been going together for almost a year. When we talked about not seeing each other anymore, we promised each other we'd always be friends. I found out that's very hard when you first break up. It hurt whenever I saw him. Going from being his girlfriend to just being his friend was a strange feeling—and it wasn't an easy transition. When I'd see him at school or places the two of us used to hang out, I didn't know how to act around him—especially if he was talking with another girl. Or, if I was with my friends and then discovered he was nearby, I'd pretend not to notice him—yet I'd hope he'd see me. At school, I'd even walk by some of his classes again and again just so he'd catch a glimpse of me. But if I would find myself in the same hall with him, or in the cafeteria at the same time he was, or when I saw him with his guy friends at the movies or someplace, I'd try not to let him see me. But then after he was gone or out of sight, I'd look around for him, or ask my girlfriends a thousand-and-one questions about where he had gone! I just felt so crazy. I didn't want him to see me, but the moment he was out of sight, I wished he had seen me! I didn't want to talk to him—but I *did* want to talk to him! I began to think I was crazy. It was really a confusing time. Falling out of love, I've learned, takes longer than falling in love!

I've also learned something else about love. It can change your perspective on things. For example, as you'd expect, my girlfriends tried to make me feel better and encouraged me to "move on." At first they'd say rotten things about Josh in order to make me feel better. They'd say things like, "He's such a jerk for not wanting to be with you, but don't worry, you can do better than him." Even though they meant well—they were just trying to soothe and comfort me, and of course, to help me feel like I was still a cool person, worthy of finding love with someone else—their comments didn't make me feel better at all. In fact, they did just the opposite. They made feel bad about myself, wondering how I could like someone they thought was such a loser. And their comments didn't take into account that I knew my boyfriend better than they did—even if he is my "ex." He's really a nice person, a genuine good guy. I didn't like my friends saying that he wasn't. This was a new feeling for me, because before when I'd decided I no longer wanted to like a guy, I'd join in on "trashing" him. But with Josh, it just didn't feel right to do that. I was, after all, once "in love" with him. So one day, after a friend made a derogatory comment about him, I said, "I know you're only saying that to make me feel better, but I'm not going to trash Josh just because we're not dating anymore. Even if we have broken up, he'll always be my friend. Just like you're my friend and I wouldn't go along with anyone talking bad about you."

My friend looked really surprised. "Wow," she said. "That's cool. I hadn't thought of it that way, but I really do get it." I don't think your friends expect you to defend an ex-friend, much less an ex-boyfriend. And that's when I learned yet another lesson. My friend became an even better friend. Why? Because now she could admire my respect for Josh and trust that I'd always give her that same kind of awesome respect.

I'd say love is a good teacher.

Helena Longfellow, 16

Nice Guy—Out There

You come into my life,
Accepting me for who I am
Liking everything about me
Cheering me up when I'm feeling down
Giving me courage to go the distance
Helping me when I need it
Becoming my faith in love.

You're a nice guy out there,
Somewhere.
One day we shall find each other
Until you come into my life,
You remain,
A dream.

Kayleigh Minutella, 14

Love Is . . .

Love is
>   being happy for the other person
>   when they are happy
>   being sad for the person when they are sad
>   being together in good times
>   and being together in bad times
>   Love is the source of strength

Love is
>   being honest with yourself at all times
>   being honest with the other person at all times
>   telling, listening, respecting the truth
>   and never pretending
>   Love is the source of reality

Love is
>   an understanding that is so complete that
>   you feel as if you are a part of the other person
>   accepting the other person just the way they are
>   and not trying to change them to be something else
>   Love is the source of unity

Love is
>   the freedom to pursue your own desires
>   while sharing your experiences with the other person
>   the growth of one individual alongside of
>   and together with the growth of another individual
>   Love is the source of success

Love is
   the excitement of planning things together
   the excitement of doing things together
   Love is the source of the future

Love is
   the fury of the storm
   the calm in the rainbow
   Love is the source of passion

Love is
   giving and taking in a daily situation
   being patient with each other's needs and desires
   Love is the source of sharing

Love is
   knowing that the other person
   will always be with you regardless of what happens
   missing the other person when they are away
   but remaining near in heart at all times
   Love is the source of security

Love is
   the source of life

Susan Polis Schutz

A Flower in Her Hair

She always wore a flower in her hair. Always.

She was a young woman, an aspiring graphic designer who worked with me in a large, busy office. Every day she sailed into the office with its ultramodern crisp decor wearing a flower in her shoulder-length hair. Usually color-coordinated with her otherwise suitable attire, the flower bloomed as a small parasol of vivid color, opened on a large backdrop of dark brunette waves. To my knowledge no one questioned the young woman as to why a flower accompanied her to work each day. In fact, we probably would have been more inclined to question her had she shown up without it.

One day she did. When she delivered a project to my office, I queried her about the missing flower. "I noticed there is no flower in your hair today," I said casually. "I'm so used to seeing you wear one that it almost seems as if something is missing."

"Oh, yes," she replied quietly, in a rather somber tone. This was a departure from her usual bright and perky personality. A long pause followed, prompting me to ask, "Are you okay?" Though I was hoping for a "Yes, I'm fine" response, intuitively I knew I had treaded on something bigger than a missing flower.

"Oh," she said softly, with an expression encumbered with recollection and sorrow, "today is the anniversary of my mother's death. I miss her so much. I guess I'm a bit blue."

"I'm sure it's very difficult for you to talk about," I said, my heart feeling for her.

"No. It's okay, really. I know that I'm extraordinarily sensitive today. This is a day of mourning, I suppose. You see, my mother knew that she was losing her life to cancer. Eventually, she died. I was fifteen at the time. We were very close. She was so loving, so giving. Because she knew she was dying she prerecorded individual birthday messages. I was to watch one every year on my birthday, from age sixteen until I reached twenty-five. Today is my twenty-fifth birthday, and this morning I watched the video she prepared for this day. I guess I'm still digesting it . . . and so wishing my mother was alive."

"My heart goes out to you," I said.

"Thank you for your kindness," she said, smiling sadly. "Oh, and the missing flower you asked about? When I was a little girl, my mother often put flowers in my hair. One day when she was in the hospital, I took her this beautiful rose from her garden. As I held it up to her so she could smell it, she took the lovely flower from me, pulled me close to her and, stroking my hair and brushing it away from my face—in the exact manner she did when I was a little girl—she placed the flower in my hair, just as she had done so many times. . . ." She paused and, as tears clouded her eyes, added sadly, "Mom died later that day. I've worn a flower in my hair since—it made me feel as though she were with me, if only in spirit."

To keep from crying aloud, she sighed deeply before continuing. "Today, as I watched the video designed for me on this birthday, my mother said she was sorry for not being able to be there for me as I grew up. She said she hoped she had been a good parent and asked for a sign that I was becoming 'self-sufficient.' That's the way my mother thought—the way she talked." She looked at me, smiling fondly at the memory.

"What a very loving and touching living memory," I said sincerely.

"Yes," she agreed, nodding her head. "So I thought, a sign, what could I do to communicate that I had learned to be self-reliant? It seemed it was the flower that had to go. But I'll miss it and what it represents." As if momentarily transported to a memory that held much strength and dignity, her melancholy eyes transformed into a gaze that was both serene and brave. "I am so lucky to have her . . .," she said. Her eyes met mine again. Intuitively trusting what she saw there, she pressed a tissue softly against her eyes and unapologetically allowed herself to shed her sadness with tears.

Her strength refortified, she said, "I don't need to wear a flower to be reminded of these things. I really do know that. The flower was just an outward sign of my treasured memories. Mom left a legacy rich in love, and it will take more than an absent flower to dim its presence. Time can never take away her gift of love—nor diminish the manner in which she shared it." Her voice trailed off again before finally saying, "Still, I will miss it. . . ."

She sighed deeply and, changing emotional gears, shifted from her private self into her professional self. Assertively she said, "Oh, here's the project. I hope it meets with your approval." She handed me the neatly prepared folder, signed with a hand-drawn flower—her signature trademark—below her name.

Now I knew the flower this young woman wore in her hair was symbolic of her outpouring of love—a way for her to stay connected to the mother she had lost.

I looked over the project she had completed and felt honored that it had been treated by one with such depth and capacity for feeling . . . of being. It was with respect and esteem that I now saw clearly the enormity of her ability to bring the past into the future, integrating it as a way to give meaning to the present. No wonder her work was consistently excellent. She lived in her heart daily.

I hoped I would always do the same.

Bettie B. Youngs
Excerpted from Gifts of the Heart

Part 5

Expressions of Love!

You will do foolish things in the name of love, so you might as well do them with enthusiasm!

—Colette

A Word from the Authors

Love. Just saying the word conjures up a sense of wonderment, an exciting feeling that fills life with elation and joy. It's so important to feel love and to give it. It's been said that our lives are shaped both by those who love us and those who refuse to love us! "I love you": Three little words that hold a lot of power.

Expressing your love verbally is a great way to communicate, but as teens everywhere know, so is expressing your love in writing. "The art of the love letter is going the way of the condor," said University of New Orleans historian Douglas Brinkley, in an interview (February 2000) with *USA Today* interviewer, Karen Peterson. "It is becoming an endangered species."

Well, we don't think so. Teens write, and write, and write. "In love" teens are simply compelled to express their feelings—some of it by way of the timeless standard letters, and much of it in poetry, as well.

"Mom, it's kind of funny, when you think about how many teens detest creative writing, but love to write letters to their friends. And knowing the love letters I've written, sent and received, I can tell you love letters are very *creative!* Think about how much time teens spend writing to their current flame in school. I know I spent my share of time thinking of the right things to say in a love letter—and I still do! No writing is more inspired than a love letter, or even than a 'let's make up' letter. For that matter, even the 'get-lost' letter in love's demise is pretty inspired!"

"Love: getting, giving, getting right with it. It's all pretty heady stuff, Jennifer! I'll bet that every custodian at a junior high or high school can tell you about all the love letters they find every day on the floor, dropped from inside books and note-books, tossed beside trash cans."

"Do you think they read them?"

"I'm just venturing a guess here, Jennifer, but my sense is that they read the first two million they come across, and then after that, they probably just read a line or two. From that, they pretty much know where things are going from there, and so they don't bother to read further. But while the finder may not read each one, I'm betting that each time they find one, their heart smiles, *remembering*."

Love letters! Imagine the letters we've sent that should have never been sent, the ones we've written and never sent—but wished we had, the ones we wished we'd written, and the ones we've received and those we've saved for years! Whether you write them because you're upset or burning with the desire to express your passion, if you're writing them to or about your love, they can certainly be a powerful way to communicate!

You teens proved that love inspires creativity! You said love was definitely on your mind, and the letters you shared with us confirm that when it comes to love, Romeo and Juliet have noth-ing on you. Whether it was to let your girl or guy know it was over, or to ask your boyfriend or girlfriend for another chance, whether you wanted to profess your eternal passion, or to ask your loved one to go steady—or to marry you—your letters spoke volumes about how seriously you take romance. Poetry definitely seems to be a way that many teens express their deep-est and most inspired feelings. We were really impressed by how many of you also shared love poems you'd written to send with your letters—and beautiful, heartfelt poems they were—whether the romance was long-standing, had just begun that day, had already ended or was only taking place in the poet's mind.

Your poetry and your letters proved that love, whether taking place only in fantasy or in a "steady" relationship, has the power to give people, young and old, dreams for the future—dreams of connection and passion, romance and greater meaning in life. And they showed that love adds new dimension and brightness to your days, which you deeply value: so much so, that you sometimes have trouble letting go, even when you know it's the illusion of love, more than real love, that you are holding onto. So much so, that you are able to forgive, and able to beg forgiveness and feel just awful when you've made a mistake and hurt love. So much so, that even when you cringe or blush as you look back at some of the crazy things you've said and done in the name of love, you then do it all over again when you're in love once more!

In addition to all the heart and passion that the following expressions of love communicate, many of them also help prove you're not alone when it comes to literally "going crazy" over your latest love—which is always a nice thing to know. We hope you're "crazy in love" with the following expressions of love!

Alexis + James

Alexis + James
James + Alexis
Alexis Hall & James Bradley
Alexis Anne Hall & James Jeffrey Bradley

James Bradley
James Jeffrey Bradley
James J. Bradley
J. J. Bradley

Alexis Bradley
Alexis Anne Bradley
Alexis A. Bradley
A. H. Bradley

Ms. Alexis Bradley
Mrs. Alexis Bradley
Ms. Alexis Hall-Bradley
Mrs. Alexis Hall-Bradley

Mrs. James Bradley
Mrs. James Jeffrey Bradley
Mr. & Mrs. Bradley
Mr. & Mrs. Hall-Bradley

Alexis loves James
James loves Alexis

Alexis Hall, 15

Killer Fashion Sense

Dear Love of My Life,

I once thought that I knew what it was to love a girl, but what I felt was a pale comparison to what you inspire in me. When I think of you, when I see your picture, my breathing actually stops momentarily, arrested under the weight of all my feelings of love and passion. Words will never be enough to tell you how I feel. My love is deeper than the sea, higher than the highest cloud, a force greater than thunder, lightning and the mightiest hurricane. You've become my reason for living—for existing. I would gladly lay everything I own—and everything I will ever own—before your feet if you would only give me but a portion of the love I am willing to give you, an eternal love, I am certain.

When I wake up in the morning, my first thoughts are of your smile, and because I'm filled with anticipation of thinking of you all day, the sun comes out, the skies get blue and flowers bloom. When I go to sleep at night, visions of you lead me into a world of the sweetest dreams. Knowing that you live and breathe and sleep at that moment, here in the very same universe as I do, gives my life greater meaning, my soul greater purpose. Say that you'll be mine, and let's build those dreams together. If you would agree to be my one and only love, I would commit my entire life, my heart and soul, my very being, to showering you with love and devotion.

I know many others must love you for all the reasons I do—your beauty, your smile, your killer fashion sense—but I am absolutely certain no one will ever love you as much as I do. When I think of the immeasurable depth of my love for you, I can't believe that I first saw you only three short months ago! Yet, I really believe I've known you for an eternity. I know we are destined to be together, because we are soul mates, who have always been together in a realm outside of time. With that first

look at your picture in my sister's *Seventeen* magazine, I just
knew we were fated to be together.

You've yet to meet me, and I realize I don't have a great career
like you do as a model, but I do have great potential. I get good
grades, know my way around the Web and plan to go to college.
More importantly, I would bring you more happiness than anyone else in the world could ever hope to. I can only ask with all
sincerity, will you please go out with me?

All My Love, I Give to You Forever,
Peter

P. S. *Seventeen* has returned my letter, so I sent it in to be pub-
lished in this book, hoping you would read it. When you do, you
can write me care of the authors. I'll be waiting!

Peter Colucci, 15

Richard, Richard

Richard, Richard on my mind,
I think about you *all* the time.
I dream of you every single night.
Thoughts of you flood my days with light.

Every day my heart grows fonder.
Even so, I have to wonder,
Is this true, is this real?
I can't control the way I feel.

I've ridden my bike down your street,
Hoping just by chance we'd meet.
How can I make you clearly see
How I feel about you and me?

I'd love to hold you oh so near,
And softly whisper in your ear.
Can we hug? Or take a walk?
Go on a date? Or just go talk?

Can I kiss you? Can I call?
Say yes, and I'll give you my all.
The pain I feel when we're apart
I'll tell you now, it breaks my heart!

Richard, Richard on my mind,
I think about you *all* the time.
I dream of you every single night,
I LOVE YOU, so love me, too—all right?

Thelma Wright, 14

Absolutely P-r-o-m-i-s-e-d

Dear Grant,

Just so you know, I'm never speaking to you again! I can't believe that you could stand me up after you promised—*absolutely promised*—that you would meet me in the library after school. I'm through—and I mean *through!!!* I warned you yesterday when you didn't meet me outside my last-period class to walk me to the bus, and now this! Both times you said you'd be there, but you weren't. You promised—p-r-o-m-i-s-e-d—you'd be there! I don't even know how you can live with yourself!

Obviously, your word, your promises, mean absolutely nothing to you. So they mean absolutely nothing to me from here on out. Just like *you* mean absolutely nothing to me from here on out. I am not the kind of girl who can be taken for granted. You'll see; I'm not going to speak to you ever again. Don't even bother trying to speak to me. I don't even want you looking at me. You just live your life and I'll live mine, because we are definitely over. Our relationship is a thing of the past. Just pretend I'm invisible, and I'll pretend you are invisible. Just pretend we are on different planets—obviously *you're* from a different planet. That ought to make it easy enough not to speak to me, because I am never going to speak to you again. Ever!

I'm beyond apologies, so don't even try. No excuse or apology could be good enough to explain away your standing me up yesterday and now again, today! Just so there's no doubt, I'll say it again: I'm never going to speak to you again. Don't think I'm not serious, because I've never been more serious.

Once Yours, Now Forever Silent,
Heather

P. S. If you want to talk about any of this, you can meet me after sixth period or call me after school today. And if you would like to start our breakup after Saturday night, that would be okay with me, too—since there is the dance and you know they'll play our favorite song. It would probably also be good for us to have just one more kiss. You owe me.

Heather Solice, 15

My Hands They Quiver, My Feet They Quake . . .

Last year I wrote a poem for Aaron, a boy in my class. I had a huge crush on him. I found the letter the other day and was so happy and relieved I hadn't given it to him! I'd be so embarrassed! Thank goodness I never got up the nerve to actually give him the poem. Here it is:

When I See You

When I see you my heart it thumps,
My body is covered with little goose bumps,
My hands they quiver, my feet they quake,
And I feel like I'm a chocolate milkshake.
You may not believe I can love you this true,
But that's how I feel when I see you.

I can't believe I was actually going to send this to Aaron! One of the nice things about growing up is you can see just how silly some of the things you did when you were younger really were. Giving the poem to Aaron would have been a very stupid thing to do. I mean, you can't waste a good love poem on a short-lived romance, and I don't like Aaron anymore. But I am a proud survivor of heartbreak, and this year I like his best friend Tommy Moran. I'm sure glad I didn't waste my masterpiece on Aaron, because I'm planning on giving it to Tommy instead!

What I've learned is love can come and go, so you have to be really careful about sending out your best romantic notes. (Or, you might want to make a copy so you can use it again when you fall in love with somebody else.) Good inspiration is a terrible thing to waste.

Kristi Powers, 14

Wear My Ring to Prove It's True

Dear True Love,

Where to begin to try and reveal to you my heart?
Perhaps telling you I love you is the best place I can start.
My soul was like this page before I wrote a word,
Empty, blank, it was a void until my love for you occurred.
The first time I met you, and my eyes drank in the sight,
My world broke into vivid color, where it had once been black
and white.
From that very first moment, my whole being came alive,
And I knew the feeling you inspired would eternally survive.

Each time we share a glance, a wink, a word, a kiss,
It always feels so right; it is nothing short of bliss.
You cause me to sing and to reach for the unknown,
Oh, just look at the tender fruits the seeds of our love have
grown.

The blossoms of happiness and stems of unity and peace,
Fill our true love's garden with contentment that will never
cease.
You've given life to all my dreams; for they are manifest in you,
Now please say "yes" and wear my ring to prove our love is
true.

Derrick Whitney, 16

Just You, Me . . . and Jenny Gentry

Dear Leanne,

Oh, please, please forgive me! Please tell me you didn't mean it when you said you never want to see me again, because I don't think I can live without you in my life. I admit I was wrong to go out with Jenny Gentry when you and I had an agreement not to go out with anyone else. But I want you to know that our love is the most important thing in my whole world. Jenny Gentry means nothing to me. The whole time I was with her, you were all I thought about. I don't know why I even did such a stupid thing, but it'll never happen again.

I know it's hard for you to believe that I won't go out with her again, because I've told you this before and still went out with her another time, but I mean it this time. I'm really sorry you found out about it because I know how it must have hurt. I told Brad to keep his big mouth shut, but he didn't. I love *you*, just *you*. You are there, deep in my heart.

Leanne, you are the kind of girl who can give me the inspiration to live up to being the person who you deserve. Just give me one more chance, and I'll prove I love you. You'll see. The five things I want the very most out of life are: a four-wheel drive, a palm-pilot, a new surfboard, a new stereo system and to prove to you how much I really do love you. Leanne, all the things I want in life mean nothing without you. I beg you to give me another chance—please? What more can I say besides I love you, I love you, I love you. I have a couple of things to do this weekend, so what do you say we start up our love again on Monday? Please say yes.

Stevie Medina, 17

. . . On the Phone Last Night

Dear Michael,

Why did you have to flirt with Annie Janson, and right in front of me and all my friends? Everyone knows Annie has a bad reputation. If you love me like you said you did on the phone last night, then why would you embarrass me that way? I really want to understand how you can love me, yet treat me the way you do. Why do you have to make it hurt so much to love you?

But I do love you, and I can't help loving you. I love you for who you *really* are, not for the way you act. And I love you for who you *really* are and not for the way you treat me. But I still want to know, why do you treat me the way you do?

If you love me the way you say you do, why do you say you want to break up with me when your friends are around, and call me later and act like everything is just fine? It seems like it's almost always only on the phone, or when we're out all alone, that you say all the nice things you say to me—like I looked really hot that day at school. But when we were at school you acted like I was only an acquaintance or something. When I tell my friends that you like me, they say, "No way! Look at how he treats you! Get a clue!" You see, they don't know that you have two ways to treat me: One when we are at school, and a different one when you talk with me on the phone at night. So what's it going to be? I'm voting for the Michael-on-the-phone-at-night person.

So please be *the real you*—the one I know you *really* are. You are *that* person, aren't you?

Lisa Morrison, 16

Suggestions for Meeting the "Right" Girl

Dear Raymond,

I know you're ten years older than I am, and you're my big brother and all. Still I've learned a few things through my junior high years that are sure to be helpful to you when it comes to looking for "the" girlfriend. (I'm not saying you don't know these things already—but, seeing as how you're not married yet, I wanted to tell you them, because they are sure to be very helpful.)

1. Love is a beautiful thing, and when you have it, you should just decide to be very happy.

2. When you look for a girlfriend you should look at the good things the person has done, not all the bad things other people say the person has done—because you never know if the other girls are just jealous because they want you for themselves.

3. You shouldn't pick one person over someone else just because she is cute or beautiful. A cute person could turn out to be mean or quarrelsome, if not to you, then maybe to other people. So pick a girl with a good attitude and nice personality over a girl who is just good-looking (not that it's not even better if the girl has a good attitude, is nice AND good-looking, too).

4. When you decide to ask someone out, it's a nice gesture to give them something like a flower or a small box of candy. But don't give her stuff all the time, because it won't be love she wants—it'll be your money.

5. When you're in a public place and you want to know if a girl is married or not, you have to watch closely and see if

she and another man yell at the same children—if they do, they're married.

Believe me, I know each and every one of these things are important and true, and I learned them all the hard way (even if I learned the last one from watching Mom and Dad)!

Mike Wright, 14

Star Power

Dear Travis,

At the end of this past summer, I sat in my backyard one night just looking up at all the stars and thinking about the new school year. While I was searching the skies, I hoped this year I would find someone special just for me to love. As I was hoping this very thing, a falling star shot across the sky. Right then and there, I wished for a special guy.

Then when I came back to school, my wish was realized when I met you. I'm so glad you moved here from out of state. And I'm so glad I wished on that falling star.

You are that special someone. So, I've written you this poem. . . .

You Are My Star

I gazed out on life's darkened sky,
One bright and shining star to spy.
That star was you—a ray of light,
To guide me through the darkest night.

Your love it shines, your love it glows,
My heart it yearns, my heart it knows,
I wished for you, my shining star,
Wished for your love from afar.

All those magic wishes have come true,
With your love for me and mine for you.
I guess all they say of falling stars is so,
On my wish we fell in love, I know.

Camilla Ronson, 17

It Seems You've Gone
and Left Me Lonely

Dear Jean,

It seems you've gone and left me lonely,
So I write this plea for your heart only,
Please remember all that was once ours
And accept the message of these flowers.

Red and yellow roses for the words so hard to find:
Red for the passion and the tender ties that bind,
Yellow as an offering to right all the things gone wrong;
As a symbol of apology, assuring my remorse is strong.

The thorn on every stem represents the pain in my heart,
As every cruel word I spoke now pierces me apart.
The sweet scent of the blossoms speaks of all the fun we had,
And begs a chance to restore that good and to erase all the bad.

Take my bouquet of apology with my words so sincere,
Know the feelings they express are very real and clear,
And forgive me please I humbly beg, and let me prove to you,
My love is real, forevermore and will be forever true.

Phil Salley, 18

Will You Marry Me?

Dear Danny,
You,
The Love of my life,
With a smile on your face,
Asked, "Will you marry me?"
My answer:
YES YES YES YES YES YES YES YES YES YES YES YES YES
YES YES YES YES YES YES YES YES YES YES YES YES YES
YES YES YES YES YES YES YES YES YES YES YES YES YES
YES YES YES YES YES YES YES YES YES YES YES YES YES
YES YES YES YES YES YES YES YES YES YES YES YES YES
YES YES YES YES YES YES YES YES YES YES YES YES YES
YES YES YES YES YES YES YES YES YES YES YES YES YES
YES YES YES YES YES YES YES YES YES YES YES YES YES
YES YES YES YES YES YES YES YES YES YES YES YES YES
YES YES YES YES YES YES YES YES YES YES YES YES YES
YES YES YES YES YES YES YES YES YES YES YES YES YES
YES YES YES YES YES YES YES YES YES YES YES YES YES
YES YES YES YES YES YES YES YES YES YES YES YES YES
YES YES YES YES YES YES YES YES YES YES YES YES YES
YES YES YES YES YES YES YES YES YES YES YES YES YES
YES YES YES YES YES YES YES YES YES YES YES YES YES
YES YES YES YES YES YES YES YES YES YES YES YES YES
YES YES YES YES YES YES YES YES YES YES YES YES YES
YES.

Daniella Wells, 15

With Me . . . with You

Sometimes when we are on the outs
I don't really mean what I say or do,
Acting indifferent or turning away
Makes me feel sad and incomplete.
Sometimes I act out of pride
afraid to admit I am wrong,
fearful that if I reach out
you might see my tears—or have none of your own,
when at these times, all I really want is to hold you
and for you to hold me.
I do want to love you
and have it be your heart's desire to be loved by me.
I want you to love me—and care that I do.
Thank you for being patient with me
as I learn to be more honest
with me . . . with you . . .
more honest in expressing what I feel
more honest in expressing what I need
more honest in expressing what I fear
more honest in showing you the kind and thoughtful person I
     know I am
more honest in speaking the words of love I feel within my heart.
I believe with all my being
that this hurt and sorrow I'm feeling now
lets me know how important you are to me
and how I am succeeding in learning this language of love.
I promise to trust love
. . . mine . . . yours . . . ours,
and to savor the experiences it brings,
to learn the lessons it teaches,
and to *become* that which love is—honest . . .
with me . . . with you . . . with us.

Bettie B. Youngs

"The" Letter

Dear Craig,

You said you'd meet me at one o'clock
You never showed up at the agreed-upon place
So then you wrote me "the" letter
Because you didn't want to tell me to my face.

It didn't make me feel much better
That the breaking of my heart
was something you couldn't do in person
And therefore not your art.

All I thought as I read your words,
Alone, torn and blue
Obviously, I don't matter
So I guess we're really through.

Leila Sams, 16

Just Tell Me, "I Love You!"

As a child, selecting a Mother's Day gift for my mother was always easy: a box of candy, a bouquet of picked flowers, a lovely card with a heartfelt verse. No matter what size the box of candy, what pedigree the flowers or what color the card, she always expressed surprise and gratitude. But a gift for Dad on Father's Day—now, that was more difficult.

"What do you want for Father's Day, Dad?" I asked my father when I was fourteen. His answer was the same one he gave when I asked him what he wanted for his birthday. And for Christmas. And on Valentine's Day. "Oh, I don't need anything," he would reply nonchalantly.

So badly I wanted to say, "Well, maybe you don't, but I do. I want you to tell me—in words for once—that you love me. I know that you love me, but I want to hear you say it." But, because my father was such an all-powerful person in my life and because as a child I was too timid to say this to him, I didn't. Instead, one year I bought him a red plaid flannel shirt—one so lovely that it cost nearly eleven weeks of my carefully saved allowance. That was a long time ago.

Home on a family visit recently, I found myself sitting on my parents' bed, chatting with my mother as she cleaned their closet. She reached into the closet, fetched a garment, hoisted it into mid-air for inspection, then either whipped it back into the closet or tossed it on the pile of giveaways mounting on the floor.

Out came a tattered shirt—in terrible condition: faded, elbows with patches on top of patches, collar and sleeve cuffs badly frayed. Why even the neckline was completely worn through, few buttons matched and the faded fabric was so antiquated that it hung limp and lifeless on the hanger.

Mother quickly hung it back in the closet.

Curious, I asked, "Mom, why did that shirt make its way back into the closet?"

"Oh, this darned old thing," she said, rolling her eyes. "It's not even fit for a dust cloth! Your dad doesn't wear it, of course, but he would ask me where it was if it were missing. I don't know what it is about that old thing," she said, and in a spirit of fun quipped, "just one of your father's many quirks."

"Mom," I asked, "do you remember anything about that shirt?"

"Not a thing," she said dispassionately. "I don't even remember patching it, though that's my stitching, all right. When I ask your father why he keeps it around, he says, 'Oh, I don't know.'"

"I want it," I said. "I'm going to ask Dad if I can have it."

"Well, don't get your hopes up," she laughed. "He won't part with it."

I won't part with the memory of it:

One evening I was having stomach cramps. Soon the pain was fierce. At first it felt like a blender at high speed, chopping around inside my stomach. Then it worsened. As the excruciating pain became more intense, the interval between spasms shortened. My parents put me to bed with a warm water bottle— this made it even worse. When it was apparent the acute pain was not going to subside, my parents took me to the emergency room at the local hospital. Within minutes I was wheeled into surgery for an emergency appendectomy.

As I stirred from the sedation and moaned in pain, I felt the soothing presence of my parents beside me. "We're right here with you," my mother said as she stroked my face and brow. "We love you," my father said. Smoothing my hair, he clarified, "*I* love you." Not even the remaining Demerol in my bloodstream could drown out the addendum my father had added to the proverbial "we." It was the first time he had spoken these words to me.

The importance I had assigned to hearing these words from my dad crystallized the moment and made everything about it memorable—most especially the red plaid flannel shirt my father was wearing—a gift to him from me that Father's Day.

"Mom," I said, watching as she continued sorting through clothes, shoes and other items, "why does it take some fathers so long to feel comfortable telling their children that they love them—to actually say the words, 'I love you'?"

Looking thoughtful, she offered, "Love is an interesting word. It can mean so many things—anything from, *It feels so good to be together with the both of us feeling good about each other,* to the feeling between you and me right now. Why it can mean simply, *I'm so pleased that you're in such a good place—happy, doing well, healthy, feeling purposeful.* But it's one thing to say 'I love you,' and another to show it. You can't take away from the importance of actions as a way of expressing love. For example, making the necessary sacrifices to keep your family healthy and together, *shows* 'I love you.' Actions like that are as substantial as saying 'I love you.' While on the other hand, some children are told by their parents that they are loved, but their actions don't back their words."

She had a good point.

As I packed for my return trip to San Diego later the next day, I happened to glance out the window and spot my father doing what I had watched him do on so many occasions. He was stooped over my (rental) car, the hood up, looking at the engine. I stopped to watch the familiar ritual. First he checked the water level, then the oil. Then he wiggled every hose to detect if any were loose. Straightening up, he closed the hood then walked around the car, looking at the tires. One at a time, he kicked each tire. Apparently one didn't pass the kick test because it was subjected to yet another kick. Dad then opened the car door, got in and looked over the gauges on the dashboard. When satisfied with whatever it was he was looking for, he started the engine. Checking the brakes, he drove the car forward, then suddenly stepped on the brake. The car lurched to a stop. This same test was repeated as he put the car in reverse.

The scene was so touching, so familiar, that I had to laugh out loud. How I loved this about my father, the caretaker, the protector.

"Dad," I said, approaching him, "throughout my childhood I've watched you kick the tires on Mom's car every time she went somewhere. Over the years, I've watched as you do this to your grown children's cars, including your sons—all of whom, I might add, are nothing short of master mechanics. You also kick the tires of all the grandkids who are driving. I don't need to ask you why you do it, but I'd like to know what it means to you."

Deep in thought, he looked first at the ground, then at the car, and gave his customary explanation, "Oh, I don't know."

"Dad," I said, realizing he wasn't going to offer a more profound reason, "I love it when you kick tires. It reminds me how much you love and need your family. And speaking of love and need," I said, producing the red flannel shirt that I was holding in my hands behind my back, "I love this shirt and really need it. May I?" Looking at the shirt brought a big smile to his face. "Oh, yeah," he said, eyes misting over. "That was a pretty scary evening. For a moment there we thought we might lose you."

Momentarily disappointed at the thought that his words that evening had been triggered by fear of loss, I said, "No, Dad, I was just trying to scare you into saying 'I love you.' Do you remember telling me that evening that you loved me?"

Thinking it over, he said, "Funny at what we remember, isn't it? That night when you were in surgery I recalled how excited you were as you watched me unwrap a gift you had given me for Father's Day. Obviously I didn't show as much enthusiasm as I should have because a look of sheer disappointment washed over your face. As I watched your labored breathing while you were in the recovery room, I kept praying that I wouldn't lose the opportunity to make it right."

"Dad," I said, loving and respecting this tender brute of a man, "it's a cherished experience at the soul level to be told by your father that you're loved. But if you hadn't kicked those tires all those years—and worn that red flannel shirt to the hospital—I would never have known the depth and breadth of your words. Thank you for loving me so much—and for all of the ways your actions say it." Pointing to the red flannel shirt, I said, "I'm transferring this shirt from your closet to mine."

Tears came to his eyes as he said tenderly, "I've been saving it for you."

My mother knew intuitively that you could never say I love you too much. My father had learned it.

Looking at the old shirt I held in my hands—a precious token, symbolic of my father's words and all the ways he showed them—I was reminded that for children young and old alike, parental love is a powerful anchor, offering untold support throughout our lives. A loving anchor none of us ever wants to give up—nor the tokens that represent that it is so.

What tokens do you have that represent love? Aren't they also poignant expressions of love?

Bettie B. Youngs
Adapted from "When a Father Says 'I Love You'"
in Gifts of the Heart

Part 6

My Greatest Hopes and Fears

*One does not discover new lands
without consenting to lose sight
of the shore for a very long time.*

—André Gide

A Word from the Authors

In a recent workshop we did for teens, Jacob LeMarr of Brandon Parks, South Dakota, remarked, "Some people think it's a snap to be a teen, but it's not. It's a complicated time. There's so much to sort out." As Jacob is all too aware, adolescence is a challenging phase of life. Others might like to think that teens have a fairly easy, fun-filled life. In fact, teens are often told, "It's the best time of your life," or "I wish all I had to do was go to school, study and hang out with my friends." Yet, teens know well that life isn't all a bowl of cherries.

"One of the tough things about being a teen is all the uncertainties, the ups and downs. Fear and hope are emotions that run my life—*every day*," seventeen-year-old Jason Gilbert of Columbus, Ohio, explained. "Take yesterday as an example. Suzee Thomas, a girl I'd been hoping to ask out—but hadn't because I wasn't sure how she felt about me—casually sat down next to me in the library. It was the perfect chance to ask her, so, I worked up the nerve, faced my fear of rejection and asked. She said yes, and it was like all my hopes had come true! I felt like I'd conquered the whole world. Then, less than one hour later, I learned my SAT scores weren't high enough to get me into the college I was hoping to attend next year. Instantly, all I felt was fear: 'Now what?'

While I can take the SAT again, it's a real bear of a test, and I'd really boned up for it: Why would taking it again mean I'd do so much better the next time around? It sure took a toll on the elation I was feeling from the date I was already planning with Suzee. Now I have to face the fear of taking that test all over again, because more than anything I hope to go to college."

"Jennifer, with all the possibilities and uncertainties teens face, no wonder they feel as if they're walking a tightrope when it comes to holding onto any balance in their lives."

"*Balance*, Mom? I don't think the word is even in a teen's vocabulary. As the many teens we worked with confirmed, there's a lot at stake with the issues they face—perhaps much more than we may think. Take peer approval, for example. It's not as benign as it seems. Winning approval of one's friends is not only a personal gauge of fitting in and being one of the group, but a social test—are you a part of the whole, or the odd man out? Do you have Socialization 101 down, or not?

"And being around others is not only about gaining acceptance and fitting in, it's also about making decisions when it comes to the nature of others. After all, school is a source of both hopes and fears since young people can attend school with classmates who are simply awesome people—and some who are in need of counseling, even therapy for frail mental health.

"Then there's the hopes and fears in deciding what do in life for work. Certainly the years in school should lead you to some sort of conclusion about who you are and what your talents, interests and attributes are. But while you take a lot of classes, there is that red flag in the back of your brain that keeps letting you know that getting good grades in your courses may not exactly be relevant to helping you hone in on knowing just exactly what your interests, talents and attributes are. The chance that it will is the hope part. The fear is that maybe all your years in junior high and high school won't result in gainful employment—that is, after getting into and successfully making it through college (another hurdle that involves plenty of hope and fear). Just as there are fears, the hopes number in abundance. There's that whole array of your dreams of a job leading to independence and everything you envision that to mean: your own apartment, putting on nice clothes every day and going to work, a paycheck of your own, new friends, vacations. Now, for hopes and fears for your love life, being a good citizen and being a social activist . . . I think you get the idea."

"Your point is well taken, Jennifer! After all of that, suddenly I'm happy to have the hopes and fears of adolescence behind me!"

As was the case with the many teens we heard from, the hopes in your lives often create the fears. But be that as it may, teens know the antidote to dispelling such fears. What works? Among your suggestions:

- Seek friends and others who are positive and optimistic people. When the cup is half-empty, it is also half-full. Hope is a matter of seeing the cup half-full, which includes being with those who likewise see the cup half-full.

- Do the things that help you face your fears head-on and increase the chances of having your hopes realized. If you're hopeful of passing a big test, and it has you worried, lessen your chances of doing poorly: Prepare for the test. Get a good night's sleep the night before. If you're going to talk on the phone with friends before going to bed, don't dwell on your worries of not doing well on the test, because doing so will only get you worked up and keep you from falling asleep—and then you won't be your best the next day.

- Talk with others about those things you hope for, and the fears that paralyze you from doing your best. If you are about to take your driver's license exam and you're unclear what it entails, ask those who have gotten their driver's license what you should expect when you take your test.

Not only does reaching out to others give you support and direction, it also gives you the chance to examine the assumptions you hold, which can help take the power out of your fears.

- Know that you'll survive and can even thrive in spite of life's high hopes and uncertainties. If things don't work out the way you had hoped between you and a friend, don't give up altogether on having friends; instead, go on to form other friendships.

- Know that everyone has hopes and fears—not just you . . . even adults. Wishing, wanting, hoping and needing collide and mesh with each other, which can lead to very confused feelings. Coping with ambiguity is a fact of life at any age.

If meeting fear on a daily basis is a reality, it is greeting hope that brings the balance. As we walk the tightrope of fear, we would do well to think of hope as the balancing pole in our hands. Then, keeping our eyes on the goal, believing in our ability to reach it and refusing to be halted by any doubts otherwise, we must walk through our fears by placing one foot in front of the other, until we reach our goals.

Almost every great hope carries with it at least some degree of fear, since it's not yet a reality. Our hopes and fears move us forward in life: Our hopes give us a vision, a reason to strive, a reason to try, a goal to move towards. And through facing our fears we gain the experience, confidence and strength of character we need to keep striving to see our hopes become realities. And perhaps most important, we learn that the more of life we master, the less of life we fear.

In the following stories, you'll meet teens who share their hopes and fears as they seek daily to master more and more of life—a most noble and worthy goal.

Holes in the Sky

Last summer my mother's family had a reunion. All of my cousins and second cousins were there. The teenagers all hung out with me; they were really cool. We listened to CDs and talked and laughed and had a really good time.

There were also about a billion old people there—and all of them were related to me, too! What I noticed about these "old geezers" (as we kids secretly called them) was how different they all were. There were some who sat around and didn't look much interested in each other or much of anything—and especially didn't look interested in us younger kids. Some of them commented on the way some of the teens dressed and wore our hair, and they weren't very nice comments. It was obvious they considered it their role to "tolerate" us, but probably only because the day would be over and they wouldn't be seeing us until a year or more later. You just knew they didn't really accept us, or even necessarily like us. I'm not trying to put them down; it's just you could tell they hated the music we played. They even complained about the state of the world—as if our music created it.

Then there were some of the older set who smiled and seemed interested in us. You could see they came to the reunion with the intention of being open to the things that were going on, and to everyone who had come. I appreciated how nice they were.

Then there was old Aunt Lottie (who is really my great-aunt)! She has to be about eighty years old. "Great song," she commented once, smiling real big and shaking her head to the music. "I love music that can put holes in the sky!" I thought that was a cool comment. "Don't you ever forget how to love music and dancing," she commented. "It's the wind that sets love to spinning the world around!" Now I think that is a perfectly hip thing to say. I knew right then and there that I didn't ever want to get old the way some of my relatives had. I'd like to stay forever young at heart just like my Great-Aunt Lottie.

When I get older and wiser, I hope I'm as full of life and fun as she is—and not old and grouchy like *some* old people. And I'm starting to think "young" now, because I think grouchy old people are grouchy young people—and people who are full of life and fun when they are old were full of life and fun when they were young, too. My hope is to be forever young at heart—like Great-Aunt Lottie.

Lerissa Dennison, 15

The Love of Justin Vance

I know it would sound really good if I said my greatest hope was that world hunger would be annihilated, or something selfless like that. But if I'm being totally honest, I have to say that my very greatest hope in life is that Justin Vance will ask me out. I've loved Justin Vance for as long as I can remember—probably ever since the seventh grade. I've never told him—but that may change.

This year, it seems like Justin has finally noticed me. He talks to me at lunch sometimes, and sits next to me in Spanish. Still, he hasn't gotten around to staring at me, or doodling hearts on his folder of our initials—like I do. And, as of yet, he hasn't asked me out. But I'm hoping he will. If Justin Vance were to ask me out, I know that once he got to know me, he'd see I was meant to be his girlfriend.

So my hope is that Justin Vance will take notice and decide to be in love—with me, I mean. Being in love can be a good thing, and not just for the two people who are in love. When people are in love they make the whole world a better place! And, when it comes to Justin Vance, I'm sure willing to do my part.

Janine Ito, 15

"Dr. Santos"

When I was seven years old, I got spinal meningitis and was really sick in the hospital. While I was there, the doctor not only saved my life, he was also really good to me. Every day, he took the time to make me smile and was always friendly. He never treated me like I was too young to understand what it meant to have spinal meningitis and what he planned to do to treat it. He also didn't think I was too young to have an opinion about my treatment. That made me feel like a real part of the team, and I'm sure it was important to my getting well.

It also was a big factor in my decision to become a doctor when I got better and finished school. I knew I wanted to be just like him. Then for a long time, I forgot all about it, until I was in high school and it was time to decide what classes I needed to get into a college. This forced me to think about what I was going to do with my life. I knew I wanted a career where I could really make a difference in the world, one where I knew I was doing something that would help other people—and I recalled the doctor who healed me, and decided practicing medicine would be a wonderful way to use my life. So I renewed my desire to be a doctor.

I believe it's good to visualize myself doing what I hope for most in life, so now I picture myself in a white coat with a stethoscope hanging around my neck, my diploma on the wall, and being able to help and heal others. Remembering my doctor, his kindness as well as how he healed me by being a great physician, gives me a perfect role model for moving toward my goal. My excitement for being a doctor is at an all-time high. I'm in my first year of college working toward that goal.

Being a doctor and healing others is what I hope for most in life.

Craig Santos, 19

The Power of One

When I was a little girl, I always used to think I was going to grow up and do something really big—something that would make a difference in the world. What I would do to make that difference changed over the years: When I was in the second or third grade I was sure I was going to go to third-world countries and feed starving children with the Peace Corps or the Red Cross. By the time I was in sixth grade, I just knew I'd work with Amnesty International to free political prisoners and expose atrocities and corruption in far-off governments. I never had any doubts that I would do something great, something that would make a big difference in the lives of others. Then, slowly, almost subtly, I began to doubt myself and my ability to ever make a difference. I began to doubt the world, too—because, to me, it just seemed to get worse and worse. The older I got, rather than feeling more brave, I became more fearful. There was more hunger, more corruption, more atrocities—or, maybe, I just discovered what was always there. I began to doubt that anyone could make a difference, let alone me.

I wonder what's going to happen to our world by the time I'm an adult. In science class, I hear about the ecology, and how there's a hole in the ozone layer. The rain forests that give the Earth its oxygen are all being cut down; the rivers and oceans are polluted. There's acid in the rain, and nuclear waste drifting around. Our air's not fit to breathe. So, of course, I wonder whether or not the world will still be able to support human life, plant life, animal life—any life! Thinking about that scares me. I worry that I won't be able to make a difference, I even worry that nobody can really make a difference—and what if we don't even try? I hope that I will not stop believing in the power of one person to make a difference—and that that person is me.

Merrilee Moens, 16

No Threats, Please

Sometimes we hear that the world is moving toward being free of nuclear weapons, but it's not true. There are tons of nuclear weapons in the world—enough to destroy the world many times over. We hear about the wars of the past century—including two World Wars. I watch news reports about the conflicts and wars going on in other countries today, and realize that the threat of yet another Cold War looms larger than we might like to believe. Not only that, I also see reports of what could be called different kinds of wars—street wars: gangs, drugs, violence—they're all over. I think any kind of hate and prejudice could also be thought of as a war—maybe not with guns, but still it's a destructive force that rips lives apart. And of course, news about all the families being torn apart by conflict is everywhere; domestic abuse happens in homes in every community, rich or poor. So you could say that domestic abuse is a war . . . a family war.

My hope is for true world peace, and then there would be no need for nuclear weapons. I see a world where there would be no conflicts, no violence on the streets or abuse in families. The world would be a more beautiful place. That's my greatest hope: world peace. And it's more than an empty hope. I know world peace starts with me living at peace with everyone in my life and being a model of how people my age can work toward the dream of world peace for our planet. I'm hoping to keep that dream alive and always work toward it.

Hugh Benton, 17

Looking for Love

More than any other thing in life, I hope that I will never be all alone, without someone who loves me. Just thinking about that situation makes me sad. A person can be afraid of all sorts of other things, like pain, or poverty or failure, but if you face any of those things alone, it becomes so much worse. But if you walk through any of them with the love of someone else to support you and comfort you, it is so much easier to survive.

My grandparents are so happy. Even when one of them is sick, the other is there; they take such good care of each other—"in sickness and in health, for better or for worse," that's my grandparents, all right! When they're both feeling fine, they go just about everywhere together. They know each other so well and love each other so much. On the other hand, I also have an uncle who never got married. He has no children of his own, lives all alone and travels all alone. When he gets sick, no one is there to take care of him. And even when he comes to some family event, he's alone, looking somehow left out. Something about him seems so sad.

I just know that I don't want to live my whole life like my uncle—being all alone.

Amber Innis, 14

Globe-Trotting, Jungle-Braving, Tundra-Probing: Boyd Matson!

When I grow up I hope to be like the globe-trotting, jungle-braving, tundra-probing Boyd Matson! As the host of *National Geographic Explorer*, Boyd Matson's whole life is like one big adventure after another—and he gets paid a lot of money for it!

Just look at all the wild animals he gets to play with: snakes, bears, bats, mountain lions, chimpanzees. And his job includes traveling everywhere in the world—the Sahara Desert, Chile, New Zealand, Patagonia, the Sierra Nevada mountains, the Amazon, New Guinea, the Arctic. My very greatest hope is to travel like that when I grow up. Everywhere he goes is an adventure. He went cave-diving in underwater caverns in Wakulla Springs, Florida, and climbed Africa's highest mountain, Mount Kilimanjaro in Tanzania. In the Dominican Republic, he swam with humpback whales. In Hawaii, he stood on the rim of the active Kilauea volcano.

He's always facing extreme-edge, thrilling adventures—like the time he hand-fed sharks in the Bahamas, or the time he was charged by hippos and elephants in Botswana. Once he actually rappelled into the Devil's Sinkhole in Texas, which is filled with six million bats. He's even journeyed across the outback in Australia with no food or water. All the things he gets to do are so cool.

Besides having all that fun and excitement, Boyd Matson also gets to help the planet in a lot of ways, such as helping biologists tag polar bears in the wild, piloting the Sustainable Seas Expedition's experimental one-person submarine, and joining crews from around the country to fight wildfires in Florida.

Imagine living a life of adventure, traveling all over the world while doing an important job that's a real taste berry to the planet—just like Boyd Matson. It's exactly what I hope for out of life!

Joshua Thomas, 15

Would You Like to Win My Car?

My greatest fear is that I'll do something really stupid in front of a lot of people and they'll all make fun of me. I know if I did something stupid (like say, fall down in front of a huge crowd of kids at school and rip out the seat of my pants so that my underwear was showing), I wouldn't necessarily lose my friends or anything. But I also know everyone would make fun of me forever. From that day on they'd say things like, "Hey there, Slick," or they'd point at me and sneer, "He's the one with all the moves," or maybe they'd just laugh when I walked by. It would be terrible. I would be so humiliated.

So I have this huge fear of being forced to stand up in front of a large crowd, like my class. (After all, it's the perfect setup for the humiliation I just told you about.) When I have to give an oral report, I get sick to my stomach. This fear has even kept me from running for student-body office. I think that even if I could win the hottest car imaginable if I'd just get up in front of an audience and give an acceptance speech, I'd let someone else win the car. My cousin said what I have is a lack of self-confidence. Call it whatever you want, it just feels like being scared to me. I'm working on getting over it by taking a speech class next semester. I hear I'll have to stand in front of everyone in the class and give a speech a few times a week. They say when you face your fears you get over them. I'm not convinced that this is true, but we'll see.

Torey Thompson, 16

Sea Cucumbers Forever

I'm lucky—lucky enough to have grown up with the ocean as my playground! Since I was old enough to remember, my parents took me to the beach to swim and spend family time together almost every weekend. This is where I learned to read the currents and ride the waves with my father, and looked for seashells and built sand castles with my mother. My older brother Benji would take me out to the tide pools where we searched for starfish and sea cucumbers. We would have contests to see who could build the biggest sand castles, but mostly we built them so we could knock them down while wrestling. When we got older, my brother showed me how to surf and skin-dive. Because of all this, I've grown to love the ocean; I feel it is part of who I am and part of why I see the world as a vast place, filled with wonder.

I dream of a time when I can share my love of the sea with my children when I have a family of my own. I dream of teaching my kids how to build sand castles and showing them how to surf the waves and read the currents. I want them to understand and appreciate the ocean—to know how important the sea is to mankind, and to honor and preserve it. I'll show them how to take care of the great ocean by keeping its waters and beaches clean. So I'd say my biggest hope is to pass on my love of the ocean to all of my friends, and most especially to a family of my own.

Ethan Olivera, 20

Three Bathrooms

One day I would love to accomplish some really important work for all of mankind and the planet, but I don't know if that's my greatest hope. The really big important work is awesome, but I think that what can make the most difference in the world is doing the small day-to-day work with the same sort of dedication.

My grandfather once told me that if he had a chance to live his life over, there are some things he would do differently. For example, there are two bathrooms in my grandparents' house: one upstairs and one in the basement. My grandmother always wanted a bathroom built on the first-floor level of the house. But this seemed unnecessary to my grandfather, especially since the house had two bathrooms and there were just the two of them. Not long ago my grandmother passed away. Now my grandfather feels awful about never having built her that third bathroom exactly where she wanted it. Now he's the first to say, "It's the small things." He'll get no argument with me on that—I think he's right.

My biggest hope is that I'm a person who thinks about my life, day by day, making wise decisions, being honest and doing my best, especially in the small things. My greatest hope is to make a difference in the lives of those I love—my family and my friends—by doing the small things that can mean so much.

Jennifer Leigh Youngs

Fearless Passion

My older sister, Robin, had a friend, Stephanie, who wanted to be an actress. This was a passion that you could almost feel whenever she talked about it. Well, my sister and Stephanie graduated from high school three years ago, and Stephanie drove all the way across the country to Los Angeles, where she started attending classes at a junior college and got an agent. Her goal was to break into the profession and be an actress.

Stephanie's passion for doing things didn't allow any fear or uncertainty to get in the way of following her dreams and goals. To me, that is the way to look at life. Now Stephanie has been in a number of commercials and has had a couple of small roles in a bunch of TV ads. My sister told me just last week that Stephanie is expecting to hear back on a regular role in a sitcom she auditioned for, and she's also auditioning for a minor speaking part in a huge movie. I say, "More power to you!"

I think Stephanie's really going to make it BIG one day.

If people live fearlessly—I don't mean recklessly, I mean fearlessly—wholeheartedly going for their dreams without wavering, then they're going to love life and have a better chance of achieving things. My greatest hope is that whatever dream or passion I have in life, I go after it fearlessly—like Stephanie.

McKenzie Loughlin, 16

I Need a Date for the Prom

My greatest fear in life right now, today, is that I won't be able to find a date for the prom. I know it may not sound as noble as hoping for world peace or something as important as that, but believe me, not having a date for the prom can seem like the world is coming to an end.

Besides, all my friends already have their dates set for the prom.

I'm nice-looking and smart, so why haven't I been able to find a date yet? It's bad enough I haven't dated a girl throughout my whole senior year; will I have to miss out on my prom, too? I know some people don't think that guys care about those things, but we do. At least, I do—and so do most of the other guys I know. And I really, really hope I find a date for the prom.

Tommy Jorgens, 17

Diplomaville

I was raised being told over and over again how important it is to get a good education. So I guess that's why my greatest hope is to get a degree from a good university. Both my mother and my father are the first people in their families to go to college and get degrees. As a result, their whole family was proud of them, and they were able to do much more in life than they would have been able to do without a college diploma. They both talk about all the opportunities it opened for them, and all it has done to make their lives and their children's lives better.

Practically since I started kindergarten, they've driven home the message that I was on my way to college. Every class I took and every school I went to before then were just stepping stones on the journey—college was definitely the destination. At first, it all sounded okay. I mean, going to college seemed like a great idea—until the seventh grade when I started hating homework. That's when I decided going to college probably meant homework forever. So I decided then and there, no college for me. Besides, I loved skateboarding. By the time I was in ninth grade, I had even designed one for me and one of my friends. My design was so cool that pretty soon other friends wanted a skateboard rigged up for them, too, one that was uniquely decorated just for them—like the ones I'd made for me and my friend. I built and decorated a few more, and pretty soon, I had parents calling me to ask me if I could do one so they could give it to their child as a surprise present, like a birthday gift. And that's when I realized I could actually make a living from doing this. But pretty soon, I had orders for thirteen skateboards and all my free time was booked up for practically the next whole year. So that got me thinking that I'd like to have a skateboard company, where the boards and designs would be done by a production team. And then, you know, as strange as it might seem, I decided

I'd need a college education to run a big company. So, I want to go to college again. The goal is to get a business degree so I can have a really successful company.

My biggest hope is to get into a good university and do really well while I'm there. I really believe a good education brings a lot of rewards—a better career, better family relationships, more self-confidence. Especially now that I'm thinking about my own life, a "quality life" as my mother would say, I've focused on the things that help me reach my dream. I realize that just because my parents "made it" doesn't mean I will—unless I get busy and do it for myself, which means keeping on those tracks headed for "Diplomaville."

Travis Terrance, 16

Pretending Impostor

I feel like I'm this loner who is an impostor pretending to belong. It's a scary feeling. I have a lot of friends in different cliques at school, and I get along really well with all of them, but inside I don't really feel like I belong in any one of their groups. I feel like an outsider all the time, even when we're all going somewhere or doing something fun.

I don't know how many times I've felt out of place, even when I've been at a party in the middle of a whole crowd of people who are having a lot of fun. I'll be making jokes, listening to the music, dancing, keeping up on all the latest gossip—you would never guess I felt totally alone. You would think I was really having a good time.

I'm afraid I'll never find where it is that I really fit in. What if I go through life always having to pretend I feel like I belong? What if I never feel completely comfortable with any group of friends? What if something is really wrong with me and that's the reason I don't belong anywhere? There's nothing lonelier than feeling lonely in the middle of a crowd, and being scared that you're always going to feel that way. For right now, I just continue to "act as if" I belong, and hope that I really do belong, and the real illusion is my feelings of not fitting in.

Desiree Huerta, 15

Now What?

With graduation just a few weeks away, I'm facing my greatest fears. *What am I going to do next? Should I go to college right away, even when I have no idea what I want to do in life? What kind of job can I get until I decide what kind of career I want? Should I move away and try living somewhere else?* Suddenly, I have all these decisions to make, all this new freedom, and it doesn't seem like freedom at all. What am I going to do? It doesn't help that all my friends seem to know what they want to do in life. At least they know whether or not they want to go on to college next semester and what college they want to go to. I just don't know if going to college right away is the right thing for me to do right now; it's not like I don't think I'll go some day. But if I actually don't go, what will it be like working full-time? Will I end up feeling like I made a huge mistake by not going straight to college? I'm not the greatest student. Maybe that's why I shouldn't wait—no use letting my study skills get rusty. Then again, maybe that's why I should take a little break, and go back with a total commitment towards some goal.

I'm afraid I'll never find out what I'd like to do. At my age how am I supposed to select a job I'd like to do for the rest of my life? I mean, I change my mind about almost everything so fast now. Sometimes I'm interested in all kinds of things, and sometimes I'm bored with it all. My uncle is fifty-five and plans to retire when he is sixty-two. If I were to retire at sixty-two, that means that I'll be in a job for the next forty-five years. Sounds depressing if you ask me! I mean, that's such a long time, especially if I make a mistake and choose the wrong sort of job.

My uncle is the principal of a school and loves his work, so he's lucky. He started out being a classroom educator and later became a principal. He loves working with kids. He says that his work is one of the great loves in his life. My father, on the other hand, has had six jobs in his life. Some of the jobs he's liked, and others he hasn't. My dad says he considers them "jobs" and not "career work." Dad says that a career is where one job is related to the next, and probably in the same industry. Right now my father works in the office at Camden Industries. He's not all that happy in his work, but it's a job. He took the job because he can make more money than selling real estate, which he did last year. Before that, he worked in a company where he had to travel, and he was gone a lot, which is why he took the job with the real estate company in town.

My dad tells me that when it comes to deciding what I want to do in life, the sky's the limit. All this leaves me a little confused. Is finding what you're good at like love, where there's supposed to be that "one special" someone? Is there that "one special" job or career? Does everyone have just one soul mate? I don't know. I'm interested in a lot of things, but that doesn't mean I'd like to spend my life's work on one of them, and it may not mean that I can make a living doing them, either. But I do know that I'd like to be happy doing my work, whatever it is, and that I'd like to have the same excitement about my work that my uncle has about his. Today, my biggest fear is not finding what it is I should be doing with my life after graduation—but I intend to keep right on looking until I do find it.

Jeff Daniels, 17

French Kisses Forever

Sometimes I worry that there's never going to be a guy out there who really interests me to the point of really falling in love with him. More than anything else, I hope to be "in love"—and hopefully, at least once while I'm still in high school. I've had a few crushes over the past couple years, but never anything serious. I mean, I've never been involved in any great romance. I never felt like I was "in love." I've never French kissed, or even been someone's girlfriend. This is not the case for my friend Jessica—she has had at least six great loves since seventh grade. I mean, these were boyfriends who she was absolutely, positively convinced she was in love with and who she was sure she would always be in love with. I know that it's natural to be in love a lot, but some day, I'd like to have just one permanent love. I'm concentrating on finishing high school, then college and then getting a good job after I graduate, so I can have a great family, one whose members really love each other.

I'd like a handsome husband, a kind man who loves me. I want us to have two children (hopefully a boy and a girl), who we both love and take care of. I want all of us to be good to each other and love each other no matter what. In our home, we won't have screaming matches, even when we get angry. We'll have respect for each other and sit down and talk things through. Things in my home will be very different from how they are in my family now. My parents seem to fight a lot, mostly about money. Knowing things will be different in my home helps me get through the times when my parents are fighting. I'm sure there's a better way and that there is such a thing as a loving family—and some day I'll have one! I know that struggling financially can cause a lot of fights between couples. Since I don't want to have to do that, I plan on going to college and getting a good job.

I'd also like to live on a ranch where my kids can grow up playing outside with a bunch of golden retrievers, or even horses! On the other hand, I want to live near the city so my husband and I can go out to dinner and spend some nights out on the town enjoying ourselves. It's important to live somewhere that's convenient to both my family and work lifestyles. I understand that a loving family doesn't necessarily mean a "Seventh Heaven" type of life, it just means that everyone thinks of everyone else in order to get along better. Someday, I'll have that kind of family. Along with having French kisses forever!

Alicia Powers, 15

Ducking Bullets

My mother is working really hard and saving every penny she can to get us out of the neighborhood where we now live. There are a lot of gangs and drugs around this neighborhood, so there's a lot of violence, too. At night you can hear gunshots sometimes, and my mom always has to make sure me and my younger brother and sister come inside before it gets dark out.

I hate that my mother, my brother and my sister have to live in a place where people have so much hatred and so little respect for each other. I don't want my younger brother or sister to ever feel like they need to belong to a gang in order to feel safe or to feel like they're cool and have friends who care about them. Living here makes me scared for them most of all, because I'm afraid that since they see so much of the "street life," they'll decide it's the way the world is supposed to be. I know that I have to continue to be a good role model for them, since they look up to me because I'm their older brother. When they see how I don't have anything to do with gangs, hopefully they will follow my example.

My biggest fear is that a stray bullet from some drive-by shooting could hit my mother, brother, sister or even me. Hopefully, we'll be able to move to another neighborhood before my little brother and sister get much older, or the gangs get any worse. No one should have to worry about ducking bullets. And that's why I'm making sure that I'm a good kid—I don't want my mom to have to worry about more than she does. I also try really hard to be good to my younger brother and sister and to encourage them to be good kids and to earn good grades like me, so that our lives will be different in the future, whatever the "future" means. I'd like to say that in the future I will make enough money to buy my mother a great house, kind of like the athletes and movie stars do when they strike it rich, and maybe

I will. I hope so. I know that I really want to make sure that I am able to afford a nice home in a safe, decent community for my family when I get married. And I plan to raise my family, and not leave my wife stranded with children, like my father did.

Garrett Jones, 14

The BIG Test

I think the goal is not just to be good and stay out of trouble in life (which can be a lot of effort as it is), but to make your life a positive example for others while you are on Earth. I think being down here is a test. Even though we think it's our own life, it isn't—we're all taking a test. Everything you do and say is important because it influences others, and it comes back to you: You give out good, it comes back to you. You dish out bad, well, that comes back to you, too.

I don't think it's enough not to break the Ten Commandments (which is a good thing, because I don't think some of my friends could tell you exactly what all ten of them are). I think you need to really care about others and do things that show love and goodness to each other. Sometimes, I think you even need to be each other's guardian angel when you can, and help each other get into heaven (which is what I hope for). When I get into heaven, I bet there are even more people there than most believe, and it's because they've passed that important test of loving God and showing it in all the things they say and do. I think getting into heaven is the most important thing anybody could ever hope for. It definitely is my biggest hope.

Lennie Frazier, 14

A Taste Berry for Life

From what I've seen, pessimists don't get very far in life. So I'm an optimist. My friends all say I am, and my greatest hope is to remain an optimist. It just makes sense to be one. If you look at all the great inventors, the great leaders and humanitarians, all the people who made the biggest difference in the world from the beginning of time all the way until today, they were optimists, not pessimists. They believed and hoped for the best, even when things didn't look to be going that way. In doing this, they got what they expected. Some even got more! Like Goethe's famous saying, "Destiny grants our wishes, but in its own way, in order to give us something beyond our wishes."

I remember when I wanted a puppy, and my dad brought me home a three-year-old dog. Her previous owners had named her Dancer. What I really, really wanted was a cuddly puppy, so I was disappointed, because not only did I want to name the dog myself, I also wanted to make sure the dog was trained to do things that would be fun, like play Frisbee. I had heard that it's best to teach dogs tricks beginning when they're young, because this is when they learn things best. So when I saw that the dog my dad got me was already grown, I thought I wouldn't be able to teach her the things I'd wanted. But I decided to try anyway. That's when I discovered that not only could my Dancer already play Frisbee—and she's really, really good at it, I might add—but that Dancer actually knows how to hop up on her hind legs and dance when there's music on. I would've never thought to teach her that myself. And she can do some other really cool tricks. She's really, really talented. So I received my wish, and even beyond.

My friends tease me about being an optimist. When they grumble that we're having a final, I say something, like, "Sure it's a final, but look on the bright side: Aren't you glad it's an essay?" They groan a little at first, but I can tell they appreciate my attitude, too. After all, it gives them a more hopeful perspective. So I laugh with them and just look at my optimism as meaning I'm moving toward my goal to stay a taste berry for life!

Anika Aviara, 16

Tortoises Among Us

He was seven years old at the time—and a guest on *AM Philadelphia*. Smiling with enthusiasm and confidence, the smartly dressed little boy with the large round eyes sparkled as he counted in twelve foreign languages, and then used his hands to count perfectly in sign language. What an incredibly delightful and smart kid! Imagine his parents' pride!

But then, since the day he was born—June 27, 1974—Jason Kingsley has always been extraordinary. When he was only fifteen months old he made his television debut sitting on Buffy Saint-Marie's lap on *Sesame Street*, and he was a regular on that show until he was sixteen. Not that he settled for just being a star on an award-winning television program attuned to its global audience. In addition to having parts in a number of television movies, including *The Fall Guy*—for which he learned a sixty-four-page script—Jason attended school, remaining on the honor roll throughout. There, the young man with a wondrously curious mind and a playful sense of humor excelled in math (he says he is "mathemagical"!), though he was mostly interested in the study of other cultures—especially Latin America, South and Southeast Asia, Africa, Afghanistan, Lebanon, Israel, the Middle East, Western and Eastern Europe, China, Japan and Russia.

Not that academics consumed him. He was also active in Wig 'n' Whiskers, a drama club, and he worked part-time. Oh, and while still in high school, he coauthored a book (*Count Us In*) with his best friend, Mitchell Levitz. Their work was so impressive, both boys were invited to appear on *Dateline NBC* to discuss it! What promise!

To keep himself fit and full of an unquenchable energy, Jason hikes, swims, likes to fish and enjoys group sports. He is also a pianist who plays a bit of Mozart and Bach. And he *loves* Broadway musicals! Though inner-directed, he's not selfishly self-absorbed. In fact, he's a sensitive young man with a real concern and compassion for others—especially those suffering from war and starvation. And, if you engage him in a conversation about how "Planet Earth is faring ecologically"—yet another of his favorite topics—you'll learn that he can talk hours on end on this subject, too.

What a multifaceted, interesting, talented, goal-setting and achieving guy!

In view of the extraordinary scope of Jason's interests and achievements, it's nothing short of disappointing—if not shocking—to learn of the doctor's words just hours after his birth: "Your child is mentally retarded. He'll never sit or stand, walk or talk. He'll never be able to distinguish you, his parents, from other adults. He'll never read or write or have a single meaningful thought or idea. Place him in an institution immediately, and go home and tell your friends and family that he died at birth."

Jason Kingsley has Down's syndrome.

At the time their son was born, Jason's mother, Emily, was a writer for *Sesame Street*, a popular national television program created to help young children develop basic skills. Mrs. Kingsley's chief responsibility was to help an audience of children in seven million homes in more than 140 countries learn their letters, numbers, shapes and the rules for playing fair. What good fortune for Jason: His mother was in the business of helping children learn how to learn! Jason was quickly added to her audience. With all the resolution in the world, Mrs. Kingsley—a mastermind of children's learning—set out to help Jason learn. From sewing quilts of different fabrics, to putting Jason in tubs of flavored Jello to stimulate his learning, Emily Kingsley was bound and determined to help her son develop skills that could help him achieve and succeed in the world, most especially to have a full and happy life.

Not only did Mrs. Kingsley unlock the door to Jason's

learning and developing a wide array of social and life skills, she also discovered that finding out *how* Jason learned was useful to her work on the show. If Jason could grasp a concept and retain it, then so could other children. And so Jason's "point of learning" served as the baseline for selecting the methods to teach the children who tuned in to enjoy and learn from *Sesame Street*. Not only did Jason open up new possibilities for the series—*Sesame Street* opened up new possibilities for Jason as well.

How fortunate for Jason that he was born to parents who feared what kind of a life their son would have should he be condemned by the doctor's prognosis, and hoped that with their love, they could help Jason move closer to having a "full life." Today, as his remarkable achievements attest—with a special thanks to his parents and his pal, *Sesame Street*'s eight-foot, two-inch "Big Bird"—Jason has a full compliment of skills. Moreover, he has an interesting and meaningful life.

How fortuitous that Jason's sense of self persevered against those dire predictions as well—and hoped to prove them all wrong. But we must not think it's been easy for him. Jason struggled arduously to overcome the obstacles inherent in the biological nature of Down's syndrome.

Still, Jason's life is a bigger legacy than his lucking out by having parents whose struggles moved between hope and fear and, in the end, helped him become a capable and achieving young man. And it's more than an account of his journey to overcome the obstacles and struggles inherent in being born with special needs. The real value of tallying the ledger of Jason's accomplishment is not just to admire his phenomenal personal achievements, but rather, that by confronting hopes and fears, we chronicle the *real worth* behind the words *each person is special and unique*. Admiring Jason is to look through the lens that brings into view not just that we are special, but that the mark of a successful life is in finding how we are special. For Jason, Down's syndrome is the vehicle on which he rides into the sunset.

Because of it, he has found purpose and direction. It is his *calling*.

The trouper has gladly put on the yoke of wanting a chance to live among family and friends, a chance to live a full and happy life. And so he has become a tireless crusader, intensely insistent that others born with Down's syndrome have the chance to make a meaningful contribution to family, school and community. Jason wants all of us to know that despite their intellectual limitations, children with Down's syndrome have a great capacity to give and receive love. He believes that whatever their ultimate level of achievement, they must be allowed to live a full and productive life, to have an opportunity to go down the same road in life as he has.

He couldn't be more suited for his work. Though busy doing many things, none give Jason greater pleasure than talking with parents of children born with Down's syndrome. It's his passion, one that has become his avocation. "When parents first learn their baby has Down's, they are anxious, and a little nervous about this 'different' baby," he tells me. "So I help."

"How do you do that, Jason?" I ask this hard-working, good-natured, goodwill ambassador.

"I let them see—in person—what Down's syndrome looks like," he tells me, smiling his usual charismatic grin, and then in the same breath adds, "The parents look at me and see how tall I am, how smart I am, and how nice I am and how friendly I am, and when they learn about all the things that I've done, they decide that it's okay for their baby to come home with them. Because of me, they'll be good parents to their baby, and they feel happy and not sad about their baby. That makes me feel proud that I helped them. And I've helped their little baby, too. The little baby will be loved and not left alone or have to live without his parents and brothers and sisters and friends. And now the little baby will get a chance to be taught things, and to learn things, because the parents will expect their little baby to be a real person with a normal life. And then, one more little baby will get to have a great life. That's what *I do!* It's my job!" With ever-gleaming eyes, he adds, "What I'm doing is *really* important."

Its importance is evident in his explanation: "When they see me, parents aren't so worried they won't be able to love their baby." Pausing, Jason grows reflective, then adds, "especially if the doctors have told them things that make them feel the baby will never be able to do anything."

"What are the magical words you use to open them up to all the hopeful possibilities, Jason?" I ask.

"I tell them to not call it 'Down' syndrome but rather 'Up' syndrome, because then they can stay focused on being up and positive," Jason answers. "They have to teach their child to be proud and not ashamed of himself. The parents have to be proud of their child so they will teach him, and their child has to be proud of himself so he can learn and be happy." Soulfully, he adds, "Just because a child has Down's syndrome doesn't mean he can't do things. It just takes a little longer."

"So you tell them to be patient," I say.

"Sort of," he replies. "I remind them of the story about the tortoise and the hare. You remember it, right?" he asks, laughing merrily and not waiting for a response. "Being born with Down's syndrome means you're the tortoise because you do things more slowly. I'm a tortoise because I have to work much harder at things than other people do, but still, it's not bad to be slow. You learn a lot when you are slow like the tortoise. And you see a lot of things other people don't see, so you really know the scoop on things!" Now dead serious, he leans forward and enunciates each word slowly, "People aren't *losers* just because they're slower than others." Without pausing, Jason lightens up and cheerfully informs, "Don't forget, the tortoise won! Like the tortoise, I'm a winner!—just like all the other people with Down's syndrome."

"I'd like to do a story on you, Jason," I say. "May I?"

"Oh, sure," he approves with genuine enthusiasm. "That'd be

great!" And then, reflecting on our conversation, he instructs, "Be sure to remind doctors that if you send a baby with Down's syndrome to an institution, the baby will miss out on his family's love. And be sure to tell the family that they will miss out on all the love that their baby can give to them. Oh, and one more thing. Tell them the story about the tortoise and the hare. And, don't forget to remind them that the tortoise won!"

Jason Kingsley. A person who entered "the race" and won.

Today Jason Kingsley works tirelessly and enthusiastically for the rights of those with Down's syndrome—a condition that affects one in every eight hundred births. Thanks to Jason, parents with children born with Down's syndrome have a model—a vision of the possibilities of what their child's life can be. Jason wants us to honor whatever that potential may be. Though some children will never learn to read, much less write a book, they have no less value and dignity than another child who performs on a higher level. We must celebrate their more modest accomplishments and deem them purposeful.

The commitment of Jason's parents to layer love and teaching upon layer of love and teaching is a powerful example of what can be accomplished by confronting fear and holding on to hope. That Jason finds meaning in helping parents of children with Down's syndrome pays tribute to *using* the life you are given, the highest homage we can make to fulfilling our purpose and calling. Jason's life is inspirational because through him we can see more clearly that though we are each unique and special, more than this, we are each *called*. As Jason reminds us, regardless of the nature of our lives, and the obstacles we face, we must each choose to enter the race and to live life to the fullest—even if at the pace of a tortoise. As Jason reminds us, it helps to remember that "the tortoise won"!

Bettie B. Youngs
Excerpted from A String of Pearls

Part 7

Tough Stuff

The unspoken thoughts of even the most private heart can be seen.

—Isumi

A Word from the Authors

"Editing the stories for this unit was particularly bittersweet, wasn't it, Jennifer?"

"Sure was, Mom. The letters teens sent telling us about the tough stuff they faced were so heartfelt, you couldn't help but be touched by them."

It's interesting that of the literally hundreds upon hundreds of letters we receive each month, the subject matter teens write about seems to be split right down the middle. On the one side, there are accounts of the many teens doing extraordinary things to help others deal with tough stuff: teens like Allison Wignall, eighteen, from Newton, Iowa, who helped raise $350,000 to fight AIDS and HIV; and Lauren Detrick, fourteen, of Tulsa, Oklahoma, who personally raised $50,000 for cystic fibrosis research in her town. That's a lot of money—and effort! Ariane Wilson, eighteen, from Menlo Park, California, created a Spanish-language guide to help non–English-speaking people get quality health care services, and Elizabeth Cable, fifteen, from Mountain City, Tennessee, designed and created cloth "caddies" for wheelchair-bound people that adds a great deal to their comfort and ability to have fun and stay fit. Meanwhile, Andres Allshouse, sixteen, from Honolulu, Hawaii, collected a million books for underprivileged kids; while in Essex Junction, Vermont, Brad Luck, eighteen, founded a teen center in his town to keep kids off the street while having a fun and healthy outlet for their energy. Gabriella Contretas, thirteen, in Tucson, Arizona, organized a community service club to help teens stay drug-free. If we were to list the many teens doing great things for others, it would make up a book in and of itself. It's heartwarming to know that teens are involved in awesome ways, helping, and doing positive things for others.

The second stack of mail is from teens who are also doing extraordinary things—but their involvement is in struggling, to get through tough stuff of their own, some of their issues so trying they require a tenacious spirit just to cope with them. This chapter is about issues teens from that second stack of mail face. In these letters, teens opened their hearts about everything from the pain they felt at the death of a loved one, a grandparent, a parent, coach or a classmate, to the struggles they faced with friends—even themselves—dealing with a personal illness. You teens talked about parents divorcing, which you acknowledged as incredibly painful for you and everyone in the family—and even voiced concern for your (or their) mental health. Some of you had struggled with all the challenges that came with your family relocating to another state—and therefore having to leave dear friends, schools, neighborhoods and other familiar things; the stress and anxiety of school; or the uncertainty about what to do in life after graduation. And of course, there were your many letters letting us know how awful it felt to be dumped by a guy or girl, or betrayed by a friend.

From your letters, and from our years working directly with teens and their families, we know how tough it is to emerge on the other side of such trying times. Coupled with the normal strains of growing up—and the day-to-day pressures that entails—facing these kinds of tough issues can make it all overwhelming at times. Yet it is precisely at times when things seem tough that it's important to exercise care and compassion for yourself and choose healthy solutions and not make unhealthy decisions—in a nutshell, choose positive ways to cope.

In this unit, we highlight a sampling of your stories. We remind you that if the issues addressed are also the kind of things you are going through, know that you are not alone—and please be encouraged to reach out for help. Sometimes the challenges you face are simply too big for you to handle alone. Asking for help is a sign of strength. So if you are facing struggles that seem overwhelming, rather than suffer alone or resort to doing things that are self-destructive, confide in people you trust. This is especially true if you are afraid of someone, feel depressed or suicidal, have an eating disorder, are pregnant (or suspect you are), are using drugs or alcohol, or like so many teens, if you are dealing with the loss of someone dear. Don't feel you have to go through these times alone. They are too much for even the strongest and most brave among us. Remind yourself that many people find great satisfaction in helping and comforting others; it's how we show our finest hour of being human. Allow those you trust to direct you to where you can get the help you need. (Some suggestions are included in the last story in this unit.)

You can do something else as well. When we are in the middle of our problems, it can be easy to forget all the many good things going on in our lives. But it's important to recall what's good in our lives. Not only does this help us through the hard times, but it can help us accept that there are going to be times of trial and tribulation—and that these, too, are a part of life.

And, when in the midst of turmoil, ask yourself what good can come from searching for positive solutions and making it through to the other side of a tough time. As Albert Einstein said, "In the middle of difficulty lies opportunity." Sometimes our problems seem so tough that it's nearly impossible to think that anything good can come out of it, yet, many times this is the case. Consider how a beautiful pearl is the outcome of an intrusion of a grain of sand within the oyster's shell. Likewise, the intrusion of disappointment, heartache or a particularly difficult time can be transformed into a thing of value in our lives, as so many teens reported. For example, Cammy Reece, a high-school dropout, now runs one of the most successful centers for school dropouts in her city, including writing a number of manuals that are used by those working toward a GED. Her story and those profiled in this unit, as well as the millions of others out there, show that we humans are more resilient than we imagine, that we can survive tough times. What's more, we can use them to not only set goals for ourselves, but spur us on to complete noble goals, such as Craig Santos, nineteen, from San Diego, California, chose to do. Craig was seven when he came down with spinal meningitis. After recovering from his ordeal, Craig is now in college and hard at work accomplishing his dream of becoming a doctor so that he might help heal others with this disease.

Finally, just as we encourage teens going through hurt and pain to be extra-good to themselves and reach out to those who will offer support and understanding, we also hope that teens everywhere will be encouraged not to look away from nor down upon those going through these times, but rather, offer your comfort and encouragement. Showing compassion for those walking through their own dark moments is exactly what being a taste berry is all about.

And last, may you keep in mind what psychologists often tell those going through tough stuff: "We are hurt less by the calamities of life than by how we perceive them," a philosophy that readily shows up in the story in this unit about the famed artist, Dennis Patton, who had one of his most prized possessions—in fact, a masterpiece—burned to the ground by three teens. Crushed and feeling forsaken, he called his best friend, literally crying. You can only imagine his surprise at his friend's jubilant laughter—which was followed by a piece of taste-berry advice from his friend that we might all do well to store inside our hearts: "Success is not measured by your victories, as much as by how you recover from the tough times in life."

Hitting Home

I lived with my parents and my younger brother until I was eleven. My dad was very abusive towards my mom and me. Sometimes the abuse got so bad that my mom would wind up in the hospital. Finally, my mom left him. Believe it or not, that's when things started to get even worse.

My younger brother ended up living with my dad; and my mom and I lived between motels and my grandparents' house. Then my mom got back on her feet and we moved into an apartment. Everything was going okay between my mom and me, but inside we were both struggling. My dad started shooting out my mom's car windows, putting nails under the tires of her car, and toothpicks in the locks of her car doors, as well as in the locks of my aunt and grandparents' cars.

To get away from my dad's harassment, we moved into a house that my mom rented from an older friend of hers. He introduced my mom to his son. They connected and started dating. At first, he and I got along because he was like one of us kids. He is only twenty-four and my mom is thirty-eight. Then, he started drinking and got abusive towards my mom. It brought back memories of my past. This went on for about two years. My mom never fought back, and sometimes he would hit her so much that I would hit him to try and make him stop. I felt so much anger towards him. And more than anything, I was so frightened for her. Sometimes I would stay up for hours listening to them fight to make sure he didn't hit her. Sometimes, I would even miss school because I was too tired from staying up all hours to make sure he didn't hurt her. I felt like I was going crazy. I tried to tell my mom how upset I was, but she just wouldn't listen. Finally, there was a night he was hitting my mother, and I jumped on him and the fight got really violent. He spit in my face and I got so mad that he started looking just like my dad. Then, I lost all control and began to hit him even more— hard enough so that I really hurt him. After that, it was decided

I couldn't live with them anymore. I was placed in a juvenile detention facility, which is where I'm writing from now.

The sad part is my mom still lives with her boyfriend. She comes and sees me on the weekends sometimes. I ask her why she is still with him, and she tells me it's because she loves him. I don't want to live with my mom if she's living with him, but I do wish I could live with her. It's hard for me to think that they're still living together, and he's probably still hurting her. I'm trying to deal with all of this, but it's hard. I have a cousin and some friends who are there for me, but it is my mother who I most want to be there for me. I still try to tell her how I feel, but she just says she doesn't want to talk about it.

I know I shouldn't have been so violent; there are other ways to deal with feeling angry. The price I paid was a very big one. I'm learning that, because I grew up never being taught to handle my problems by talking them through. I am an angry person. The good news is that I'm now getting help with my anger and feelings of loss.

I wish parents would realize how much their love lives can affect their kids. I also hope teenagers living in an abusive household will get help before it is too late so they don't have to face what I'm facing, because I'm in a world that's all so cold. Nobody is here to hold me. I stand and walk alone, hand in hand with my shadow. I feel as if I'm powerless, full of pain and fear. I just hope that one day everything will become clear for me. For now, it's like all my days are filled with gray clouds and raindrops. My eyes are shut and my heart's broken. My mind stays in the imaginable, and my thoughts are lost and cannot be found. I'm the "lost-looking" girl who is quiet and never talks. I keep my head low; if anyone were to look deep in my eyes, my tears will surely flow. All I do is cry. My tears are filled with fear, lonesomeness and sorrow. My soul is stained—stained with pain, hurt and shame. My words mean nothing; no one hears them. My tears are powerless. I'm helpless. And so very all alone.

R. L., 15

Lost in Love . . .

From the day I first saw Randy, for me it was love at first sight. Soon after that, we talked and that was that—he loved me, too. He brought a smile to my face and joy to my heart that felt good in every breath I took. It was warm, it was comforting, and it was energizing—and so incredibly wonderful to have love in my life. Because of this love, I began to understand that my focus up to that point was mostly only on me. But with Randy in my life, suddenly other people mattered more, too. I listened more closely and felt more deeply—all because of his love for me.

This point really became clear when I learned that my grand-mother was very ill. Immediately, I had a need to reach out to her, to care for her, to be there for her. Now that I *knew* love, I could give love more than I ever was able to before. Because of this, I grew very close to my grandmother and even chose to stay with her during a school break in order to comfort and care for her and give her maximum love and attention. It was a wonder-ful connection, one I know had been transformed by my love for my boyfriend.

Deep inside I began to feel like this was how *real* love felt. This was the feeling others described when they talked about a soul mate or described the incredible feelings of "being complete." So strong were my feelings that I thought about marrying Randy. I knew I would if he asked. I also thought that's where our love affair was taking us, we so completely trusted each other—which is why I wasn't all that surprised when he and I didn't keep in constant touch while I was with my grandmother. After all, we were each just waiting for my return, and then we would continue on with our lives—and our love. In the meantime, his love freed me to care for my grandmother without feeling inse-cure or jealous; without regretting that I was one hundred miles away from him.

With so much peace and love, I cared for my beloved grandmother. But then, suddenly, my grandmother died. The next two weeks were taken up by our family rallying together. It was an emotionally devastating time, and I relished knowing that soon I would be with the love of my life again, and he would be there to comfort me.

Then it happened. When we finally saw each other, Randy said simply, "It's just not working out anymore." I was amazed that he could end it all so quickly, for no reason—and at a time when I needed him so much. My heart broke into a million pieces. It's still broken.

Now, looking back, especially during this painful time of my grandmother's illness and death, I can see that I loved him more than he loved me. Like someone threw on a switch, the clues now stand out like a neon sign in the dark. If he loved me as much as he professed, then why on those few times when he called did he barely ask how my grandmother was, or how I was doing? Instead, Randy had talked mostly about what he and his friends were doing. Of course, I wanted to hear about his friends and how he was doing, but at the same time, if it had been me, I would've wanted to know how Randy was feeling and how he was holding up through such a tough time. I would've been interested in showing him I was there to support and listen to him.

As painful as it is to admit, I know that no matter what explanation I offer up to excuse Randy for not being there for me—which includes when and how he chose to break things off—the truth is, love doesn't act that way.

As you can probably tell, I'm still very sad. My heart still hurts. Having someone you love leave you is a terrible, terrible feeling. The saddest part is that my heart still loves him as much as the first time I saw him—even though it doesn't stand to reason to love someone who is not there for you. I know I'll be okay, and I know in time, I'll get over this. But I also know what I felt, and that it was real, even if others don't see it that way. Some people don't really believe that teens are old enough or "experienced" enough to love this deeply or feel so deeply about love. When you break things off, so many are quick to say things such as, "You're seventeen; you have lots of time," "You'll find someone new to love in no time," or "There will be other guys who are *more* right for you!"

But the heart, I've learned, has a heart of its own. Mending it is not about replacing one boy for another. It's about urging this huge ache within to leave, too. What shall I do with the loss of an emotion so beautiful that it can make you feel as though you can conquer the world? But then again, what shall I do with this new emotion that has just dropped me off at the end of the universe?

Whoever said, "It is better to have loved and lost than never to have loved at all," has probably never been really in love!

E. K. H., 17

The Last Gift

Have you ever conceived what it would be like to know that you are dying? My grandmother had to think about it every day for three months. I can hardly fathom how hard that must be.

One day she was healthy and then, like a thief in the night, the next day she was ambushed with a cancer that has no cure. When the doctors diagnosed my grandmother, with a great deal of compassion they informed her family that all we could do was prepare a peaceful exit for her. Like a cruel sentence, they announced the cancer was "terminal"; she would be granted two to five months if she took chemotherapy treatments, less without them. Such a blatant word, "terminal"—as in *the end*. No more. Over. Finished. Final. Gone.

When I heard this bleak report on the status of her health, I remember thinking, "Where are all these advanced medical breakthroughs, anyway?" I was so angry. My grandmother: a soul mate. This loving and giving person in my life who loves me, believes in me, supports me in my decisions—and unlike any other, ever so gently and lovingly helps me see the errors of my ways. My fan. A *huge* fan. Someone who makes me my favorite food at any time of night or day when I am visiting her. Someone always with a twinkle in her eyes when she looks at me. Why are we boasting about all our scientific and technological advances when there isn't even a cure for my grandmother's type of cancer, when the cherished mother of my mother can be taken from me as quickly as poof, and she's gone? This is a question without an answer—even in this "new millennium"!

And so my grandmother returned to her own home to be with those she spent a lifetime nurturing: her sweetheart and husband of fifty-five years, and her family of six children, seventeen grandchildren, and seven great-grandchildren. Only now we would be the nurturers. It was my grandmother who needed looking after. Day by day by day. And then hour by hour by hour. And in the end, minute by minute.

Not that I ever gave up hope. I continued to hope when there was no hope at all. At first I searched for cures everywhere—even experimental treatment programs outside her doctor's care. But a search from one end of the country to the other revealed that there was nothing we could do for the type and late stage of her cancer. I watched helplessly, trying to disguise the hurt and loss I felt, even trying to give her my energy so she might garner strength from it. But all I could do was watch over this remarkably loving and Christian woman. Even in her profound illness, my grandmother remained a magnificent person: graceful, beautiful, kind, concerned for others.

She was always so selfless. I watched now as she lay helpless to affect that which was strangling the breath out of her, dependent on others to care for her, and was reminded about all those times when she watched over me when I, too, was helpless and completely dependent on others for everything. How I cherish her.

There is so much to cherish. All my life I knew her. Twenty-five years of having a soul-mate relationship. It would be impossible to tell someone all that she meant to me, there was so much laughter, playfulness, praying together and all the many events—big and small—where Grandma sat, hands in lap, beaming at me, one of many adored and adoring grandchildren. I felt like her favorite, always, but in my heart I knew she loved us all the same, and that all of us felt as if we were each her most favored. Her love was so profoundly unconditional. How will I ever file all the memories? We built so many of them together, she and I. They are among the fondest times in my life. In fact, my entire life is feathered with such memories.

How shall I pick a favorite memory to remind me of her ever-encompassing spirit in my life? Perhaps it is the nature walks we took wherein no flower, rock or feather was too inconsequential to touch, talk over and give thanks for. Our conversations were as rich as our love for each other—always we held hands, and even as one of us would stoop to pick a flower or a feather, never did our fingers lose touch of the one we loved so much. I remember the time when I was a very small girl, walking hand in hand with her, when we found yet another feather from an old gray wild turkey. "Look!" I exclaimed, and my delight was her own, as she marveled aloud over its beauty—turning it this way then that in the light, and pointing out its shimmering colors and intricacies. Then we spoke of feathers and of wings and of all sorts of creatures that were winged—from the old wild turkey, to the angels in heaven. My grandmother left a trail of memories longer than the trail of feathers discarded by that old gray turkey. How will I ever sort out these memories, categorize them, harbor them and keep them safe? I want to. Forever!

I knew my grandmother's fate was drawing near. And I was listless, anxious, sad and happy, too, knowing that my grandmother was going soon to journey home to God. One day as my grandmother lay so very ill, I began to look at her things, and in an old storage chest at the top of the basement steps, tucked behind old flashlights and an old tin with loose kernels of corn and hats for winter's chill, found one of the feathers we had collected on a walk together. Wrapped in delicate paper—and memorialized in her sensual handwriting—were the words, "Jennifer—'84." Remembering the many soulful conversations between my grandmother and me, and remembering how she loved feathers—certainly feathers had given wings to so many of our nature-walk conversations—I took the feather and, along with a beautiful blooming bouquet of fresh flowers, presented them to her.

On this day, she oohed at the beauty of the flowers and then looked at the feather, considering the feather the most pleasing of the two offerings. I was about to remind her that a feather from a huge wild turkey was among the last gifts she gave to me before she fell ill just weeks before. But in her gaze I realized she knew these words were about to be spoken, and instead, she lowered her head and smiled knowingly. So, I held the large plume proudly in front of me and like a child exclaimed, "Grandma, look what I've found!" She lit up with joy and as if transported back to the time when I was a child and she was much younger herself, declared, "Oh, Angelface! It's the best one we ever did find!" And then, tenderly, looking over toward my grandfather, she asked, "Everett, have you ever seen such a splendid feather?" My grandfather acknowledged the deeper meaning of the wild feather by responding, "A genuine family heirloom!" *Yes, she is,* I thought. My grandmother will always be an heirloom etched within my heart. An heirloom as priceless as the most valuable treasure passed down within a family, a treasure that brings to mind memories of love and connection.

Still, the most grand and priceless heirloom of all that my grandmother left is not an outward token, but an imprint etched in my heart of the precious power and grace of her life as a simple and noble person. This is a woman who quietly—and staunchly—began the foundation of our family. She created the spirit of the Burres family home. For more than half a century, she remained sweetheart to a husband she truly loved.

Yet another facet of this heirloom is a deep and abiding faith. My grandmother loved God and lived her life around her uncompromised spiritual principles. Aside from living these principles as a pillar of character within a community she cared about so much, she was also a shepherdess of Christian ministries the world over. Only after her death did my family discover that my grandmother had been supporting nearly thirty missionaries for nearly two decades, and over time, some twenty orphaned children from all corners of the world.

Always the eternal optimist, always the caretaker, always the nurturer, my grandmother gave so many the gift of love, the word of God, and a feeling they had met an angel, which I'm sure she is.

As I left my grandmother's graveside with feather in hand, I thought about how difficult life will seem without her. And of the vacuum that her passing has left within my life. Perhaps it's because the legacy she leaves behind is her courageous example of just how pure and simple—and unconditional—her love was.

As I look at the beautiful gray feather, I realize that there will be many days ahead of me when I'll cry over having to part for now with a soul that knew my own soul so well, and loved me so much.

The beautiful feather sits now in a vase, lonely, as I am. Yet I find comfort in this heirloom, too. Maybe it's because the feather is more symbolic than I had first imagined. I now stare at the feather and think of how my grandmother always gave me wings to fly to my greatest potential. And so feathered with her love, and graced by knowing of her eternal life, I am now able to gently let go of some of my pain. A little, at least.

Jennifer Leigh Youngs

Yours—for the Asking

When I was in the fifth grade, I transferred schools. At my new school I met a girl, Pia, who was really nice and we instantly became friends. We sat next to each other in every class, spent all our time at recess together, chose each other first for every spelling quiz, and did all group projects together. We were like sisters—inseparable.

By the time eighth grade rolled around, we were even closer friends. One Friday night, she slept over, which she did often. As usual, we had a lot of fun together. Later on that weekend, when I went to use my nail polish I couldn't find it. I began searching through my drawers, and that's when I discovered I was also missing two lipsticks and an eyeshadow compact. Though they weren't in the drawer where I always kept them, I thought maybe I'd put them in my purse, and then when I went through my purse, I discovered the ten dollars I had gotten from baby-sitting just the week before was missing as well. I knew all these things were there on Friday night, and I hadn't left the house since, and no one had been over except Pia.

I considered that Pia took them, but I just knew that my best friend in all the world wouldn't steal from me. *But then, where were these things?* The idea that maybe she had taken my things was very unsettling, and my feelings were so hurt that I even had trouble sleeping that night.

The next morning I woke up not just hurt, but appalled that someone who had been a friend for so long could do this to me. So on Monday, as soon as I saw her at school, I asked Pia about the missing things. Outraged, she accused me of not being a very trusting friend, and then added, "I would *never* steal from a friend!"

I guess I was just hoping she would admit what she'd done and we could make up and go on as friends the same as always.

Even though she wouldn't admit it, and even though I knew that it couldn't have been anyone else, I still decided to just try to forget about it, because maybe there really was some kind of an explanation.

But a couple of weeks after that, I went over to Pia's house so that we could go to the mall. While she was getting ready, I noticed my nail polish sitting right there on her dresser. I recognized it because I had used the nail polish to paint my initials on the side of the bottle. When I saw this, I knew that she had taken all the things that belonged to me. I was stunned: I just couldn't believe Pia, my *best friend*, would take things that belonged to me without asking, especially since she knew that if she had asked to borrow them I would've said yes. They would've been hers for the asking—that's the kind of friend I am. That she didn't ask and just took them anyway made me feel so violated and betrayed. How could my *best friend* steal from me?

It was strange to have to come to terms with the feeling this gave me. I found myself not only insulted that she could steal from me, but saddened. Like my heart had been bruised.

And what about all those deepest and most private secrets and thoughts I'd shared with her? I told her about boys I liked, shared my fears, even things about my family. With her I had opened—and emptied—my heart. Suddenly her act of stealing from me made me feel cheated, like all these thoughts that belonged to *me* were now in the hands of someone I couldn't trust. I knew that she had forever lost the privilege of being my *best friend*. Our friendship might go on, but I'd never trust her or be as open with her as I used to be. Learning I could not trust Pia was a painful lesson, but it also gave me a clearer idea of what really matters to me in a friend.

Marie Lake, 15

Familiar Isolation

Once a week, for one hour, I am labeled a "violator" of the rules of my society. I spend that time actively challenging patterns and beliefs I have held for much of my life. But the agony of that struggle doesn't stop at the end of that hour. It continues every hour of every day, because my real violation isn't just against the legal system. I violated my faith in myself, in the values I was raised to respect and my worth as an asset to the world.

Growing up, I never imagined that I was very different from everyone around me. I am the only child of divorced parents who love me very much. Both are achievers. My father works hard at his career and spends a lot of time with his friends, very nice friends, I might add. They like and respect him and want to be in his company. My mother is less outgoing and social than he is, but she is an achiever nonetheless. I'm most like my father, but I want to be like my mother. I always remember looking up to my mother and wanting to be like her because she is someone who completely owns herself. Educated, independent, driven and physically stunning: somebody who mattered.

By all regular standards, I had a normal "good-kid" childhood. Everybody seemed to like me. I had the good fortune to live in a nice home and attend school in a very nice neighborhood. I got good grades, had great friends, took piano lessons and was tutored in any subject in which I needed a little extra help. I was destined to go on to a great college. The future was mine for the taking.

You would have thought that I had everything. But inside my head, none of it was real. I was faking the self-assured confidence I exuded. Inside, I was all alone, without hope for ever really being like the parents who had raised me and who I had idolized for all those years. I was desperate to satisfy their expectations—the thing is, their expectations of me were reasonable. They encouraged more than pushed. They hoped more than prodded. Somehow I had to work harder, I had to achieve more because it was expected—especially by me. The expectations inside my head were those that pushed and prodded. But I didn't think I could do it alone. I needed help to be more, to be better. And so I rebelled against *myself*, even more so than my parents. Knowing this added even more guilt to what I already felt. So, I'd try to do better. But it was hard.

And then came the magic potion, the easy answer. The first drug I ever tried is the reason I am now in after-care. I snorted crystal methamphetamine for the first time in ninth grade. Meth offered the superhuman energy I thought I needed to work harder to be the person I was expected to be. And it had an extra special side effect: it kept me trim, no, thin—like my classmates.

While this was the answer to my finding more stamina, drive and success in the beginning, within months I found myself a slave to the drug. Basically, I was burning myself out: Exhaustion, a quick temper and a constant bad mood were the outer results. The inner damage was to my health—physical, mental and spiritual. But since I couldn't really see it, it didn't much matter.

Quickly, snorting meth was replaced by smoking meth. The side effects intensified. Days of sleeping were followed by days of violent moods. Along with damage to my mother's home, I would break things in my own room, doing things such as throwing my phone across the room and into the walls when a conversation with a friend didn't go as I felt it was supposed to. After a streak of stealing my mother's things, I "moved" from home to an apartment with a girlfriend. I was seventeen. You would think that being on my own in an apartment with a friend would be living every girl's dream, and so I'd be happy. I wasn't and because I wasn't, I became even angrier within myself. All my friends were going off to college or getting jobs, great dates and engagement rings. I was married to meth. And so my cycle of self-destructive behavior intensified even more.

My antisocial habits and attitudes began showing up in my surroundings. It wasn't long before my roommate was unwilling to put up with my irresponsibility of not paying my share of the rent and apartment expenses. She didn't necessarily approve of my friends—who were pretty much nonachievers, as I now so blatantly was also. The toll on my psyche was enormous, and so I called upon my drug to rescue me from even my own thoughts.

I was well on my way to disassociating from life in the real world. I was neither fully living nor dying—at least not immediately. I wanted to stop using, but I didn't know how. A loud voice inside of my head shouted, "You can't stop, you can't do anything about it because you're a failure. . . . You're an addict." I was open to any solution, even to my mother's prodding to go to a drug rehab center—where I went for three weeks. And started using the very day I got out. The next family suggestion was that I move from the bad influences of my friends to another city. Maybe it was my chance to start over—once again. But it was also scary. Surely, I was bound to mess up again. I moved halfway across the country to live with my father.

The circumstances in my new surroundings and the lack of knowing any dealers kept me sober for a while. Five whole months actually. During this time, my parents loved me like an adult, treated me like an adult, and were so relieved that their daughter had joined the real world. They were genuinely happy. So now I knew I was also a huge shareholder in their happiness. Hopefully I wouldn't screw that up. But I did.

I managed to get hooked up with the "underbellies" of life, as my mother called them, and started back in the cycle of drug use. Within months, I was a full-blown user again. Only this time, it was just too much effort to care. So I tried not to. Lying seemed to be the only way that I could communicate. Having told lie upon lie, it wasn't long before I believed my own deceptions. My mental health was now so corroded that the dangerous crowd I used with just looked like regular people to me—even if they were running from the law.

Every now and then, I needed to come up for air. Plus, I was strung out and tired from living so minute by minute. Wanting to "feel better," I decided some new clothes would make me look better, hence I'd feel better. I stole the clothes, was taken to jail and put on probation with a suspended sentence. But still I wasn't slowed. By now I was a clever girl and could work my way around anyone—police officers, probation officers, jail guards—even trained psychologists. I knew what they wanted to hear, and I served it up. And when any or all of these upped the stakes of my "going straight," I simply upped my stakes of finding ways to beat them at their own tactics. You see, it didn't cross my mind that at any of these junctures of being accountable to the court system, I could have used the many people coming into my life as lifeguards to keep me from swimming further out to sea in the midst of a hurricane. I didn't think I even needed a life raft. I was invincible. Just ask my buoy, meth.

And then my probation officer got me on three dirty U.A.'s (urine analysis) and I was given an ankle bracelet to wear. An ankle bracelet, mandated by the courts, allows the police and drug enforcement agency officers to keep track of your where-abouts. Basically, you are under twenty-four-hour surveillance. Among other privileges taken away from me was being out past ten o'clock at night. Worse than a tenth grader—curfew! But how did I see it? "No biggie," I swaggered, "I'll just have the drugs delivered to where I'm staying." Which is what I did. Then I was arrested again for violating my probation when I skipped a rescheduled meeting with my probation officer. From the county jail, I was court ordered to be placed in a girls' detention and rehab center. So now I had a new challenge ahead of me: Successfully conning those around me into believing that I had changed and could now follow the rules—theirs and society's.

Six weeks later they bought my act, and I moved back into my father's house. As ordered by the courts, I got a job. Once again, while I was doing everything to look like the good girl I was expected to be, I was dying on the inside. I started to feel restless, and it only took about three months before I started using again. I began stealing mercilessly from my father, and our fights over my drug-crazed moods and irresponsibility got me tossed out of the house again.

And so once more life became a day-in, day-out battle for my own survival. I moved into a place using drugs as rent money. By hook or by crook, I barely maintained my monthly schedule of visits to the probation department. It wasn't long before my probation officer was exasperated with the games I was playing. And with my second set of violations—missing an appointment, changing my address without notice and termination from my employment—I was buried deep within my own hell. Now I was "tripped up" by the rules of the system and my own self-destructive ways. *If only* I would have been able to confess outright to my probation officer, or a drug counselor or someone I could trust—and simply admit: "I'm scared and tired and feel that any day now, I'm going to die from an overdose, or from a stray bullet from gunfire on the street outside. Could you please help me? I don't know how to begin to get better on my own. But I desperately want to find my way back."

But I couldn't or wouldn't. I sat trapped in my own game—and paid the price. After thirty days in the county jail, I was sentenced to a violator's program at a women's detention center. So to my image of me, I added the reality check that here I was, two days before Thanksgiving, at the bottom yet again. I remained incarcerated over Christmas, New Year's, Mother's Day, Father's Day, my birthday and the hospitalization of my grandfather for a serious illness. All this from a girl who had so much potential, and from whom so many expected so much. All this from such an exceptionally pretty, extremely loved and privileged girl.

But maybe I was more ordinary than I had imagined. In the violator's program, I learned that I had a "criminal mind" and I really wasn't an exception to the rule. I learned a lot of things I had known before, too, but in order to get out of the program, this time I had to show that I was going to apply them. After completing violator's boot camp, I was off to the rehab and detention center where the staff didn't trust me at all this time around. They deliberately ignored me, refusing to allow me to participate in activities open to the residents. It was a terrible feeling.

Trapped in a familiar isolation, I descended deeper into depression.

Finally released, I met my new parole officer. He seemed genuine, as though he really did want me to change my life, and he actually believed that I could. All I had to do was stay off drugs, attend after-care once a week without being late, keep my job and, as he said, "Be good to yourself for a change." It seemed so simple, at least, to a normal person, but for me it still wasn't simple enough. Within seven days of release from the facility, I relapsed again. Once again, I traveled down that all-too-familiar path to the county jail, on to yet another women's facility, this time a tougher, stricter one. Then back to jail for a meeting with the judge for reconsideration. But since I hadn't served enough time, I couldn't even see the judge, so I was sent off to a detention center to wait it out. There seemed to be no end in sight.

An amazing thing happened to me on the trip back up to the detention center. I crashed into the most terrible reality yet. I became aware that, rather than being that special person I thought I was, I was just an inmate. The ropes of life inside jails had become familiar, and I realized I was becoming institutionalized. I was facing my worst nightmare—the anonymity of becoming just another person who others will never trust, never look up to or never love. On the day of my reconsideration, I truly believed I was going away again—and that it would be forever and, by now, because I had burned so many bridges, no one would even care.

Only now, I cared.

My final chance to change my life was granted with a host of guidelines and ultimatums. Electric monitoring, no dirty U.A.'s— and all the pressure of those who loved me, my parents and those who were there to help me. I made it through the first six-month period of my formal supervised probation.

I don't know if I'll ever fully recover from my descent into drugs and the annihilated self-esteem and shattered self-image it resulted in. But I hope I do. I am working on it. Today, I am more profoundly aware of who I am and who I want to work towards being. I do know that intentions and strong will only bring temporary change. Real change takes a complete shift in understanding, a new awareness brought about by choosing a different personal attitude. Negative self-talk, shame, anger, sadness and depression are all still very much alive within me today. Even so, I try not to allow them the power to decide my actions for me without being able to cast my vote on my own behalf.

I am also becoming better able to open my mind and my heart to new ideas and directions in thinking. This helps me accept new insight into a different way of life. Today, I am aware of the many emotions I inevitably go through in the course of a day, and I know that it is okay to feel them. When faced with those situations and emotions that are a part of day-to-day life, I can think about consequences, good and bad, and then choose how I want to react or not react, as the case may be. But even as I say this, the anchor that holds me each day is these words: "If your thinking is solid and clear today, you'll probably still be sober tomorrow." I do know that to the precise extent I permit this, I avoid squandering the hours that might have been worthwhile. That's my new goal, my new "game"—to try not to squander any more of my life.

Sara Jane Keller, 20

One More Thing

So many things to do,
Every single day!

One more dish to wash,
Laundry to put away.

One more paper to write,
A book to return.

Parents, teachers, classmates, friends,
Lost buttons and broken zippers to mend.

One more book to read,
Practice to attend.

One more person to meet,
An important note to send.

One more appointment to keep,
A part-time job; gotta have money to spend.

Just one more thing to do,
Every single day!

Jennifer Leigh Youngs

What You Did with You

You had "such potential" they all said,
Now, at eighteen you lie dead.
Your body drugged beyond repair.
Not long ago so young and fair.

My heart and hopes lie with you shattered,
As your grandfather, could I have mattered?
You have my pity, but there's anger, too,
When I think of what you did with you.

Why did you waste and then destroy
A life meant for greatness and for joy?
The world needed all your best
But now you've just been "laid to rest."

You could have made the world a better place
Safer for the human race.
You have my pity, but there's anger, too,
When I think of what you did with you.

Your body was given to treat with respect
To nurture and honor, not to neglect.
Your place was to reach out and to say,
"I know there is a better way!"

But, now you're dead and gone;
We're left to wonder what went wrong.
And the mourners' tears have all been spent,
As they question what your life has meant.

My heart and hopes lie with you, shattered,
As your grandfather, could I have mattered?
You have my pity, but there's anger, too,
When I think of what you did with you.

Forgive my anger, my grandson so dear,
I only wish you were still here.
I miss you more than you could know,
Wanted to watch you succeed and grow.

I just wished you had come to me,
And let me help to set you free,
To hold you and give you my strength,
I would have gone to any length.

I wanted to love you for so much longer.
My love for you could have made you stronger.
There was always help that I'd gladly give,
And always hope—as long as one still lives.

Elmer Adrian, 94

The Boys Only Wanted One Thing . . .

For some reason, right from the start in this school, I've had a reputation for being "easy." It's been almost five months since I moved to a new school in another state, and it's been a really tough thing for me to deal with. I don't know if this awful reputation is because I moved here from a big city, or because I look really mature for my age, but whatever the reason, it's just not true!

I learned that I had this reputation two weeks after I started school, when a boy from my biology class called me one Friday night and asked me if I wanted to go out with him—right then. I was a little surprised, since it was already ten o'clock and we'd only said "Hi" a few times when we passed each other in the halls. Still, he seemed nice enough, and he said we were just going to meet some of his friends for pizza. So I said okay. Well, we didn't go for pizza! And being with him was a terrible experience—like fighting off an octopus the whole time! I mean, his hands were all over me. When I demanded he keep his hands to himself, he said, "Come on, don't play innocent!"

"Innocent?" I questioned, having no idea what he was getting at. "Everyone knows what you do!" he said with a really big smirk on his face. "What does that mean?" I demanded, in complete shock about what I was hearing. "Your reputation for being easy," he replied as easily as if it were a common fact.

Over the next few weeks, I discovered this seedy information was a "common fact" around the halls at school. Maybe that explains why whenever a guy does ask me out, it's never to go to a school activity or to a movie or dinner or anything like that; it's to meet him somewhere later and go someplace where he's sure no one from school will see him with me. When I say no, they don't ask me out again.

Because of my reputation for "putting out," I can't trust any boys, because I feel sure they're only asking me out because of what they heard about me. And I don't have many girlfriends either, because they don't want to end up with a bad reputation themselves just because they're my friend. "Guilt by association," as one girl said. Well, I can tell you from experience how terrible it is to be thought of as a girl who does these things, even though I know it isn't true. And I now know firsthand how dangerous, painful and unfair stereotypes can be. It was a tough lesson to learn, one I never asked or wished for, so take it from me: Don't judge others when you don't really know them, and don't pass on hurtful information even if it is true. You may be not only contributing to someone getting a bad reputation unfairly, but also to her having to defend herself.

As for me, even though I'd never wish such unfairness on another person, I'm determined not to let it keep me down, especially since there isn't anything I've done to be ashamed of. So I just keep being respectful to others, hoping that sooner or later, they'll know who I really am.

Lisa Ritchey, 16

Would You Ask Me Out If You Knew?

For two years I had a pen pal named Michelle. She lives in Tulsa, Oklahoma. I live in Billings, Montana. We decided to see if there was a way we could meet each other, and we were working it out. Then one day, I sent her a full-length picture of me. We had already exchanged pictures the year before, but just little head shots. After I sent the picture, my pen pal wrote back and said that my visiting her probably wasn't going to work out. After that she stopped writing. That really hurt.

I know why she doesn't want to be my pen pal anymore. It's because I'm really overweight. When I told this to my aunt, she said, "Oh, no! You mustn't think that your weight had anything to do with it!" But thinking anything else would just be sugarcoating the truth. Because of my weight, I will never be a cheerleader; I will never be homecoming queen; and I will never be voted "most likely to succeed." There are a lot of awesome experiences that will never be mine, because they are reserved only for people who are "normal." Overweight is not considered "normal" in my school. Is it "normal" in yours? I bet not. My weight keeps me from having some of the things I want, like the lead in the school play. I know I wasn't selected for the part because of my weight. One other "really large" boy also tried out for a lead role and, because of his weight, he didn't get the part either.

It's just the simple truth. I am a girl who weighs more than what most people think of as being the right amount to weigh. I am considered too heavy to be pretty. I know there are even some kids at school who won't be close friends with me because of my weight. And I've never been asked out on a date by a boy who knows me. The total of my entire dating life consists of two blind dates—one that was set up by my cousin, who lives in another town, and one that my friend had her boyfriend, who goes to another school, set up for me. Neither of the guys asked me out for a second date. So now when anyone asks to set me up with a blind date, I always ask, "Would he ask me out if he knew I was fat?" Naturally, they then say, "Of course. You are a very nice person," and, "Of course, you have a great personality." But I know what's up.

I guess some people are uncomfortable being around someone who is overweight. They just think that you have no one to blame but yourself for being overweight. The way they see it is, "If you just stop eating you won't be fat." Unfortunately, it's not that easy. I've been overweight all my life, and I can tell you that the explanation is not a simple one. For one, my mother has taken me to the doctor and I really do have a thyroid condition. I'm being treated for it, but still, it's a struggle. Then, there's genetics; I come from a family that has big bones. My mother is five feet, nine inches tall, and she works out a couple days a week at the family fitness center. Still, anyone who saw her would say she's a "big woman." My mother is a real inspiration to me. She has a really healthy image of herself. She loves her job, has a lot of great friends and she loves her family. While I work at being healthy and fit, my real goal is to see myself like my mother sees herself.

But I do have a bone to pick with those of you who feel it's your obligation to comment on someone's weight—and some advice. Keep your comments to yourself. When you go to school with others who are smaller than you, some who are even small for their age, it's really hard not to be down on yourself, so don't make it any tougher than it already is. And besides, look at Xena the Warrior Princess—she's big and beautiful, just like I am.

Amy Manning, 16

The Yaqui's Counsel

A year and a half ago, I transferred from one school to another. It was a voluntary transfer, a choice I made, hoping to graduate from a school with a reputation for excellence! It was my senior year, a time when many of the kids already belonged to a group, and so membership was already a foregone conclusion. Still, I had high hopes of being accepted by the other students, of making some friends and being a part of things. Of course, I also intended to continue being a good student, and being on the honor roll, just as I had been at the school from which I was transferring. This was a really good time for me. I was happy and feeling confident about the things going on in my life. My transcript said that I was a well-rounded student, so about my only worry was getting into a good college; I had yet to take my SAT, but was hopeful I'd do okay on it, and I knew that my being a good athlete would bolster my being seen as "college material." I was sure the great reviews I was bound to get from any of my handful of coaches over the past five years would clinch my being accepted to college somewhere. And then suddenly, everything changed, and SATs and athletic letters from coaches were the least of my concerns! Wouldn't you know that my stepfather would decide to have a midlife crisis that would coincide with the first week at my new school! With a final bitter and ugly argument firing up between my mom and him late one night— one where the police came to arrest my stepdad for being under the influence of alcohol and cocaine—a divorce quickly ensued.

The divorce was a brutal force between the two of them. It was made even more painful by the fact that they both loved each other, but with his prized ego intact, my stepfather refused to get the help he needed, and my mother stood her ground until he did. Their split was deeply painful for me as well. When your parents are divorcing, you quickly learn that you, too, are involved, even though you don't want to be. Certainly I was stuck on the battlefield of divorce warfare, where each pitted me against the other. Both saw me as some sort of messenger go-between, as though I was the personal reporter for each of them of how things looked from the other side of "camp warfare." It was a confusing time because though I was loyal to my mother, I was angry at the both of them—especially my stepfather, whom I had come to call "Dad." Certainly, I wanted him to be. He was handsome and cool, wore the latest Polo trends and drove a new 735i. When he rolled into the parking lot at my school, my own reputation as "someone" went up a notch. And when he stepped out of the car to wait for me, *all* of the girls remarked that he looked "really hot for his age, a real dude." That didn't hurt my standing either! Now, right when I really needed him to work his personal magic as I bounced in the lap of a new school experience, his not being there really was betrayal. But it was more than just that he was handy for my own sense of "cool." I loved him—or thought I did. All my emotions were confusing and now colliding. I couldn't believe the man I truly cherished and adored could in seconds become my mortal enemy: How could he leave us—especially someone as awesome as my mother?

The divorce derailed my whole life. I lost my edge at school, not really caring where I fit in the pecking order of things. And grades, well, who could study at my house with a Jerry Springer cast of characters—only without Jerry Springer refereeing and his troupe of bodyguards making sure things didn't get completely out of hand—as if that was possible.

I lost my direction and hope of going on to college. I was consumed with sadness and feelings of self-doubt. My life was a wreck. And it was his fault—I felt. I lost sight of who I was and who I wanted to become. What's more, I was fairly scared of who I *was* becoming. The pull between where I thought I was going and my sudden state of stall triggered a depression within me, one I couldn't seem to pull out of, one that my normal optimism couldn't balance out. Angry and bummed out, I blamed my parents, especially my stepfather, a man from whom I had been craving and striving for acceptance for the six years of his marriage to my mother—and I thought I was so close to achieving.

Rather than getting close to other students at school, I turned to my boyfriend, a guy who was four years older than I and already out of school. While I couldn't necessarily articulate it at the time, not having friends my own age, with interests and goals the same as mine, made me feel not only alone, but really left out. For emotional survival I retreated to him, and being loved by him became my whole focus.

I thought putting my heart into loving him would offer respite from my woes and sorrow. Loving him and being loved by him seemed to be an escape from the confusion and heartache I was feeling—temporarily at least. I was smart enough to know I was running from myself, and that hiding in the pocket of someone else isn't where you're likely to find yourself. But at the time, it was a safe harbor. At this point, I felt I had no control over life—and I was a girl who normally had everything under control.

Six months into the divorce between my mother and step-father, my sense of self was so lost that not only had I given up on myself, but now, rather than having friends who would help bolster my self-confidence, I chose those who didn't have their lives together themselves either—those whose own self-esteem was badly eroded, those who were insecure and unsure of them-selves—as I was. All in all, it was a cycle perpetuating self-destruction. My identity at this point was all up in the air—it seemed I had lost the me who was happy and funny and the person I was so proud of, and the person I trusted most. I didn't think about the future anymore at that point. But an even sadder reality is that even if I wanted to regroup, I didn't know how. Whereas before I wouldn't even tolerate some of the halfhearted goals of my friends, here I was, accepting them for my own. Basically, I had given up.

I definitely needed a complete emotional overhaul, a change, a shift of paradigm. I needed an incentive to begin to take those painful steps back to health, hope and love for my self, *for* myself. I had to start living a life plan that was true to me, one that was meaningful and purposeful to me in all ways. But how?

I began to clean "my" house. I stopped seeing my boyfriend, for starters—it was to be the start of a renewal, a spiritual journey that brought me back to me. The encouraging push back into reality came from a trip I took with my new boyfriend to visit his mother, Jadelina, in Sedona, Arizona. Jadelina suggested I exchange my "done in" attitude for a "fulfilling my promise to *destiny*." This idea was new—and revolutionary—to me: Life wasn't only about getting caught in the web that others spun, it was about claiming my own journey, a journey in which I could choose to be as powerful (or powerless) as I was willing to be. Embracing this philosophy was an intense turning point; it energized me in a positive way. I was introduced to the Native American spiritual path, a natural law that respects all of Mother Earth and honors all creation. I found this path soothed the part of myself that ached for goodness, peace, focus and affirmation. And so I found the weekend pure magic, and Jadelina became a source of inspiration in a whole new dawning of self, one that created new goals for me, and awakened my spirit. The renewal I had been searching for was found, and I was ready to make up for some time lost. I no longer needed to search for myself outside of myself. I returned home and began again.

Looking back, I cling to the words of a Yaqui Indian who I met exploring on the red plateaus; I cherish how true these words proved to be for me: "The moment one commits oneself, then angels guide."

My experience has filled me with compassion for those who find the courage to confront the behaviors that don't serve them in positive ways. It's been a long trip from the divorce of my mother and stepfather for me, but I made it back to me. So I want to share what I learned with those who are still grappling for a pathway out of their own days of darkness: Once you find the courage to commit yourself to taking action—those first steps toward change—it's really true: Angels will guide you on your path to higher ground. I know it was true for me. I did the right things and all the right things started to happen—my path became clearer as guides were given to me for just that purpose.

Jenny Bilicki, 19

Don Quixote's Horse

"It's been burned!" the man on the other end of the phone wailed. "They've burned *Don Quixote's Horse!*"

"It's good to hear from you, my friend!" Vic cajoled, not at all caught up in his friend's sense of tragedy. He then calmly asked, "Who did it?"

"Teenagers. Three teenagers," the distraught man sobbed. "It's gone. Everything. Everything I've worked for. Do you realize the time I spent on him? Gone." Dennis Patton, the famed artist of *Don Quixote's Horse* literally wept. His magnificent, sixty-foot-tall, lathe and tin-laid masterpiece had been touring the country, opening to rave reviews. *Don Quixote's Horse* had graced the cover of nearly every important art and trade publication. Though Dennis had been a serious artist for nearly fifteen years, it was *Don Quixote's Horse* that finally earned him not only renown as a contemporary artist, but much-needed income as well.

After long minutes of listening to Dennis's dire mourning, his good friend and confidant, Vic Preisser, interrupted. "Oh, Dennis, I am absolutely thrilled to hear this! I couldn't be happier for you! And, think of all the publicity you'll get—free, no less!" A moment of stunned silence followed Vic's congratulatory remark. "Happy for me?" Dennis questioned blankly. "It's easy for you to be sunny about this, it didn't happen to you!"

"That's right. It happened to you! You can view this as a catastrophe or an opportunity, my friend," Vic told Dennis, adding, "I see it as an opportunity."

"But, Vic," Dennis moaned, his words still dripping grief for the destroyed artwork that had taken nearly two years of his life to complete. "Finally, finally, I'd created a piece that brought the kind of recognition and money I've dreamed of. Now it's gone. Gone. For you to say that nothing could be better for me is crazy. You're crazy!"

"Crazy all right! Crazy about your work," Vic roared. *"Don Quixote's Horse* was a masterpiece to be sure, but you've been dwelling on him too long. Now you can be fresh again. Nothing could be better than this for starting the creative juices flowing, for creating, for trying something new. What an opportunity you've been handed. You've got important work ahead of you, my friend! The world is waiting for your next masterpiece. Better start working on it!"

"Oh, you're right," Dennis conceded. "I haven't done anything new in quite some time. It's just that piece was so loved, and of course, I've been counting on it to make me successful. I want to be a success." This comment was met by an instant retort by Vic: "Yes, well, just remember that *success is not measured by your victories, as much as by how you recover from tough times.*"

Breaking out in laughter, Dennis surrendered. "Why didn't I know I'd hear something like this from you?" His voice more confident and hopeful, he added, "You're right, of course. There must be something good that can come of this."

True enough, and Dennis just needed to be reminded of that. Perhaps that's why he had turned to his friend after a loss of such magnitude—his precious masterpiece that he had toiled over for so long, one that was finally gaining him a respected reputation in his field. Perhaps the famed artist counted on the fact that his friend Vic would help him see the possibility of something good emerging from his catastrophe.

Which is exactly what happened. Dennis moved beyond his despair over the destruction of *Don Quixote's Horse*. Over the course of the next year, he created many new beautiful works, including a new piece that would become his signature piece— *Woman's Head*. This exquisite statue of a woman, almost a half-block long, features real-life tree branches for her hair. The piece is that large!

By the time *Woman's Head* was completed, the burning of Dennis's sculpture—which tens of thousands of daily commuters saw and loved as they passed by it each day—had generated enough publicity and public sentiment to support rebuilding it completely in metal. Building the statue in metal was something Dennis had yearned to do in the beginning, but he hadn't been able to afford it at the time. Now he was given carte blanche to recreate *Don Quixote's Horse* the way he had dreamed it could be.

Seven years to the very day after *Don Quixote's Horse* was burned, a man called Dennis and asked if he could come see him. As it turned out, the young man was one of the three teens who had set *Don Quixote's Horse* ablaze. "I've come to plead for your forgiveness," the man said to Dennis. "I was one of the three teenagers who burned down *Don Quixote's Horse*. We did it on a drunken dare. I feel so badly for what I've done, and I've made such a mess of my life. I want to turn my life around, beginning with making things right with you, if I can. I want you to know how sorry I am, and I'd like to ask you what I can do to have you forgive me." Dennis looked compassionately at the young man and said, "Well, I guess you know better than anyone the many curveballs and challenges life presents. I'll tell you what you can do to make it right with me: Promise me that you will be diligent in your desire to turn your life around and make it mean something. When you come upon those times that make you want to throw in the towel and just quit, remind yourself of your promise to me to do something purposeful with your life. When things are tough—whether an internal struggle or a worldly challenge— vow to see it through. It's the tough times, more so than the easy times, that show proof of our willingness to lead our lives in the most positive way we can. Let me remind you of the words a dear friend once told me: *Success is not measured by your victories nearly as much as by how you recover from tough times.*"

Bettie B. Youngs
Adapted from Taste-Berry Tales

Where to Get Help

You don't have to face the tough stuff alone! If you'd like to get help (even just information about something you're wondering about), but don't know exactly where to turn, the following list of hotlines of organizations may be able to provide it, or refer you to someone who can. Hotlines are a great resource when you need to talk about something confidential, or need a referral for a particular problem. Listed according to the problems they deal with, you will find both the names of organizations that are there to help you and how you can reach those organizations. Most of these hotlines have 800 numbers, so that you can call them free of charge from anywhere in the United States. For those that don't have 800 numbers, we've included addresses, so you can write to them. This list is just a sample of what's out there—there are any number of local and national hotlines available to help you through almost any crisis or the tough issues you may be facing. You can find other hotlines in your Yellow Pages directory. You can also turn to a school or church counselor, a school nurse or teacher, parents or other adults you trust. Remember, they have your best interests at heart.

Abuse (Domestic Violence and Sexual Abuse)
Childhelp USA
24-hour hotline: 800-4-A-CHILD
(English/Spanish)
or
Rape Crisis Center
800-352-7273

AIDS
AIDS Hotline for Teens
800-234-8336
or 800-440-8336

Cancer
American Cancer Society
(can refer you to local support groups)
800-ACS-2345
or
National Cancer Institute/
National Childhood Cancer Foundation
800-4-CANCER

Depression
National Depressive and Manic-Depressive Association
800-82NDMDA
Provides information about teenage depression and provides referrals for local physicians who can help.

Disabilities
National Information Center for Youth with Disabilities
800-695-0295

Drug and Alcohol Abuse
Youth Crisis Hotline for Teens
800-448-4663
or
24-hour hotline: 800-622-2255

Family Recovery
AL-ANON and ALA-TEEN Family Headquarters
800-356-9996

Eating Disorders
American Anorexia and Bulimia Association
293 Central Park West, Suite 1R
New York, NY 10024
212-501-8351
or
Anorexia Nervosa and Related Eating Disorders
P.O. Box 102
Eugene, OR 97405
503-344-1144

Pregnancy (and Prevention)
Planned Parenthood
(Listed in your local telephone directory)
Planned Parenthood provides reproductive health services. Teens can go to Planned Parenthood centers for birth control, pregnancy tests, STD testing and treatment, and counseling.

Runaway and Homeless Teenagers
National Runaway Hotline
Counseling and referrals for runaways and homeless teens.
24-hour hotline: 800-621-4000
or
Runaway Hotline
800-231-6945

Sexuality
Sexuality Information and Education Council of the United States (SIECUS)
30 West 42nd Street, Suite 350
New York, NY 10036
212-819-9770

Suicide
National Commission on Youth Suicide Prevention
67 Irving Place South
New York, NY 10003
212-532-2400

Bettie B. Youngs and Jennifer Leigh Youngs

Part 8

Faith at Work in Our Lives

People are like stained glass windows.
They sparkle and shine when the sun is out;
but when the darkness sets in their true beauty is
revealed only if there is a light inside.

—Elisabeth Kubler-Ross

A Word from the Authors

"You know, Mom, I love being outdoors. Being in the midst of nature is good for my heart and soul. Nature helps me get in touch with the bigger world we live in and makes me realize that, as much as we like and need our family and friends, no amount of exciting times with them can compensate or take the place of finding the meaning of our own existence."

"I agree, Jennifer. Even when we are with others, we experience our lives one-on-one. I really like the following passage from your book, *Feeling Great, Looking Hot & Loving Yourself! Health, Fitness & Beauty for Teens*, where you offer your readers your sense of the importance of faith in their lives."

Picture that you and several of your best friends have ridden your bikes to the top of a steep hill, where you stop to rest. You look outwardly into a vast blue horizon where clouds that look like tufts of cotton balls lounge like lazy alligators sunning on a riverbank on a hot summer's day. You look down into an immense valley of lush green trees and hearty ground-shrubs sprinkled with patches of wildflowers, a picturesque landscape—a sharp contrast to the teeny-tiny flowers decorating the ground beneath your feet. You are filled with an appreciation for the wonder and beauty of nature, one that leaves you with a feeling of awe and serenity.

As though she notices your appreciation—perhaps by your tranquil smile or from the lengthy breath of fresh mountain air you've drawn deep into your lungs—Mother Nature, having already flaunted her beauty, decides to please you even more. Intricately colored butterflies flutter to and fro and from flower to flower, each exquisite bloom generously offering up its sweet fragrance. Bees buzz by, busily sampling the sweet nectar, then carrying it off to distant places. As though to complement the phenomenal array of activity going on around you, a medley of tunes begins to play: There is the clicking and chattering of busy-bodied chipmunks and bushy-tailed ground squirrels as they scurry about foraging for food. There is the cheerful chirping of birds, their melody of happiness as evident as the other multitude of inhabitants of this hill who, though unseen, make their presence known.

In this moment, all call out to each other. What a choir! You can't help but feel the powerful stirrings going on inside of you. You marvel at all this intoxicating splendor, and ponder what it must be like to be a butterfly, willfully following a sweet scent, or a bird free to surf the warm winds at will. You feel a kinship with all the other little creatures making their way through the day, most especially that little rodent playing hide-and-seek with the shadow overhead in hopes he doesn't become a hungry hawk's timely, tasty lunch. And in that moment, you realize that everything in the universe works in harmony; we are all interdependent.

"Such a beautiful visual, isn't it, Mom?"

"It sure is, Jennifer. It reminds us that we live in a universe buzzing and humming with life. We live in a world of creation, one where a universal energy permeates all living matter. Whether we are marveling at an intricate flower in full bloom, or feeling at peace within because we're in a good space, all are reminders that we live in a universe that breathes its wonders into daily life. Acknowledging a force greater than ourselves is the foundation of faith. And faith is the wellspring from which hope, peace and love flow."

Be it facing a new situation or confronting an obstacle, be it searching for an answer or giving thanks, many teens said they believed a Higher Power operated in their lives. While some expressed this as "a voice within" my "conscience," "divine guidance" or "God," all said it was a source of thanksgiving and guidance.

As with so many other parts of their lives, teens examine for themselves the workings of faith and think about what it means to them. At times, they can see no other reason (other than God's doing) for why things are as they are, or happen for the reason they happen. And sometimes teens doubt faith, wondering why God would let bad things happen to good people. As you will see in the stories in this unit, teens explain how they came to believe in what they do and why, and how they reclaimed their faith or lost and rediscovered it.

Added to your many stories, we conducted a workshop for teens and we asked them to share with us one of their typical prayers to God. They did, and we've included some of them in this unit. While we were initially surprised that the prayers seemed so lighthearted, you teens told us that it's because your relationship with God is "user-friendly."

"You can talk with God about everything," said Sandra Moss from Tucson, Arizona. It's an opinion shared by many teens who said they considered God: "on my side," "loving," "understanding," "compassionate," and "since God knows all anyway, why not be open? You can't lie to God." Maybe this is one reason teens talk with God about the things that are very real for them: daily life—the ups and downs in relationships, what to do about their future, how to deal with everyday problems. As teen Brian Erwin said, "There is virtually not a day that goes by when I'm not either saying, 'God, please help me with this,' or 'thanks for helping me pull through on that.' For me, faith is believing I'm not alone and that as I make my way through life, I have an omnipotent source of love within that is a beacon showing me the way. It's a source I can turn to whether I'm feeling down in the dumps, feeling misunderstood or I am grateful for something. Faith is a natural feeling. Without it, what's the point?"

Because of their beliefs, many teens said they felt "connected." Certainly, faith can sustain us when we feel alone, fearful or overwhelmed—as so many teens discovered when overcoming challenges. Whether getting off or staying off drugs, facing changes—like moving to another state, the divorce of parents, a major illness, the stress of getting into college—or sorting out love or mending a broken heart, teens confirm faith is a source of comfort, strength and leadership.

As you will see in the following stories and prayers, teens have a lot to say about how they view God, and a lot to ask of him, as well as much for which to thank him. May you be inspired by their discovery that faith ties us to the timeless truths of all humanity.

I'm Listening

Dear God,

It's been a long time since we've communicated.
I meant to keep in touch
but I've been busy keeping up the payments
on my house, the cable, electricity and such.

Guess I'm one reason why your world's a mess.
Didn't help you much to make it better;
so I'm ashamed to ask you to even
read this letter.
But . . . I'm writing because I need your help.

I have teenage great-grandkids,
who I love as you well know.
I want them to have all the joy
and good as they live and grow.
I wonder what their world will be
if most of us have been like me.

And though my promises
are long past due,
please God, for them
help me to help you
make this world a place
where peace and beauty shine.
My love for them assures
I'm listening this time.

Elmer Adrian, 94

Faith and Rice

Over the summer of 1999, I traveled a long distance from the west coast of America to Thailand on a mission trip with a youth group to visit some of the orphanages there. Thailand is a country of great beauty, but it is also a country where a good many people are suffering—or at least that was my experience. On the border of Burma, I saw a man crawling on his hands and knees because he had deformed feet, begging for money. I saw many diseased children with large sores all over their bodies. I saw countless women, most of whom were cradling babies, their eyes filled with a yearning for relief from their hunger and suffering—their gaze bore deep into the souls of those brave enough to make eye contact with them. I was saddened by these deprivations—and at the same time, felt helpless in the face of all of it.

While in the country, I visited several orphanages, one of which was near the hills of Chaing Rai. Many of the children here faced poverty and deprivation as well, but these children were different. They knew Jesus. In Thai, they called him *Pra ye su*. The orphanage had taught their children about the great love of God, and so there was a particular joy and happiness within these children.

Happiness is one thing; food is another. There were one hundred hungry mouths to feed at the orphanage, but on this particular day, there remained but one last handful of rice and no other food to feed them. There is a saying in Thailand that states: "If you have rice, you have everything, but if you do not have rice, you have nothing." Would it be a day these little children would go without food?

Ever sure of God's abundance, the pastor turned to God in prayer for guidance on what he might do to secure food for his dependent children.

Little did he know food was on the way! At that exact moment, four unannounced visitors from California, one of which was me, drove up the narrow little path to the orphanage, each of us bearing a large sack of rice. We had absolutely no knowledge of the orphanage's desperate need for food; we had merely thought it would be kind to bring something with us as a gift to offer upon our arrival. And without any prompting, we had decided on rice—even though we didn't know at the time that it was the most perfect gift we could have brought.

Upon seeing our gifts of rice, the pastor called the children together to give thanks to God for loving his children so much.

Some experiences in life are so perfectly timed and well-placed that there is no way to shrug them off as chance or coincidence, times where even luck and fate are ruled out as possibilities. I believe with all my heart that on that day divine intervention was in play. I also believe it is a common occurrence, one that is readily seen in the activities of our day-to-day lives. It is in our everyday lives that God shows his love—just like he did that day at the orphanage—times when he reaches down to us all and whispers softly, "I love you." What a kind and loving God, always looking out for his children—always arranging perfect ways to help them.

It just goes to show you that all we ever need in life is faith. Well, faith and rice.

Megan Haver, 16

Dear God, About My Boyfriend/Girlfriend . . .

Dear God,

I always feel so much more calm and serene when I ask for your help. This feeling was especially helpful when John Duncomb dumped me for my best friend, Rachael. Thank you for comforting me so I didn't cry all day long in front of my friends— especially Rachael. I didn't want to ever return to school. I just knew it would be awful seeing them walk down the hall together, standing together, talking together and sitting together in the cafeteria, all the things John and I used to do. But you showed me I could get through it. You really do have everything under control. Please help me remember that, especially in times like this. Amen.

Jennifer Lyndon, 15

Dear God,

Every time I have a girlfriend, I seem to make some sort of mistake. I know you forgive me, but my girlfriends don't seem to. Please help me to learn from my mistakes, so I can get this having-a-girlfriend thing right! I really like being in love, so I want to get it right. Please help me. Amen.

Jeremy Lessman, 17

Dear God,

Having a broken heart is sure draining. I feel so sad and lonely. Please help me get back together with Trey. If that's not what you have in mind, then help me forget about him. When my heart hurts like this, I don't seem to be able to do much else. Thank you *so* much for caring about me.

Chelsea Barton, 16

Dear God,

I realize with people praying about world peace and things, this may not seem all that important, but it's practically a life-and-death matter to me: Please let Mickey ask me to the dance this weekend. I promise to abide by the curfew my parents have set, even if it is much earlier than other kids my age have. I'll even be ready and willing to help out more around the house. I really do appreciate your loving me and helping me with these issues. It's just that when it comes to love, I feel so much better and so much happier when I have a boyfriend. And I know that's by your design, or love wouldn't feel as good as it does. Anyway, I really do honor you. It's a great world you have set up here, one that will be even better if Mickey asks me out. Thanks *so* much for *all* you do for me.

Penny Moore, 16

Scuba Man

Bouncing off the rocky bottom of the reef, I scratched my way towards the surface for air, gasping for breath as my head broke the water. Looking around for my surfboard, I began reeling it in by its leash. My brother and I had gone surfing, and I'd been flying across the face of an overhead wave when the wave pitched, hurling me into a shallow water wipeout. Now, as my surfboard grew closer, I saw what looked like a heap of kelp dangling over it. But when it got close enough for me to grab, I discovered that what appeared to look like kelp was in reality a hideous creature! Yanking back my hand, I stared in wide-eyed horror at the sea serpent clinging to my board. A closer look revealed that it was a huge octopus. Octopus or not, it had staked its claim to my surfboard, and I wanted it to get off! Cautiously gripping two edges of the board, so as not to touch the slithering mass, I tried to shake the slimy monster off.

It didn't budge—ironic, because as another wave assailed me, I did. Being in the "impact zone"—where the waves are continuous—I knew the ocean wasn't about to grant me a calm stretch so that I could settle my property dispute in a stress-free way. I clawed for the surface again, again spitting out salt water and swallowing gulps of air and again reeling in the leash—only to find the creature *still* wrapped in place.

A new tactic was in order.

Gingerly, I attempted to pluck the animal off. Tentacle by suction-studded tentacle, I tried to get this creature to give me back my board. But yet another crashing wave put a tumultuous end to that strategy (which hadn't been meeting with any great measure of success). This time when I returned to the surface, I saw my brother, David, paddling towards me. Momentarily relieved, my heart swelled with hope and gratitude. Sudden sentiment filled me—my younger brother had come to rescue me!

Imagine my frustration when he eyed the situation, then threw back his head in laughter and paused just long enough to call out, "Hey, scuba man!" before paddling off to catch his next wave. To my great anguish, he hadn't realized how dire my situation was, and in fact, he had seen my predicament as humorous!

My "near rescue" took place just seconds before yet another wave battered me. This time when I panted to the surface, I grabbed one end of the board and threw my legs around it, using my feet to try to push the octopus free. I actually had it halfway off, but then the next set of waves knocked me completely off the board and sucked me back under water, where I skidded painfully across a treacherous reef.

Flailing my way towards the surface again, I was totally exhausted. And frightened. Beaten, I surrendered. I couldn't do this on my own. "This is it, God," I thought. "If you want me, I'm all yours!" The moment I thought these words, I had a renewed surge of energy. My head crashed above water again. Hand over hand, I wrenched painstakingly on the leash until my board came into reach of my fatigued arms. Flailing towards it, I collapsed on its surface—only to find the octopus was gone. Listlessly draped there, my heart pounding, lungs burning and all my muscles screaming, I couldn't help but imagine the time and energy I might have saved if I had turned it over to Spirit to begin with!

Pastor Christian Sorenson
National President, United Church of Religious Science

Dear God, Some Things Are Really Tough

Dear God,

I know that you know how hard it was for me having my dog, Elvis, die last week. Thank you for making me feel just like you've been checking in on me. I can feel that you know how much I miss Elvis, and how lost I feel without him. I know you have Elvis there with you now, so give him a pat from me—the same kind of pat he'd get from me. And thanks for bringing him into my life. He was a great dog. Boy, do I miss him. As you know, my parents are trying to make me get another dog, but I don't want another dog. No other dog could replace Elvis, and having one would only make me miss Elvis even more than I already do. So could you be sure that my parents don't surprise me with a dog for my birthday next week, because I think that's what they might do. I just really want to remember Elvis for a while. And thank you for all the ways you are good to me. Amen.

Jackie Garza, 12

Dear God,

There are sometimes when I just feel like I'm all alone, and it can happen even when I'm in the middle of all my friends or the entire school. Please just tap on my heart at those times and remind me that you're there with me. I would *really* appreciate that. Love to you, Annie.

Annie Calderone, 17

The "Third Column"

Just like it does every fall, football season returned. And yesterday was just another Friday—except for one thing: It was *game day*.

Climbing off the bus that carried my team to the game, I stood looking off at the opponent's field. In this peaceful moment, all was well. Just another ordinary moment filled with the usual pregame jitters. Yet even though I couldn't have known it at the time, it was to be anything but an ordinary game. In fact, it was to be one of the most challenging games I would ever play.

Immediately after school, my team had boarded the bus and headed to this town nearly forty-five miles away to play our third game of the season. We'd won the first two games, and were hoping to make it 3–0.

We arrived at our opponent's school at about five-thirty, a half-hour ahead of time, which was fine by me. It's always nice to have a little time alone with your thoughts before you have no time for thoughts at all. Playing football is a team thing, and once on the playing field, you start thinking like a team—there is no time for any thoughts other than the moment at hand.

But for now, I let myself feel a peaceful moment as I stood looking at yet another football field in yet another city, where I'd be playing yet another group of guys in football uniforms. Taking in a deep breath of fresh air, I knew that the peace of this moment would soon be interrupted by the home-team advantage our opponents would have in being spurred on by fans, zealous cheerleaders and their parents and friends in the stands. Then would come the usual taunts and macho chants from guys on both teams as they took the field, guys like me, who hoped to walk off the field a hero or, at least, not get carried off the field on a stretcher. Better yet was the possibility of making the papers—being mentioned in one column would be great, making plays worthy of two columns was every player's dream. Three hours from now, we'd all know our fate—and just how much our muscles, ligaments and tendons would ache. For now we could only hope our pride wouldn't be aching, too. After all, no team likes to go home having lost the game.

The game that turned out to be anything but ordinary certainly started out ordinary enough. The other team arrived and both teams headed to their individual locker rooms to change into football gear. When announced, each team took the field. That's when I saw how huge the other team's players were! I knew our opponents came from a school that had a larger enrollment than ours, so it was only natural their school had more guys to choose from. I knew the team would be put together from the best of the best athletes. Although I knew going into the game that the other team was big, just how big never really sinks in until they are a couple of feet away, waiting for you to flinch, so they can shred you in two. These guys were forty and fifty pounds heavier and two years older than me. So, I decided I'd just have to buck up and concentrate. I had no sooner thought these thoughts when the band started playing, so I knew it was time to rock-'n'-roll. The next thing I knew, the ball was flying and so was I.

The first quarter was the "same old, same old" of both teams trying to size up the strong points of various players while working up their own ferocity. I was playing pretty well right from the start, and by the start of the second quarter, I was feeling even better. This was going to be an even better game than I had first thought. But then, things started heating up. Suddenly, like a grinder had been switched on, foul language filled the air and all kinds of illegal hits and pushes began to take place. That was when I realized that the other team was trying not only to hit hard, they were trying to rip our heads off. One of my teammates got hit so hard he lost one of his shoes. I got hit really hard from behind by number thirty-four. He was called five times for late hits—but he did it so many more times, it's amazing he didn't get thrown out of the game. Foul language, trash talk and threats of "I'll hurt you" and "I'll get you" now dominated the game. In addition to their taunting, they resorted to things like kicking a grounded player or twisting an ankle of a player down on the ground in a pileup.

To be honest, I was shocked. I couldn't believe such poor sportsmanship was actually going on in a school game. It was worse than anything I'd ever seen in a game before—worse than all of it put together. It was like suddenly none of the players on the other team had any honor at all. I was even more surprised at their behavior because, just as we were from a Christian school, we were also playing a Christian school. This made the behavior from the other players all the more unexpected, to say nothing of completely out of character. Or so I thought.

By the end of the third quarter all this had escalated to the point where we felt we had to tell the coach that we thought he needed to do something to intervene. He assured us he'd been watching and had already issued several warnings to the other coach—as well as the referees. "Should we return some rough play, Coach?" I asked.

"Absolutely not," replied my coach.

"But how can they play like this if they are from a Christian school?" I asked. And then the coach explained something that has made all the difference in how I look at people—and Christianity. "If you are at the mall and you spot someone wearing a San Francisco 49ers jersey, it doesn't mean that person is a 49ers fan. It means he is wearing a 49ers jersey. Likewise, just because you attend a Christian school doesn't necessarily mean that you are a Christian. Like the old used expression, 'You carry your sunshine inside,' faith begins on the inside and radiates out. You must always play to 'win in the third column.'"

While every player wants to win big enough to merit two columns in the paper, my coach was saying there was a column beyond that to strive for—a column unseen in print, but one that shows up nonetheless. *Playing to win in the third column* means that who you are always shows up in your actions, no exceptions. It's the column that includes how you represent your spiritual principles. And so my team played a good and fair football game. We "won in the third column."

Back home, everyone learned that we lost—and how the other team hadn't practiced good sportsmanlike conduct. Some of my friends asked me why we didn't just "give them a taste of their own medicine." But aside from not relishing the idea of being in a dirty fight, it is as Gandhi said, "If we practiced an eye for an eye, the world would all be blind!"

We lost that football game, but we won in the most important column, the "third column." You just have to do what you know is right. It's the only way you can respect yourself. And the coach is right. The example you set is the one that teaches the best lesson of all: You have to win at the game of life—at all costs. Besides, in the end, your "score" is always tallied in the third column.

Brian Slamon, 16

Dear God, Can We Talk About My Friends?

Dear God,

Thanks for getting me through another year of school. Wow, it was really tough. I thought I was going to flunk English, but you helped me make it through. Finally the summer is here, and boy am I looking forward to it—even if I won't be with a lot of my friends. Since I won't see them, I'd like to ask if you could please watch over them and keep them safe until we're all together again in September. Joshua Logelli is going whitewater rafting (with his older brother) in Colorado, and Suzette Harrison is going with her family to Madrid, Spain. Between the two of them, they will take a total of eleven different flights, so that's a lot of risk. I'm terrified of flying. They are the best friends any guy could have. I'd feel so much better if you could look out for them and keep them safe. Thank you and amen.

Jason Zachary, 16

Dear God,

As you know, Becky is having a lot of problems. I'm just talking to you for her because I know she needs you. But most of all, please help me to have patience listening to her, because she really can get on my nerves. Thank you for helping me not to snap at her or anything like that so far, because I really want to be a good friend. And like I said, she really needs help. I'm not certain, but I think she's anorexic. Or bulimic. One of those. Whichever one it is, I hear it's very dangerous. Thank you for making sure I don't have an eating disorder. I really like my body and wouldn't do anything like that. I'll be listening for what you have to say about what I should say to Becky. Thanks and amen.

Letticia Rosen, 13

Dear God,

Sometimes I forget to be grateful for my friends. My grandma always said that friends are one of life's greatest treasures. I used to think it was some hokey thing she said to keep me from fighting with my friends, but now that I've gotten older I can see that she's right. I really appreciate the friends you've given me. Thank you for them.

Caleb Jameson, 15

Dear God,

Thank you for all my friends. Life seems great when we're all laughing together. Laughter is probably one of the best ideas you came up with—along with friends to share it with. You're so cool!

Martin Michaels, 14

Last Good-Byes

When I was eleven years old, my sister got to go on a trip to Cabo San Lucas with her friend from school. That sounded like a very grown-up, sign-of-independence thing to me, and I wanted to go on a trip someday by myself, too. I asked my parents if I could do something like that by myself and they said, "When you get older." But I didn't want to wait until I was older.

All I could do was think about how I could go on a trip. Any trip.

After a great deal of thought, I came up with an idea: I'd ask to go visit my grandpa in Utah. "We'll think about it," my parents said. Realizing they needed a little convincing that it would be a nice thing for Grandpa (which would improve my chances of going on a trip), I said, "I could help Grandpa clean up his garage. And he's been saying he needs to sort things out in the attic. I could help him with things like that. And I know Grandpa would like my company." Then, to get at their heartstrings, I added, "You know how lonely he's been since Grandma died— he's all alone. I bet he'd like the company of his grandkid."

"Maybe that's not such a bad idea," my dad said to my mom. "Maybe not," my mom agreed, then added, "Besides, it might be nice for all his aunts, uncles and cousins who live there to see Andrew, too."

And so the trip was planned! My trip—all alone! I was on my way to Salt Lake City, Utah—all by myself on a plane. I don't mind telling you that I was plenty happy having been clever enough to think of how I could accomplish my goal of being on a trip of my own.

I met my aunt at the airport, and she took me to my grandpa's house. I love Grandpa a lot and was so excited to see him, even though he looked a little more frail than I remembered. He needed help getting around, but I was fine with helping him do that. It was a very old house, one that had been built in 1932 and was in the family for a long time. With him living there alone, the house seemed even bigger and really empty. It creaked so much that I was afraid to sleep in a room of my own, so Grandpa said I could sleep on the floor next to his bed. I thought that was a really good idea, and each night my grandpa would make me up a soft bed out of many blankets and pillows.

I really enjoyed my time with my grandfather, even more so than I had expected. I helped him in every way I could. It took us two full days to clean out the garage, and Grandpa said he didn't feel up to tackling the attic, so we didn't get to it. But every day we talked and talked about so much. And I enjoyed the time with my relatives, too. We did a lot of fun things, like picnics and going out to dinner and renting movies. Honestly, I didn't want my time there to end. Soon though, I knew it would have to. Everyone thought I was such a good guy for coming out to see my grandpa; now I was so glad that I did.

On the day before I had to leave, I felt that something was wrong. So I sat down by his garage and for some reason started to cry. I didn't even know why. Then, I just sat quietly, thinking. Intuitively, I knew God was trying to tell me something, like this would be the last time I would be here with Grandpa, and the last time I would see him alive. Of course, then I cried harder because I didn't want to believe it. Other than being old and frail, there was nothing wrong with Grandpa. I mean, he was in good health.

Sadly, the next day I had to leave. But I went home truly knowing I went there for the right reasons—even if I hadn't known them at the time.

Several days later, my family was called and told that Grandpa had suffered a stroke and wasn't expected to live. I didn't want to believe this. After all, he had two strokes before this and recovered from them just fine. My father flew to be with Grandpa immediately, and I joined him three days later.

I was too late. Grandpa died the night before I arrived.

The feelings that my visit there would be the last time I would see him had been correct.

I cried and cried over my grandfather's death. Yet, I was so grateful for the chance to be with him and to say, "I love you, Grandpa, and thanks for loving me like you do."

Maybe the reason for my wanting to travel had been to feel grown up like my sister. Still, in the end, the real reason I made my trip was to be with my grandpa, a guy I love so much. I will always believe that my trip was meant to be. God knew how much I loved my grandpa, and that was his reason for making sure I got to spend time with him before he took my grandpa home to heaven.

Andrew Meyer, 16

Dear God, Help Me With . . .

Dear God,

Thank you for giving me intuition and intelligence, and for letting me choose so many things in my life—like whether to go out with Danny Schull or with Raymond Paul this Saturday night. Please help me to know in my heart which of these two I should go out with and help me tell the other one in a way that doesn't hurt his feelings. Also, thank you for making both of them so cute—very good work. Life really is about making choices, and while sometimes I think it would be easier if things were a little more cut and dried, I can see why you gave us free will. Please give me the insight to choose wisely in all things. Even in choosing between Danny and Raymond. Amen.

Natasha Vesna, 15

Dear God,

Thank you for all the ways you make my life so good. I know that sometimes I forget to be grateful, or I start to doubt whether or not you're really there, or whether you really care about what's going on in my life. Help me stay strong in believing that there's no time you're not with me, even when I'm all stressed out or in big trouble and I feel like I'm all alone. Let me believe with all my heart that there's absolutely nothing that can take away your love.

Janelle Paquette, 18

The Candy Bar

I'm Jewish, and my family is very involved in the local synagogue. My parents and my rabbi made certain I was taught not only the precepts (laws) and creed (beliefs) our faith is based upon, but its traditions as well—including how to read and speak in Hebrew. And, they instilled in me that it was important—and right—for me to follow the tenets of my faith, and for added measure to make sure I would, informed me that God "knows everything."

I had my doubts about God actually knowing *everything*. I mean, why would God even care to know *everything?* Then there was this one incident that ended all those doubts forever.

This happened a few years ago, when I was only twelve years old. I was on my way home from school, when I decided to stop in a local convenience store to get a snack. I wandered around the store a little and found myself in front of the candy. I wanted a candy bar so bad. I checked to see how much money I had on me and discovered it wasn't enough to pay for the candy bar. Now, I had never stolen before, and I knew very well that stealing was wrong. Still, this candy bar had my name on it! I looked around to make sure *no one* was watching. Then, with my heart pounding in my chest, I slyly stuck it in my pocket. I left the store as fast as I could, quite sure that only my feelings of guilt had witnessed my theft. But I was wrong.

I hadn't gotten ten steps outside of the door, when suddenly my rabbi was right there standing before me. "I know what you've done, Mikial," he said calmly, then added gravely, "You must take the item you stole back in the store and return it. Then, we'll go to the synagogue and have a talk." I could not believe my rabbi had seen me! I felt terrible that such an honorable man, and family friend, had seen me do such a criminal thing! How he had been passing by at just that moment, I didn't know. So, feeling very embarrassed, I returned the candy bar, and just as he'd promised, my rabbi took me to the synagogue for "a talk."

To tell you the truth, I can't even remember everything else the rabbi said. But I do remember the *entire* time I was sitting there, I was thinking about how my parents had been right about God knowing what I was doing—all the time. By way of the rabbi, I was sure that God had sent me guidance that day—just like he did for all the Children of Israel. Yes, God really does know everything—and he seems to let my rabbi in on a whole lot of it, too.

Mikial Hirshorn, 16

Dear God, Forgive Me For . . .

Dear God,

I lied to my parents about Saturday night, and they found out. Now that I have a little extra time on my hands (I'm grounded), I'm getting to the heart of the matter. I really do feel bad about not being honest with my parents (and even worse not being able to be with my friends), so I'm hoping you could help me out a little bit more, and a little more often. Strengthen my spirit and guide me toward the right decisions. Also, I have four more days to spend "quality time" with my parents. Do you think you might help them forgive me for betraying our trust? It sure would make the time with them easier. I'll do my part, too. Like I said, I really am sorry, and I promise to work hard at convincing my parents I am, too. Thanking you in advance.

Lydell Watson, 17

Dear God,

I thought today would never end. One thing after another just kept loading me down. I was a little moody when my mom asked if I had much homework to do . . . and I flew off the handle and took my stress out on her. Please forgive me because I didn't mean it, and my mom was only trying to help out. I'm not really sure why I'm so quick to fly off the handle, especially with my mom. She's so good to me, and I love her so much. She is just a great mom. Please help me understand myself better, and please forgive me for doing and saying things that hurt the feelings of others. Amen.

Sienna Jones, 16

Traveling the Red Road

I'm Native American. While there may be other teachings in other Native American Nations, I was taught that there is One Creator, the Grandfather, who is alive in all life—in all animals: "the winged, the four-legged, the two-legged, the ones in the water, and the creepy-crawlies." I believe the Creator is in all the plants, the trees, the sand and the air. So, I believe we should care for all life, because we're all related and we all have our place on Mother Earth.

My parents taught me how important it is to stay on the "red road"—which means to act according to the principles of my faith, doing the right things—in words and actions. I don't go to a church like most of my friends, but ever since I was little, my parents have taken me to the reservation to "sweat"—a ritual that is very important to our faith in the Creator. The reservation we go to is kind of far away, but we get out there about once a month. This is not my family's tribe, but we're still welcomed to be a part of their sacred ceremonies. The primary purpose of the "sweat" ritual is for purification and prayer. For me, prayer is about connecting with the Creator and extending my own sense of spirit and connecting it with and for other people. Purification, for me, is about getting rid of the toxins in my body (including negative thoughts). It's like cleaning away all kinds of negative energy.

Everything about doing the "sweat" puts you in a frame of mind to focus yourself toward achieving connection and purification. A sweat lodge is very small and shaped like a dome and about the size of a camping tent—but with a low roof, so you can't stand up. You always crawl into the sweat lodge, because this shows you are being humble before the Grandfather. Once you go through the door of the sweat lodge, you are one with the world. You've gone into the womb of Mother Earth, where there is no color, or prejudice or hate, because when you're in your mother's womb all you know is warmth and love and kindness.

In the center of the sweat lodge there is a hole, like a shallow pit, where the burning rocks are placed. The rocks are called the *tutunkas*, which means the elders or the ancestors, because they've been here on Mother Earth for so long. Once everyone is circled around the burning rocks, the sweat leader begins the rounds of prayer. The sweat leader is usually an elder who has gone on vision quests and done other sacred rites. The sweat leader uses sage to sprinkle water on the rocks and make the whole sweat lodge fill with steam. During the sweat, the *firekeeper* sits on the other side of the sweat lodge door, making sure that the fire is keeping the rocks for the other rounds burning.

The sweat is made up of four rounds for the different generations: One round is prayers for your elders (for your parents, your grandparents and all your ancestors); one round is for the men, the fathers, grandfathers and brothers; one round is for the women, the mothers, grandmothers and sisters; and one round is for the children, praying that they stay on the red road. The sweat leader begins the prayers, then clockwise each person takes their turn in prayer, one by one, around the circle. If a person doesn't have a prayer or doesn't want to pray out loud, they can just say "all my relations," or they can sing a song. (The songs are sung in the language of the ancestors.)

In between each round, the firekeeper opens the door to let air in, and then puts new rocks in the center of the lodge. It gets really hot during the sweat, but you have fresh sage that you can breathe into to cool down a little. Sometimes, some sweat leaders will feel there's a need for more heat for purification, so they'll take out their feather fan and fan the steam coming off the rocks towards the people in the circle.

Even though all the heat is hard to go through, when I come out of the sweat lodge, I'm *always* filled with this really good feeling—like I just *know* the Creator is real and exists in everything. It's hard to describe precisely how I feel, other than to say I feel *new, innocent, pure,* and that in that moment, I have a chance to begin fresh and new in everything I do and say. It's such a spectacular feeling. Best of all, in those times when things aren't going my way, I just remember *that* moment when I first emerge from the sweat lodge. When I do that, all the positive effects of doing the sweat return and I am able to face the pressures and stress of my life with more calm and control. For me, faith is about traveling "the red road." It's a faith that works in my life in all ways.

Eric Hunter, 17

Dear God, Thanks For . . .

Dear God,

Sometimes my days are so full and busy, I forget about you. I'm sorry. I'm the one who loses out, because thinking of you brings greater goodness and beauty to my whole world. Thank you for that—and please help me to remember you're there, even when I have no excuse for forgetting other than thinking about other things. But thank you for the reminders: Friends, flowers, a beautiful sky and sunset. And Brad Summers, too!

Suzanne Charles, 15

Dear God,

I know I often pray for more of all the good things I can think of, but this time I want to thank you for all the good things you've already given me. So please feel my thank you because it is very sincere. Amen.

Sid Holmes, 17

Dear God,

You've given me another beautiful day full of opportunities. Thank you. Please help me to listen to you throughout the day so I make the most of it. It's a wonderful world and a beautiful one. Good job! I'm happy, and I know it's because of your love. So, I'm not asking for anything like I usually do. This prayer is just to give thanks and glory to you. Loving you and the world I live in.

Alma Russ, 18

Dear God,

Thank you for teaching me that when I keep you in the middle of my life, my whole life is just filled with *more* life! Thank you for the way you guide me through life. Help me listen to you, so that I can make you happy with me. Amen.

Ronnie Lee, 18

Dear God,

Lots of times I fail to notice all the good things in my life. You give me a lot of happiness and gifts every day—like good health, family, friends, food, clothes, good grades and good music. Thank you! You really are *awesome*.

Stevie Mead, 18

Dear God,

When I open my eyes I can see all the beauty you've surrounded me with; and when I just listen, I can hear all sorts of beautiful sounds. Please keep my eyes and my ears open so that I can experience all the beauty you've created. It's breathtaking, really. Thanks for doing it for us all. You are totally cool!

Maria Cruz, 16

Dear God,

Thank you for helping me to say "no" this weekend, because no is really what I wanted to say. Give me the courage to do what I know is right all the time.

Nancy Robins, 14

Sometimes, Life Just Sucks!

The past couple of weeks have not been the best in my life. Actually, they've been pretty close to the worst. It began the night my parents seemed really edgy at dinner. As I was about to leave the table, my dad asked me to sit back down. So I sat back down with a nervous stomach: I could tell he must have some bad news. He then announced he had come to the conclusion that he and my mom should live apart for a little while; their differences had grown so great, it was just too hard for them to continue living together.

I didn't know what to say—it was so totally unexpected—so I asked, "Can I go now?" and he nodded that I could. I went back to my room and, feeling really sick to my stomach, just cried and cried. So many questions came into my head. *Why did this happen? How was I going to tell my friends?* And then, *How will I deal with their reactions?* But most of all, I wondered why something this terrible should have to happen to *me*. I was in my junior year in high school and having a really stressful year; I didn't need anything more to worry about.

One day as I sat in school, with large quiet tears streaming down my face, and with absolutely no energy or care to wipe them away or stop them from dripping off my cheeks, the girl behind me, a classmate I really didn't know all that well, passed me a note that read: "If I can help you, then know you have a friend."

Good grief! I thought, *I'm falling apart, and it's evident to everyone.* Even those who didn't know me were taking pity on me. I didn't want anyone to pity me. Besides, I had a right to be mad. Having your parents divorce is a tragic thing, something that is inflicted upon you. No one asked my opinion. Worse, I didn't even see it coming. And I was hurt. *I* didn't want a divorce from either of my parents. I couldn't imagine not having them under one roof, and

I didn't want to have to choose who I was going to live with. And, I didn't want to shuttle between the two, packing half of my belongings and taking them with me, as I went from his house to her house and her house to his house. I have friends who do this, and it really sucks.

But maybe I was pitiful and so should be pitied. I wasn't coping well; maybe I didn't want to. I had a right to be sad. My smiles went away with my happiness, and soon everything in my world seemed bleak. Bleak brought darkness. Before this talk of divorce, I believed in God, but the more I thought about my parents divorcing, the more depressed I became.

I started slowly turning away from believing in God.

Then I saw this television show that had a similar plot to the one going on in my life. Like me, everyone was having a really tough time of things, especially the teen in the family, and like me, she was using it to discount God because of the pain of the crisis at hand. Rather than calling on faith at this sad time in her life, she abandoned it. I thought about that, and how it was exactly the opposite of the point of faith. God wasn't to blame for my parents splitting up. God was a source of comfort, not discord. Getting clear on that was an epiphany for me.

So I decided not to give up on my faith. Through faith what I saw was two parents who had tried to work things out and who, after much pain, made a decision they thought was best. They were not fighting or making things difficult for each other; and they certainly tried really hard to be extra kind to each other and to us kids through it all. Our family didn't stop loving and caring about being a family—even though we lived together differently than we once did.

And it was God's love that caused a girl I hardly knew to reach out and offer compassion when my life seemed so dark.

I don't have two parents under one roof. Even though I'd love it if I did, that's not the way it is at our house. Though we don't live under the same roof, we have managed to stay a family. I think our love for each other is the key to that—we didn't take out our pain on each other. And I believe our faith was the reason we were able to make the best of a terrible situation.

Paige Williams, 17

Dear God, So, About My Parents . . .

Dear God,

The best gift from you is my parents because of the way they love me. I especially want to say thanks for my dad. He's funny and is really a cool guy. Kids don't always remember to say "thanks" for parents, but I'd like to thank you for mine.

Nicky Lloyd, 16

Dear God,

Please help me to be brave enough to go to my parents when I'm hurt or confused. Let me remember that they're not mind readers (and I'm sure glad of that). They can't know that I'm having a hard time unless I tell them. Maybe they can't give me any great answers, but at least they can listen and be supportive. Sometimes that's enough.

Brent Tyson, 15

Dear God,

When I'm really upset at my mom or my dad, please help me to chill out. Help me to be glad that they care, and to realize they aren't trying to make my life miserable, they're just trying to do what's best for me. Thank you for parents who love me, even when I'm being moody, stressed and feeling anything but lovable. Amen.

Robin Rizzo, 16

The First Time I Got Really Serious . . .

When I was around twelve years old, I experienced something very dramatic. My family and I were all sitting around at dinner, and I felt like my stomach was literally going to explode. I couldn't eat anything that night and went to bed right after dinner. The next morning I felt like I was going to die, it hurt that bad. I couldn't even get out of bed. When my mom came to get me up, I told her I could not even walk. Of course, she looked worried and asked me what was wrong. When I told her, she pressed some places on my stomach. It was very painful. Later that day she took me to our family doctor, who suggested we go to the hospital for some tests. He thought I might have appendicitis.

Doctors ran tests on my stomach to try and find out exactly what was wrong. The whole time, I can remember shaking and being so scared that something serious was the matter with me. The nurses were very comforting, assuring me everything was going to be all right. My mom stayed with me the whole time and held my hand through every test. They took an ultrasound, forcing me to drink tons of liquids so they could see inside my stomach.

We waited in the hall for two long hours for the test results. My stomachache getting worse by the minute, I felt cramps throughout my *entire* body. Finally, a nurse with short, brown hair and a serious look on her face emerged from the enclosed doors and announced, "We'll need to prepare for surgery." I was terrified to death at this point. I had never had an operation before, and I wasn't sure what it was like. Everything was happening so fast; doctors and nurses were rushing all around me. I was wheeled into an operating room, and prepared for surgery. First came a couple of shots and then an IV, and then a strawberry-flavored gas mask over my face. It was the first time I realized I could die, and I didn't want to, so I decided right then and there that if I made it through this, I was going to believe in God—even more than I already did.

When I woke up hours later, I was in a dimly lit room with a nurse at a desk in a corner and other hospital beds in a row beside mine. I was so happy to be alive, because obviously it meant I hadn't died after all. I asked the nurse to get my mom and she left for a minute or so, and then my mom and dad came rushing in. They had big smiles on their faces, because they were so happy I was okay, too.

So the pain was gone. I no longer had my appendix, and though my stomach felt much better, I was still a little sore from the operation. For the next few days, I sat in a hospital room as a nurse monitored me and took my blood pressure every two hours. My mom slept there with me on a little chair, making sure I didn't get too bored. We read books, watched movies and talked about boys. My relatives came to visit, and so did some of my close friends from school. They brought me balloons, flowers and presents. My sixth-grade class at school all made "get well soon" cards for me. That was great!

After four days, I went home from the hospital. My stomach was still really sore and I had a very hard time walking at first, but gradually I was able to do things again. While surgery was scary for me, it turned out to be a good experience in that it gave me a chance to understand that I could die. When you face something like that, you have to give up all your arguments against whether or not there is or isn't a God, because when it's your life and it's about over, you want to know there really is a heaven. And next to life, that's the best place to be.

Kristen Mosteller, 13

Dear God, Show Me . . .

Dear God,

Please show me what you want out of me in life. Do you want me to feed starving children in third-world countries? Do you want me to help save lost souls? Do you want me to save whales or the environment, or is working on myself enough? How will I know? Please show me what I'm supposed to do, so I can make my life useful and meaningful.

Kristi Sally, 18

Dear God,

I know you created me for some really great purpose. I just feel it inside. Still, I'm a little confused about what it is. If you reveal to me just what that purpose is, I can get busy doing what I'm supposed to be doing—or at least know what direction I'm headed in. I'd love to be more clear about all that. Thank you for your guidance and direction.

David Samson, 18

Dear God,

When I start to get critical of other people, remind me it's not my job to judge them and that they are perfectly loved by you, just as they are. And when I start to get critical of myself, remind me that I'm perfectly loved by you, too. Then, just help me be a better person. Amen.

Wynnona Reyes, 15

The Truth About Truth

I was a junior at the time that some friends asked me to go with them on a four-day trip that was an outreach mission. I was looking forward to going, not only because I was with my friends, but because it came at a time when I really needed a change of scenery. I am a spiritual person, but I was struggling with my Christian walk.

I'm just a regular guy with a life pretty much like everyone else: trying to make decent grades, fit in, keep up daily demands of homework; keep my parents and teachers happy with me; get to my part-time job on time; find a steady girlfriend, and put some money away to buy a car and go to college. Yet for all these ordinary things, there were other things on my mind—dramatic things, like a good friend whose brother has AIDS, and another friend who was in a terrible car accident and was left paralyzed from the waist down. It all seemed so senseless, and I wondered why God would allow such terrible things to happen—and to young people who hadn't even had a chance to live yet. So here I was, really in a quandary about the purpose and extent of God's love, and this opportunity came along.

While we all prepared for the trip, nothing could prepare any of us for the series of events that would transpire, events that changed my passive sense of faith.

It seemed like whatever could go wrong on our outreach mission did. We went through so many bad situations—again and again. Remarkably, just as an expectation fell apart, a solution appeared. For example, we arrived at our destination one day, fully expecting lodging, only to discover there was no place for us to sleep that night. So, we packed up and headed down the road (not knowing for sure where we were going). Within half an hour, we came across a youth group from Australia, who were visiting in the area. We told them about our predicament of having no place to sleep for the night, and wouldn't you know it, they had ample room. They invited us to stay with them and we did. It was great, and a lot of fun, probably more fun than if we had stayed where had planned in the beginning.

Everything just sort of worked out with a natural grace—time and time again. For instance, one of the tasks we were given was to go to a particular church, where we would visit and share our faith with the members of that congregation. When we arrived there two days after the fiasco of not finding the sleeping arrangements we were told would be awaiting our arrival, we noticed that what was supposed to be a church was really four wooden pillars coming up from the ground with a tarp on top of it to serve as the roof. Like I said, one catastrophic thing after another happened on this trip. Sure enough, the next morning a storm hit, shredding the covering of this little makeshift church and totally ruining the structure they had in place. But once again, a remedy was instantaneous. Since our real goal on the mission was to witness our faith, we knew there was an opportunity to witness (show rather than tell about) faith in action. We quickly went to the local lumber store, rounded up some supplies and reconstructed the church, this time putting in place a permanent structure, one that would withstand seasonal rough weather and last the people for a long time to come. The new church was so much better than what they had. And so once again, things turned out for the better. Much like the incident where we found a place to stay just in the dire moment when we needed it, this incident, too, gave me cause to believe that just as bad things happen, so do good things happen.

Yet, it was after I returned from my trip that I was challenged to look beyond outward evidence of *Spirit* working, and I asked myself, "Do I *believe*? Do I have complete faith, or do I need to see in order to believe?"

One day during football season a friend of mine injured his ankle and was told his injury meant he wouldn't be playing for three to five weeks. The coach said we should all include our teammate in our prayers, and pray for his speedy recovery. I thought, "Prayers may not be enough here. This is a physical injury, and it's going to need time to heal, and I doubt that healing a muscle strain for a high school athlete is on the first page of God's 'To-Do' list." And then, just as I was thinking this, the coach said, "If any of you have any doubts—even if they are as 'small as a mustard seed'—throw them out." And I knew from the teachings of my religious upbringing that if I was truly wishing a speedy recovery for my teammate, then I needed to first remove the doubt in my own heart that it could be so. Well, I didn't pray for my teammate. I prayed that my doubt be removed and replaced by having faith that it could happen.

Though you may find this hard to believe (because I did, too—at first), the next day, my friend came back to school and told the coach he felt good enough to play the next game. And he did play. He played the rest of the season—and did a very good job, I might add. So I was happy that while I didn't pray for his healing, at least I didn't let my doubt make me someone who stopped it from happening.

So, I've concluded that being a spiritual person is really about having faith. It's not always easy to just accept whatever and believe that the outcome holds as much positive good as tribulation. But faith demands that you do, like even though stressing out over school, relationships and important decisions seem like it's just part of being a teen, in the end most of that stress ends up being pointless. It helps me to remember that good came out of bad, and I should just continue to have faith. You need to do the best you can do, and then let it go. The outcome will be the outcome. I have found comfort in the saying, "Everything happens for a reason." For every bump and obstacle along the road, I will find comfort in knowing it is all part of God's master plan.

Nick Maldonado, 16

Dear God, About the Future . . .

Dear God,

I'm so undecided about things sometimes; one day I think I know what I want to do, and the next I know I don't. Sometimes, I'm downright scared. I mean, I'm already seventeen, and still I have no idea what to do. If you can show me the way to a future I'd like, one I'm really happy in, I'll be a happier and better person. I know how important it is to be happy with my life; that way I can be really focused on making life better for those around me, which I think is a good start on making the world a better place. Please guide me.

Carey Whittle, 17

Dear God,

Finding out I wasn't going to make the football team the same day I flunked my behind-the-wheel driving test seems a little unfair to me. It feels like practically my whole world and my entire future is ruined. Please give me some perspective and let your strength fill me. I really need it. I'm really wanting to know what lies ahead for me. I know you know, so if you can reveal any of that for me, it would help me feel positive about the future, and not like such a failure—which is how I'm feeling now. I trust you to show me the way. Amen.

Alex Lawson, 17

Plano, Texas—Or San Diego, California?

When my dad told me that our family was moving to California, I was upset and end-of-the-world devastated. Why would our family move halfway across the country when everything about our lives was so wonderful right where we were? I lived in Plano, Texas, all my life, and I loved it. All my friends and relatives were in Texas. And how could my dad expect me to move right before my senior year? What about the homecoming events, the school dances, the prom, graduating with my class, my boyfriend of three weeks? I didn't want any part of moving. I thought, *If my family wants to move to California, fine. Go on without me. But I'm staying in Plano, Texas.* Leaving my life in Plano was unthinkable.

Our family talked and talked and talked about how it would be an adjustment, but a good one. And so I had no choice but to leave everything I loved. Every night for nearly three weeks, I'd lie in bed and cry myself to sleep.

Then one night after the life-changing announcement was made, I was getting ready for bed, and noticed the Bible verse my mom had taped to the corner of my mirror. She's always doing things like that, so while I take notice, it's not like I read them every day. For some reason, this verse begged my attention and I read it: "Trust in the Lord with all your heart and lean not on your own understanding," Proverbs 4:5–6. I'd read this before but I never really felt it applied to my life. Tonight it seemed to.

I decided to think about this verse and apply it to the loss and confusion I was feeling. Then I made another decision: I decided to take a leap of faith and to trust that God knew best. Maybe things wouldn't be so bad. Maybe things could even be good. I didn't cry myself to sleep that night, which was a good feeling. And a change. But everything else began to change, too. For starters, I began to look forward to life in California.

Not that it was always just that easy. Every time I had to say good-bye to some part of my life, I thought for sure that I would break out into tears. But I never did. In fact, I couldn't even find my tears anymore. That surprised me. I remember sitting in my room wondering why I didn't cry when I was in the middle of an appropriately sad circumstance, like telling my new boyfriend I was leaving, or when the teacher announced Candi Pauls would need to be assigned a new partner on the research paper (because I wouldn't be there by time it was due). Candi is my best friend, and you would have thought that the announcement to the class would have made me feel like I hadn't yet gone, but already they were going on without me. But then I remembered that verse and decided the reason that I didn't cry was because I had turned things over to God, and trusting that maybe there was an even better story of my life unfolding. Having faith in God was a decision I made, no matter how scary it seemed not knowing what my life would be like in a matter of months. When the big moving day arrived, I said good-bye to Plano with tears in my eyes. And then anticipated what lay ahead.

For three days I drove with my family across Texas, New Mexico and Arizona having no clue what to expect in my new life. I wondered what California looked like, who my neighbors would be and what my new school would be like—hoping it would be as good as what I was leaving behind.

I have been in California for nearly a year now and everything is going great. I'm glad that I didn't leave any hard feelings behind, no enemies, no homework outstanding. My transition has been relatively easy, even fun. My grades are looking fine. I like the teachers. I have great friends. I ended up with a room of my own in the house we bought. I have a part-time job at a copy center, and I've just signed up for the school softball team. I am happy! I don't have a new boyfriend yet, but the prospects look good!

I made a decision to put my trust in the Proverbs verse, to

believe these words held the power to help me in the dilemma I was facing. And it's made all the difference.

Making a decision can be a very powerful thing—like drawing a line in the sand, then stepping over and vowing to stay on that side—no matter what. It's a commitment. Having faith is a commitment you make, too.

As for me, I'm thankful that my mother taped that special verse to my mirror. Now, having made it through the move from one state to another, I know that my happiness doesn't depend on living in a certain city or a certain state, but rather on the way I choose to see my circumstances.

So, which is better: Plano, Texas, or San Diego, California? Both are just wonderful, as I'm sure I would now find anywhere I lived—especially now that I trust God with all my heart, and don't lean solely on my own understanding.

Cassie Cable, 17

Dear God, What I'd Like to Say . . .

Dear God,

Love is probably the most beautiful thing in the universe. I may not always feel loved or show love for others, but I can be grateful for knowing I'm always loved by you. Thank you for all you do for me and for showing me that doing something for others is one way of letting you act through me. Please help me to always be willing to give to others just the way you give to me.

Perry Cray, 17

Dear God,

Please help my parents to get along with each other better. I hate it when they argue, especially when they argue about me. Please help me to be the daughter both of them want me to be, so they have one less thing to argue about. You know I love them, and they love me.

Leanna Stam, 13

Dear God,

Sometimes I just think *I* have to make sure everyone is happy. I forget my friends are all capable of taking care of themselves. Please help me to quit trying to fix all of their problems. Instead, let me just make you happy by being kind to others and doing the best that I can. I'm really grateful to know that I don't have to be perfect to be loved by you.

Shawnee Golinda, 17

Mailboxes

The family mailbox stood at the end of the half-mile-long lane. In tall, proud, white capital letters it announced to all who passed by: BURRES. To us children that metal container on a post was a source of endless anticipation and a source of independence. And a promise of unconditional love.

Our mother had created this sense of adventure for us, probably not inadvertently; children needed to learn things. To Mom, everything was a teachable moment. And she was a master teacher.

Each day, around noontime, my mother would walk down the lane to get the mail. When we children saw her head for the lane on Saturdays, we would drop our activities and scurry to join her, as would the dog member of the family. Mom was a mother who found great pleasure in her children's company, happily and playfully greeting us as we joined her. The half-mile trek to and from the mailbox was a long way for short legs, but well worth it. During these trips, her mood was reliably joyous; this was an opportunity to bask in our mother's love.

Once we arrived at the mailbox, Mom would pick out the mail and while sorting through it, announce if mail had arrived for any of the children—though she wouldn't give out the names of just who among us had received mail. By doing it this way, all of us children were kept in suspense until we had reached the house, at which time we would be given our individual mail. Mother made a point of teaching us to respect each other's privacy, and to be a very good sport about who did and did not receive mail on any given day. "Here," she would say, "this belongs to you." We were all allowed to open the mail that came in our names without Mom looking over our shoulders.

Surprisingly, each child received mail from time to time. Even more surprisingly, each child received mail in fairly equal quantities. Sometimes a magazine arrived in a child's name, sometimes a note from an aunt, uncle, grandma, grandpa or Sunday school teacher (who was also our neighbor and Mom's good friend). No child was left wanting. Even junk mail arrived on cue. Written by a person or by a machine, it didn't matter; getting mail with your name on it was exciting and uplifting.

The practice of children getting to open their own mail continued from the day I was old enough to know what mail was to the day I left home. It wasn't until I was much older that I understood that while we children were caught up in the fun of receiving mail, Mother's strategy held even bigger intentions. On those brief strolls, Mom would sometimes tell us a story made up to fit the moment; at other times she used it to teach us about God. Sometimes these were the same. Mom used every opportunity to help us become aware of the obvious miracles of God's creation. There wasn't a bird or bee, flora or fauna that went unnoticed. To her, everything was evidence of God's love and involvement in the world. The fascinating habits of animals on the ground or in the air, which ones are dangerous and which aren't, and how God gave those "dangers" to animals for their protection; the intricacy and beauty in the colors and shapes and fragrances of flowers; how the bees fly to them to gather their pollen; the sun with its endless power and brilliance to warm and give light, all were pointed out to us for appreciation.

We adored her. She was our everything. This was a joyous woman, an eternal optimist, always smiling, always humming, her words punctuated with an easy-flowing laughter that caused her long, soft brown hair to be tossed over her shoulders. She was a beautiful and feminine woman with blue eyes and flawless skin. We never questioned her love for us, or her unwavering faith in the power of God and his ability to intervene in our daily lives.

One day she spoke to us about the power of prayer. "Praying is like sending a letter," Mother said. "You have to formulate your thoughts, send them to God, and then wait for a reply."

"Does God always answer prayers?" Judy questioned.

"Oh, yes," Mom said with easy certainty. "All you need to do is ask God for help, and God will answer you. The answer may not always be yes, but you will get an answer." Going for clarification, Judy asked, "Even if you are bad?"

"Yes," Mom answered.

"What if it's a really big request?" bantered Judy.

"With God's help," Mom replied, "nothing is impossible." Hearing the reverence in Mom's voice, I knew she was telling us the truth.

"How do you know if your prayer is answered?" I asked.

"Because a miracle will happen," Mom explained. "You will see a sign, or feel the answer inside."

"Where do you feel it?" I asked.

"You will hear the answer in your heart," responded Mom.

"How does your heart hear?" I asked.

"It's a certain feeling you get. For me, it's a warm sensation that I feel right here in my chest," she said, placing her hand over her heart.

"How does it feel if God says no?" I asked. Placing her hand on my shoulder for reassurance, she said, "I trust that whatever the answer is, God thinks it's the right one for me, and I thank God for helping me find the best way to do something."

As was my mother's habit, once the mail had been gathered, her attention turned to gathering flowers. Once she cut all the flowers she wanted, she would call out, "Okay, let's journey home." This was our cue to turn homeward.

I thought a lot about what my mother had taught me that particular day, not realizing I would put her words to the test so soon. The idea of not only talking to God, but also being able to ask for his help if I needed it, was a powerful concept to me, and I took it quite literally.

The following day I came across small insects scurrying about their daily business. I was amazed by the strong-man feats of a trail of ants carrying huge loads in comparison to their tiny frames, up into the hole at the top of their anthill. As I watched, I was distracted by something going on out of the corner of my eye. I turned and saw it struggling on the ground. He was beautiful, but I knew he was in trouble and something inside told me he needed my help. He was a plump, fuzzy, black and yellow bumblebee, about the size of a baby hummingbird. I tenderly scooped him up into the palms of my small hands, tightly cupped together, providing him a safe shelter. He fluttered and buzzed faintly inside my grasp. Even in my youth I could tell that he was sick and possibly dying, and I knew if anyone could make him well, my mother could. She had repaired and nursed many a wounded child, bird and animal back to health. I ran to the house with the bee. When I opened up my cupped hands to let my mother examine her newly found patient, the look on her face was one of alarm.

"Bettie, that bumblebee might sting you, put it down!" she said firmly.

"No, Mom, he's sick. We have to help him," I pleaded. My mother took a closer look at the bee and observed the tiny creature's legs just barely moving.

"Honey, God's the only one who can help that bee now. He's almost dead."

"But, Mom," I pleaded, "there has to be something we can do!"

"I'm afraid not," Mom said.

"But we can't let him die!" I cried. "You said flowers need the bees, so we can't let him just die, Mom. There must be something we can do."

"It's nature's way, honey," Mother said, searching for words of comfort. "Take him outside. Bury him if you want."

I slowly walked with my dying bee to the large oak tree in our yard and sat under its protective branches. Sitting on one of its large fingerlike roots, I leaned back on the tree's enormous trunk. My mind raced, searching for another alternative, and then I remembered my mother's words: "With God's help, nothing is impossible." I closed my eyes tightly and bowed my head, and with my hands still cupped around the bee, I prayed to God with the simple faith of a child.

"Dear God," I prayed, "this bumblebee is very sick and my mom said you are the only one who can help him, so please fix him. Amen."

Not sure what to do at that point, I remained still to allow God the time he needed. That's when God worked the miracle. And I felt it. A soothing feeling welled up inside of me, and I knew this to be the feeling my mother had talked about, the one where she said her heart can "hear." God was answering my prayer.

I slowly allowed one eye to open and then the other, and looked down at my closed, cupped hands. I cautiously opened my fingers, one at a time, and looked at the bee. Whoosh! The bee swiftly flew from my grasp. At first the bee flew only a short distance and then took a nosedive to the soft grass below. But the bee rested for only a moment before it took flight again. Then, right before my eyes, I watched as the bumblebee disappeared out of sight.

"God," I screeched in amazement. "You did it! You really did it. You fixed the bee!" Remembering that Mom had said you need to thank God, I quickly squeezed my eyes closed and said, "Thank you, God."

It was a very happy revelation. I rushed to the house and told my mother what had happened. To my surprise, she acted dismayed. To reassure her, I said, "It happened just like you said it would. I asked God to help and he did."

That sweet, familiar smile crossed my mother's face, and she said, "Yes, sweetheart, miracles do happen."

And so it is that the sight of mailboxes, especially those at the end of long lanes, retains special meaning for me. They remind me of my mother's love and the values and beliefs she so lovingly conveyed; she embodied joy, love and respect; she taught joy, love and respect.

Always mailboxes remind me of my mother's love for her children—then and now. Her love for her children was from the heart, and she found it a duty to instill in us a faith in God—a God who was a loving and benevolent father, one who joyfully, lovingly and respectfully played with all his creatures daily.

Mailboxes also symbolize my personal connection to God, and the "correspondence" that joyfully, lovingly and respectfully goes on between us—one that my heart readily "hears."

While I no longer naively believe that God can fix all dying bees, I do know that God permeates all things. Through God all things are possible. I know that all prayers, large and small, are answered. And that if you will be still, you will "hear" God answer.

Little did I know then, that on the ritual journey down the lane to the mailbox, my mother was teaching the most important lesson of all—it was about correspondence with God, and the journey home. Home, to God.

Bettie B. Youngs
Excerpted from Values from the Heartland

About the Authors

Bettie B. Youngs, Ph.D., Ed.D., is a professional speaker and the internationally renowned author of eighteen books translated into twenty-nine languages. She is a former Teacher of the Year, university professor and executive director of the Phoenix Foundation and president of Professional Development, Inc. She is a long-acknowledged expert on teens and has frequently appeared on NBC *Nightly News*, CNN, *Oprah* and *Geraldo. USA Today,* the *Washington Post, Redbook, McCall's, Working Woman, Family Circle, Parents Magazine, Better Homes & Gardens, Woman's Day* and the National Association for Secondary School Principals (NASSP) have all recognized her work. Her acclaimed books include *Taste Berries for Teens: Inspirational Short Stories and Encouragement on Life, Love, Friendship and Tough Issues; Taste Berries for Teens Journal; Safeguarding Your Teenager from the Dragons of Life; How to Develop Self-Esteem in Your Child; You and Self-Esteem: A Book for Young People; Taste-Berry Tales;* the Pulitzer-nominated *Gifts of the Heart;* and the award-winning *Values from the Heartland.* Dr. Youngs is the author of a number of video-cassette programs for Sybervision and Nightingale/Conant and is the coauthor of the nationally acclaimed *Parents on Board,* a video-based training program to help schools and parents work together to increase student achievement.

Jennifer Leigh Youngs, twenty-five, is a speaker and workshop presenter for teens and parents nationwide. She is the co-author of *Taste Berries for Teens: Inspirational Short Stories and Encouragement on Life, Love, Friendship and Tough Issues; Taste Berries for Teens Journal,* author of *Feeling Great, Looking Hot &*

Loving Yourself! Health, Fitness and Beauty for Teens; Be Cool, Not Ghoul: A Stress-Management Guide for Teens; and *Goal-Setting Skills for Young Adults.* Jennifer is a former Miss Teen California final-ist and a Rotary International Goodwill Ambassador and Exchange Scholar. She serves on a number of advisory boards for teens and is the international Youth Coordinator for Airline Ambassador, an international organization affiliated with the United Nations that involves youth in programs to build cross-cultural friendships; escorts orphans to new homes and children to hospitals for medical care; and delivers humanitarian aid to those in need worldwide.

To contact Bettie B. Youngs or Jennifer Leigh Youngs, write to:

Youngs, Youngs & Associates
Box 2588
Del Mar, CA 92014

The Taste Berries™ for Teens Series

The stories in this book will help you use the ups and downs of your bittersweet teen years to learn who you are and who you want to be.

The accounts from other teens about how they've dealt with issues will inspire you and give you hope.

Code #6692
Quality Paperback • $12.95

An awesome journal that not only helps you focus on your innermost feelings, explore unlimited possibilities and describe your fondest dreams, but also-and even more important-to turn those possibilities and dreams into reality.

Code #7680
Quality Paperback • $12.95

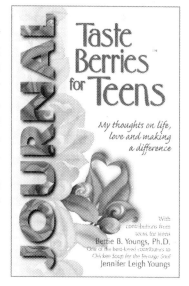

Beautiful—Inside and Out!

Jennifer Leigh Youngs, coauthor of the bestseller *Taste Berries for Teens* offers you all you need to know in this complete guidebook for every girl's teen years.

Code #7672
Quality Paperback • $14.95

"No one knows the value of 'looking hot' as much as teens do. Having it 'together' can spell the difference between being one of the crowd—or not. But the 'success potion' isn't found in a bottle or a pill any more than in a great outfit or the latest hairstyle, eye shadow or nail polish. It's also more important than winning the approval it takes to be the most popular 'in' person at school. The really 'beautiful' are those comfortable in their own skin, who make the most of their natural beauty and have learned to like themselves. Jennifer's practical advice will show you how."

—Kate MacIsaac
1997 Miss California Teen All American
Miss Teen U.S.A.

It's All About This Thing
Called Life!

HCI Titles from Bettie B Youngs

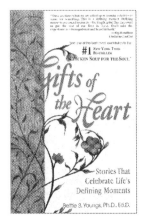

Gifts of the Heart

These 27 inspiring "parables" show us that it is often how we choose to handle a situation—not the situation itself—that infuses our lives with new meaning. These real life lessons—often passed on in subtle ways during "defining moments"—are genuine, potent and precious.

Code #4193 • Quality Paperback • $12.95

Values from the Heartland

Bettie B. Youngs shares her memories of growing up in America's heartland with loving detail—a rich tapestry that allows us to share in the warmth and balance of a principle-centered life.

Code #3359 • Quality Paperback • $11.95

Taste-Berry™ Tales

25 poignant short stories of real-life people who make a difference in the lives of others. These individuals, by their example, show us how to use the events of daily life to improve the world we live in and the lives of others with whom we share it.

Code #5475 • Quality Paperback • $11.95